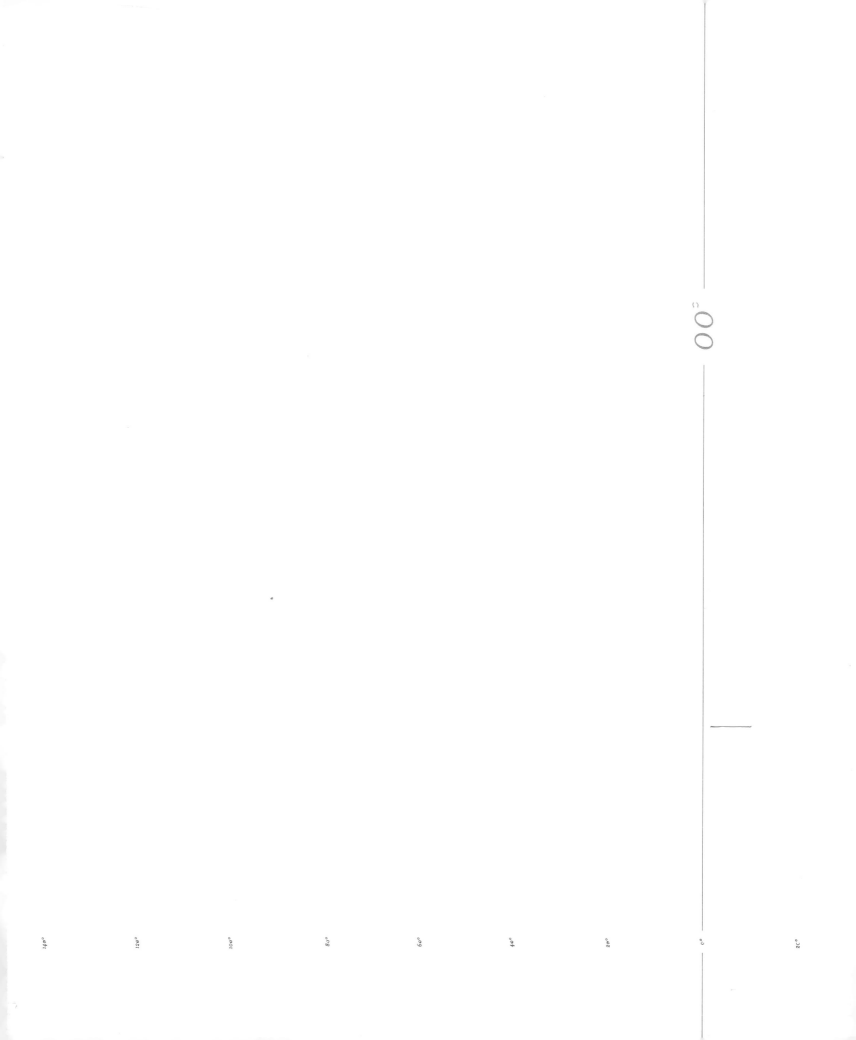

THE LONELY PLANET GUIDE TO THE
MIDDLE OF NºWHERE

Melbourne ○ Oakland ○ London

Introduction

For a supposedly social species, our appetite for space, wilderness and isolation is remarkable. The phrase 'the middle of nowhere' has wormed its way into our everyday language; we all know where it is, and we can all recount a visit there, but unlike the summit of a mountain, the shore of an ocean or a famous monument, 'nowhere' itself is harder to pinpoint. What, or where exactly, is the middle of nowhere?

Perhaps it's easiest to start with what it *isn't*. To me, the word 'somewhere' implies significance: a destination, an arrival. A place you're told about in a thousand guidebooks, documentaries and brochures – a place you already know before you've even arrived. Uluru (Ayers Rock). Manhattan. The Eiffel Tower.

If 'somewhere' is the destination, then perhaps nowhere is the journey. Featureless tundra, the unexpected detour down a dusty side street, a map crisscrossed by nothing but grid lines. Uncertainty, unfamiliarity and discovery. In spring 2004, I spent 72 days skiing solo over the frozen surface of the Arctic Ocean from the north coast of Siberia to the geographic North Pole. The pack ice of the high Arctic surely ticks a few of the 'nowhere' boxes: there are no maps as the terrain is in a constant state of flux; the ice breaks up, re-freezes and drifts according to temperature, tide and current. At the Pole itself I was the only human being in an area one and a half times the size of the United States. A long way from anywhere, and in many ways the ultimate non-destination – if only because there's nothing there. No pole, no flags, no indication that you've arrived.

When people hear what I do (and, indeed, where I go) for a living, the first question I'm asked is usually 'Why?' Why visit the middle of nowhere? One of my heroes, the pioneering Everest mountaineer George Mallory summed it up best, before his final, ill-fated expedition in 1922:

> *The first question which you will ask and which I must try to answer is this, 'What is the use of climbing Mount Everest?' and my answer must at once be, 'It is no use.' ... We shall not bring back a single bit of gold or silver, not a gem, nor any coal or iron. We shall not find a single foot of earth that can be planted with crops to raise food. It's no use. So, if you cannot understand that there is something in man which responds to the challenge of this mountain and goes out to meet it, that the struggle is the struggle of life itself upward and forever upward, then you won't see why we go. What we get from this adventure is just sheer joy. And joy is, after all, the end of life. We do not live to eat and make money. We eat and make money to be able to enjoy life. That is what life means and what life is for.*

As with all journeys to nowhere, my polar expeditions, especially the long trips I have made alone, have posed more questions than they have answered. The middle of nowhere is, in my experience, the best place in the world for reflection and contemplation. Rather appropriately, I'm writing this reflection on the meaning of nowhere from a hotel in Reykjavik, en route to a month-long training expedition in Greenland.

In 2005, I skied along a glacier last visited by human beings 38 years ago, and this year we're flying to a region called Tunu, an area so remote that its name quite simply means 'the back'. In common with the myriad nowheres around the world, I know the next four weeks amid the enormity of the barren Greenland icecap will bring the chance to consider the big questions that our action-packed, always-on 21st-century lifestyles so effectively steer us away from. An opportunity to short-circuit what Mark Slouka calls 'the cult of restlessness' in his wonderful article on idleness, *Quitting the Paint Factory*. A time to engage simultaneously with mother nature at her finest and most unfettered, and a chance to wrestle with the questions that are posed by the mystery of our existence.

We all have a middle of nowhere. What's surprising, reading the stories that follow, is how diverse the places being called that actually are. For me, the common thread is this: from rowing on Lake Baikal to bicycling in Babushkina, it's clear that we all see the middle of nowhere as a chance to reconnect with nature, and perhaps most importantly, with the soul. It is far more than mere solitude. It is reaching a place that, no matter how many feet have trodden there before you, still feels like discovery – your own piece of virgin territory. The middle of nowhere is not generic nor is it a place that can necessarily be transplanted between individuals, for we each have our own conception of it. As you read the stories in this book, remember that they represent each writer's personal middle of nowhere. They are merely signposts or moments of inspiration on a journey. And remember, that to truly understand what it means to be in the middle of nowhere, you will have to go out and find it for yourself.

I will exchange a city for a sunset, the tramp of legions for a wind's wild cry, and all the braggard thrusts of steel triumphant, for one far summit blue against the sky.
— Monica Blake

Ben Saunders, Reykjavik, May 2006

Ben Saunders is a record-breaking long-distance skier, with three North Pole expeditions under his belt. He is the youngest person ever to ski solo to the North Pole and holds the record for the longest solo Arctic journey by a Briton. Between 2001 and 2004, Ben skied more than 2000km (1250 miles) in the high Arctic.

ARCTIC OCEAN

GREENLAND

Beaufort Sea

Arctic Circle

● Cambridge Bay
Canada. p58

Watkins Bjerge ●
Greenland. p112

● Alaska
USA. p20

● Mt Marathon   ● Chugach
Alaska, USA. p16   *Alaska, USA. p24*

Aappilattoq ●
Greenland. p108

Bering Sea

Gulf of
Alaska

*Hudson
Bay*

Wester Ross →
Scotland. p124

NORTH AMERICA

NORTH
ATLANTIC
OCEAN

NORTH
PACIFIC
OCEAN

● Montana
USA. p50

Yellowstone National Park ●
USA. p46

Great Basin National Park ●
USA. p36

Las Vegas ●   ● Paria Canyon
USA. p32   *Arizona, USA. p42*

Atlas Mountains →
Morocco. p120

El Hierro ●
Canary Islands. p116

Tropic of Cancer

Gulf of
Mexico

● St Maartens
Caribbean. p104

Caribbean Sea

CENTRAL
AMERICA

Mopti Region →
Mali. p128

Darien Gap ●● Bajira
Columbia. p66   *Columbia. p70*

Equator

● Cotopaxi Volcano
Ecuador. p62

Manu National Park ●
Peru. p92

● Tuamotu Archipelago
French Polynesia. p28

The Coastal Desert ● ● Machu Picchu
Peru. p74   *Peru. p82*

● Tonga
p12

● Atacama Desert
Bolivia. p96

Tropic of Capricorn

● Easter Island
Chile. p54

SOUTH
AMERICA

SOUTH
PACIFIC
OCEAN

SOUTH
ATLANTIC
OCEAN

● Puelo Valley
Chile. p78

● Patagonia
Argentina. p88

SOUTHERN OCEAN

● Neumayer Channel
Antarctica. p100

Antarctic Circle

ANTARCTICA

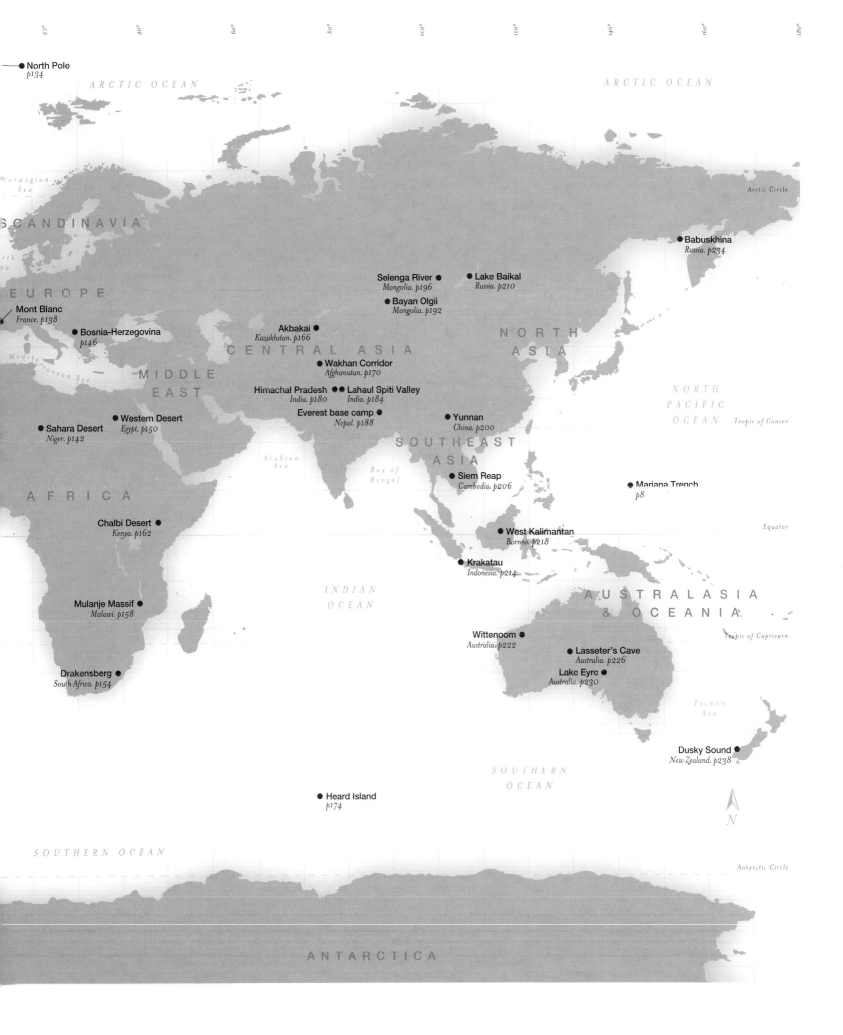

● North Pole
p134

ARCTIC OCEAN

ARCTIC OCEAN

*Norwegian
Sea*

Arctic Circle

SCANDINAVIA

● Babuskhina
Russia. p234

EUROPE

Selenga River ●
Mongolia. p196

● Lake Baikal
Russia. p210

NORTH
ASIA

Mont Blanc
France. p138

● Bayan Olgii
Mongolia. p192

● Bosnia-Herzegovina
p146

Akbakai ●
Kazakhstan. p166

CENTRAL ASIA

*Medi
ter
a*

Mediterranean Sea

MIDDLE
EAST

● Wakhan Corridor
Afghanistan. p170

NORTH

PACIFIC

OCEAN *Tropic of Cancer*

Himachal Pradesh ●● Lahaul Spiti Valley
India. p180   *India. p184*

● Western Desert
Egypt. p150

Everest base camp ●
Nepal. p188

● Yunnan
China. p200

● Sahara Desert
Niger. p142

AFRICA

*Arabian
Sea*

*Bay of
Bengal*

SOUTHEAST
ASIA

● Siem Reap
Cambodia. p206

● Mariana Trench
p8

Equator

Chalbi Desert ●
Kenya. p162

● West Kalimantan
Borneo. p218

INDIAN
OCEAN

● Krakatau
Indonesia. p214

AUSTRALASIA

& OCEANIA

Tropic of Capricorn

Mulanje Massif ●
Malawi. p158

Wittenoom ●
Australia. p222

● Lasseter's Cave
Australia. p226

Lake Eyre ●
Australia. p230

*Tasman
Sea*

Drakensberg ●
South Africa. p154

Dusky Sound ●
New Zealand. p238

SOUTHERN

OCEAN

● Heard Island
p174

N

SOUTHERN OCEAN

Antarctic Circle

ANTARCTICA

The Lowest Place on Earth

Craig Scutt

Red and huge, the dawn sun rises over the Pacific.

East of the Mariana Islands, 338km from Guam, the 50ft bathyscaph, or 'deep boat', is lowered into the water by a crane mounted on the side of its docking boat. I am the sole passenger on board. As the craft submerges, excited bubbles stream past the portholes made of reinforced glass. Through the clear surface-water I can see the sunlight glistening off plankton and plastic debris. The intercom crackles.

It is my support crew wishing me luck. They have the unenviable task of waiting for me on the surface. No matter how rough conditions get they will remain in position until I get back. They will also drive the bathyscaph remotely, guided by a combination of solar and satellite navigation systems. My life is in their hands.

Descending at a rate of 1.2m per second my journey into the Mariana Trench will take more than five hours to complete. The ascent should be quicker, when the bathyscaph does not have to stop and take samples of the water every 500m. After a few seconds I observe a school of fish being chased by a squid. Everywhere marine life appears out of the hazy blue, flitting like birds, effortlessly, serenely.

It is easy to be overwhelmed by a sense of the poetic, in awe of the perfect symmetry of life that exists below the waves. But I am too busy to devote much time to contemplation. In this environment I am reliant on technology, and on myself to monitor the technology to prevent a malfunction. Even so, as I pass through the twilight zone, the area of water where the penetration of the sun's rays is gradually reduced to zero, I notice how the light fades like a sun setting behind thick storm clouds, until finally disappearing over the horizon. As I enter the bathypelagic, or midnight zone, darkness takes over completely.

I am tempted to switch on the external lights but need to conserve power for when I reach the bottom. At a depth of 10,924m the landing spot, an area known as Challenger Deep, is literally the lowest place on earth.

The descent continues in silence, save for the throbbing hum of the engines and a low buzz emanating from the array of scientific equipment on board. As I enter the abyssal zone, more than 4km deep, my thoughts return to the surface, to those colleagues guiding me through this impenetrable black.

If they accidentally manoeuvre the bathyscaph over a hydrothermal vent, or too near a mud-spewing volcano, there is a chance the engines could fail. Even though I am wearing a suit designed to withstand the water pressure, I lack a sufficient supply of oxygen to have any chance of making it to the surface without the submersible vessel.

Finally the bathyscaph settles on the bottom. The counter reads 10,834m. This is disturbing. Either my colleagues guiding the bathyscaph have made a serious navigational error, or the surface has been covered with a fresh layer of sediment. Such a huge deposit could only be caused by a benthic storm.

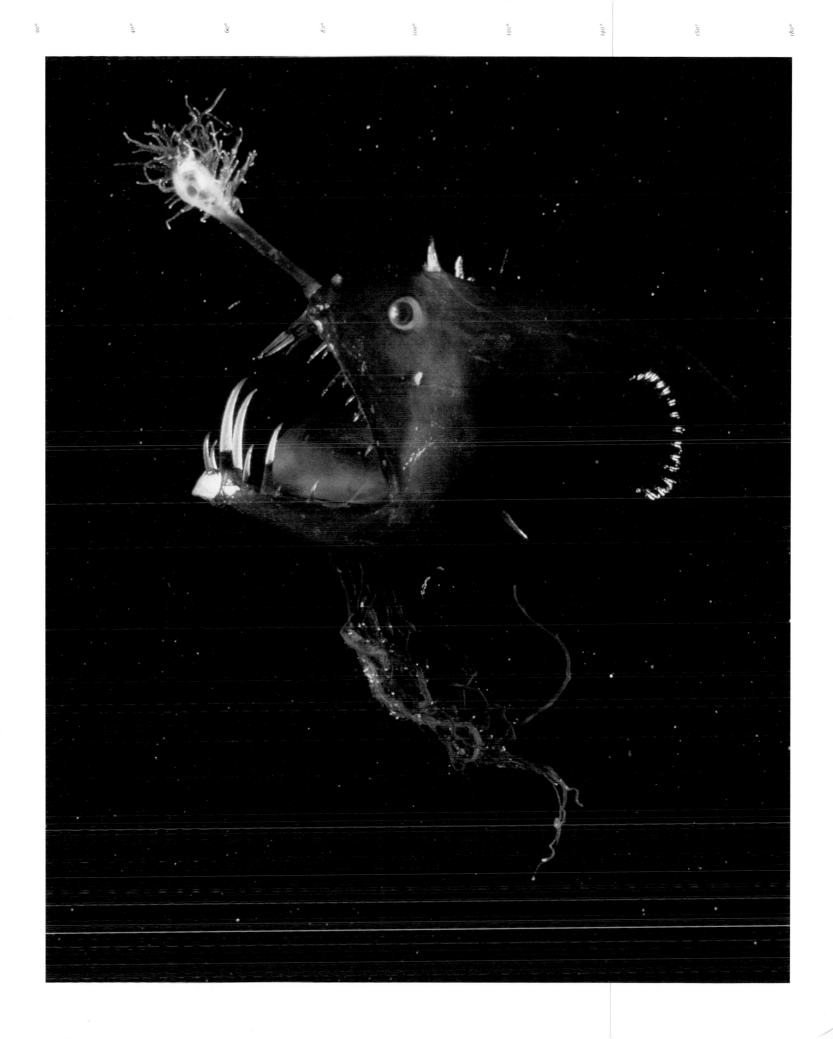

10

I strain my ears to hear the tiny, thin voices crackling through the speakers. My colleagues assure me I am in the right spot. Nobody knows what causes benthic storms, which operate much like blizzards on the earth's surface. These devastating events move fast, occur without warning, and can last for weeks. They also result in millions of tonnes of clay and sediment being displaced.

I try to picture the storm taking place. An avalanche of sediment and detritus roaring down the steep sides of the trench. If that were to happen when I'm outside the submersible then... I eliminate the scenario from my mind. Imagining it won't save me from being buried alive.

What matters is that the bathyscaph is stable. Around it the freezing, slow-moving water is calm. I focus my thoughts. I must ignore every sensible instinct and force myself to leave the bathyscaph. That's why I'm here. To conduct the final test for the deep-water suit I am wearing. In a few moments we will know whether or not it really is capable of withstanding the pressure generated beneath 11km of salt water.

The lights around the bathyscaph flicker into life, projecting unmercifully into the pitch and across the oozing mud of the sea floor. As I prepare to open the hatch the full realisation that if anything goes wrong there is no-one here to help me, slams into my brain. I have been training for this moment for three years. I couldn't be more prepared. My fear is instinctual.

The hatch opens. The water is now exerting a pressure of more than 1 tonne per square centimetre, across every millimetre of my body. Technically, I should be squashed like a bug. Much to my relief, I am still alive.

I hoist my body clumsily out of the bathyscaph. The deep-water suit is thick and restrictive. I extend the cable that connects me to the bathyscaph as I lower myself onto the primordial mud. I attach the specially designed extensions, modelled on Alaskan snowshoes, so that I can walk over the soft substrates without sinking.

The mission is already a success. I am still here. The suit works. Now I have time to engage in my thoughts. Approximately 14 minutes until the oxygen runs out.

I look up. The darkness is like being in a windowless room, blindfolded, with your eyes shut.

Suddenly a flash of colour shoots through the black wall. Green bioluminescence hovers above me, beyond the layer of light cast out from the bathyscaph. It is a creature nobody has ever seen. Its body is almost transparent. Gills shimmer in the creature's own neon glow. For an age we regard one another without moving. Marvelling, no doubt, at how alien we appear. Then abruptly, the nameless being turns and disappears, forever.

The elation caused by the encounter gives way to a sense of utter aloneness. Back on the surface my mission will earn me accolades, applause and meetings with presidents. But down here, in this formidable darkness, when there is still a chance I may not get back, I cannot escape feeling how insignificant every individual life is, in such a vast and still unexplored planet. And yet, I think, as I climb into the decompression chamber, how remarkable it is that I can feel at all.

Craig Scutt has lived on three continents and thinks everywhere's a good home. He hopes to come back as a Lonely Planet photographers' camera lens.

PREVIOUS: The abyssal zone hosts thousands of species of invertebrates and fish such as the angler fish, which uses a bioluminescent protrusion as a lure to attract its prey.

OPPOSITE: The hydrostatic pressure at the deepest point in the trench is over 8 tons per sq inch – the equivalent of someone trying to balance 50 jumbo jets on their head.

Living on Tonga Time

Gregor Clark

When Captain Cook first laid eyes on the Tongan archipelago two centuries ago, he named these the Happy Isles. Countless writers since then have remarked on the peaceful slowness of the local lifestyle. I can attest that happiness and slowness are still alive and well in Tonga, so much so that I almost didn't make it home…

My own trip to Tonga was something of a whimsical add-on, a chance for a little beachside R&R after six weeks of rugged tramping with a friend in New Zealand's back country. Neither of us knew anything about Tonga. We arrived on the main island, Tongatapu, with nothing more than a vague notion that we might find a peaceful off-the-beaten-track spot on one of the outer islands and stay there for two weeks.

Tongatapu, it turns out, was already sleepier than most places I had seen in the world, and not just because it was midnight when we arrived. The next morning we headed into the capital city of Nuku'alofa. It was the late 1990s, and thanks to Tonga's privileged location immediately west of the International Date Line, there was some buzz around town about throngs of tourists flocking here to see the first sunrise of the new millennium. But the streets seemed devoid of outsiders. Frankly, given Nuku'alofa's current somnolent state, a sudden tourist influx was hard to picture.

Could life possibly be even more relaxed on one of Tonga's outer islands? We got our answer by hopping on a little plane across to Lifuka, the not-so-throbbing hub of the Ha'apai island group. The runway was a grassy strip bordered by palm trees. After disembarking with a pair of other passengers, we walked to a nearby guesthouse, where later that evening the arrival of the twice-weekly ferry was compelling enough to hold the interest of the proprietress for half an hour. Next morning we ambled through the sleepy outskirts of Pangai, the island's only town, down to the waterfront park where the day's big event was watching the hauling in of the morning catch. Women shielded themselves from the tropical sun with brightly coloured umbrellas, while a long line of fishermen walked in towards shore disentangling their nets.

After an hour observing these local goings-on, we continued south on foot, wading across the shallow channel to the next island south, Uoleva. Here, we had heard, there were no stores, no towns, just endless white-sand beaches, coconut palms and a homespun, electricity-free 'resort'.

It didn't take us long to decide we had come to the right place. For 13 days we settled ever deeper into the soothing rhythm of the South Pacific. Each day melted into the next. Daylight hours were spent lying in hammocks, snorkelling among the kaleidoscopically colourful fish and coral at the far end of the island, walking long stretches of empty white sand, trading stories and collecting shells. Night-time meant reading by kerosene lanterns and candles, or listening to our host Soni's laughter filtering down from the kitchen as we walked to the waves' edge to gaze at the moon's reflection. We

ate foods gathered from the local sea and soil – bananas, homemade guava jam, fried fish, fish curry, fish in coconut cream, giant clams and various root crops that never tasted quite like the 'sweet potatoes' Soni insisted they were. My journal entries refer constantly to the slow-paced simplicity of it all.

A fortnight passed before we knew it. Mesmerised by the idyllic tranquillity of our daily routine, we were caught fully off guard by the need to return to civilisation. On the eve of our departure it suddenly occurred to us that the tidal gods might smile less favourably on our return trip than they had on our arrival. Soni checked the tide table and gave us the bad news – crossing back to the airport on foot the next morning would be impossible, as the water would be way too high at the time our plane was due to leave. But in typical Tongan fashion he set our minds at rest. A friend could come by with a boat, he said. What time did we need him there? 8am? No worries. It would all be arranged.

Daybreak found us standing on the beach, two sunburned *palangi* (that's Tongan for white folks) waiting for a ride. Slowly the full incongruity of what we were trying to do became apparent. We had a plane to catch, in fact a plane we *needed* to catch if we were going to make our international connection, but everyone else was living on Tonga time. Eight o'clock passed, then 8.30. Repeated questions to Soni yielded nothing more reassuring than 'he will

be here soon'. At 8.45 Soni headed back inland, and we looked at each other quizzically.

I'm normally not one to fret about arriving late for a plane. Indeed my usual mantra is 'the less time spent at the airport, the better', so cutting it close had become something of an art for me. Even so, I had never missed a flight in my life. Now for once I was beginning to worry, as we stared out into the blank Pacific, with only the distant dot of a passing boat every few minutes or so to give us any shred of hope. We really knew we were in trouble when Soni re-emerged with a pair of brooms and two large sheets of cloth. Moments later we were brandishing the broomsticks above our heads and wildly waving the cloth to signal our plight to any boat who might take mercy on us.

A passing fishing vessel finally nosed in to shore, and after some negotiation we piled our backpacks over the gunwales and clambered aboard, just in time to glimpse our plane landing in the distance a couple of miles north. Ten minutes later, as we chugged slowly across the inlet, we watched it take off again, abandoning us to an uncertain fate.

It could have been worse. After all, we were still in Tonga.

Gregor Clark's insatiable love of foreign languages and wild places has sent him exploring 'what's around the next bend' in 50 countries, including remote spots such as Easter Island, Greenland and the Galápagos.

PREVIOUS: Even in the country's capital, locals gather at low tide to gather a variety of shellfish off Tongatapu beach.

OPPOSITE: Almost two-thirds of Tongans live on the island of Tongatapu, which is one of the reasons that 73 islands within the kingdom are uninhabited by humans.

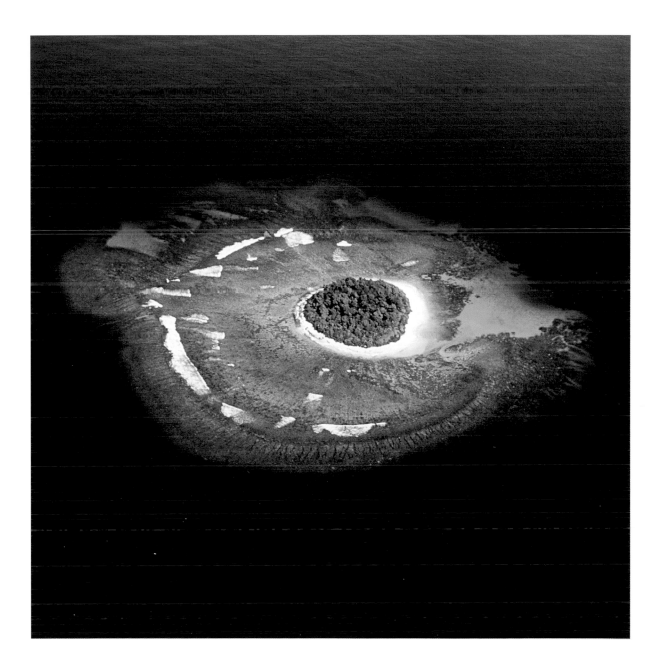

Not Lost, but Searching

Jeff Campbell

It's 3 July, and I sit halfway up Mt Marathon outside Seward, Alaska. It's 9pm, but the air is late-afternoon bright. I am with a half-Inuit Alaskan, Eric, who I have recently met, and our plan is to spend the night here. We have sleeping bags, beer, food and cameras with which to record the runners in Seward's famous 5.6km Fourth of July foot-race, which will pass right by us in the morning. Eric assures me this is the best spot; he's done this before. Fireworks explode in celebration, set not against the sky but against the blue-steel waters of Resurrection Bay.

It's a bizarre perspective, looking down on fireworks in daylight, and yet I'm thinking of my friend Chris, who is somewhere in town, looking up. Chris and I drove to Alaska from Long Island intending to help clean up the Exxon Valdez oil spill. We came because we'd heard they paid good money, and it was a noble cause, but most of all it was an excuse for adventure. I was sick of New York and had recently broken up with my girlfriend, so I quit my job and hit the road, thinking I would move to San Francisco when it was over.

We had arrived in Seward two days earlier to find that Exxon had quit hiring non-Alaskans. We were angry about this, as were locals – who suspected the company of cutting costs in the guise of 'helping' communities, since not enough Alaskans were applying to be able to finish the job by winter – but there was nothing to do except mourn our unexpected lack of purpose and income, as well as our dwindling budget.

We had met Eric that first day as well, and readily accepted his offer to join him for the Fourth of July festivities.

Mt Marathon rises like a weathered Inca pyramid above Seward. That day we had started early so we could go slow: the slope is deceptively steep. Once above tree line, the mountainside is mostly barren and exposed. Wide fields of crumbled slate shift easily underfoot, and they sent us sliding backwards with each step – it was like hiking a gravel pile. We took many breaks and struggled just walking; I couldn't imagine anyone running to the top and then, good lord, running back down. It seemed like if you tripped, you'd sail directly onto Seward, landing with a cartoon-like puff of smoke.

Stopping to admire the view, we felt suspended in midair.

The sensation became too much for Chris. He grew panicky, and then without warning he dropped to the ground and refused to go any further. We implored him; Eric's spot was just ahead. Chris tried. He gave Eric his pack and took my arm, wobbled to his feet, but after a step or two he collapsed again. He tried to force himself to get up but couldn't. Panting, hyperventilating, eyes wild, literally grabbing the earth with both hands, he pleaded over and over that he couldn't breathe – then finally he made a mad dash down the slope, tearing at his clothes, and dry-heaving into some bushes.

We sat, protected within the foliage, until Chris calmed down. Clearly, he was done – every

moment on the mountain had become torture – the only question was whether I'd go back with him. It was my first instinct, to return and ensure he was really all right, but I fought it because, underneath, I was childishly put out by Chris's inability to stay. Why had we come if not to experience things like this? Chris said he didn't want me to leave, said that if he kept descending he'd be fine, and selfishly I agreed. For the first time in three weeks, Chris and I parted ways.

In the morning, cold, thick fog blankets the mountainside. Eric and I can see only 9m or 10m, and out of the mist the runners come. By the time they reach us, they are descending. They look haggard, beaten, jaws slack, staggering in barely controlled, loping steps. Some are covered in dirt, long scrapes down their legs. At the top, to gain seconds, people are using a snowfield as a slide. I think, this isn't a foot-race, it's a brawl. I can't believe people are willingly doing this for fun. By the time they cross the finish line, numerous runners will be bleeding; some will have lost shoes, torn clothes and suffered multiple spills in scree and headlong tumbles into trees. Every year, a few dozen contestants never finish and must be rescued from the mountain.

Afterwards, when I meet Chris in our tent, he tells me he's leaving. He says the Alaska trip was a mistake. He's still agitated, talking and thinking too fast. I can have the tent and the car, he says, and he'll hitchhike back the next day. That's crazy, I argue, but I can't talk him out of it. I force him to call Long Island to tell someone he's coming. I don't want the responsibility of being the only person who knows. He only has about $50.

Something besides heights is driving Chris' vertigo, but I don't know what it is and he doesn't say. He's gone too far, too high, and he is scrambling, completely overwhelmed by a sudden desperate need to be home.

I don't know where my home is. About as far as I can get from everyone and everything I know, I am alone – not lost, but searching. I realise my 'adventure' has been a test, an effort to strip away all that is familiar to see what is left. We aren't so different from the marathon runners after all.

Incredibly, Chris hitchhikes across the continent in three days. I stay in Alaska another two months and continue to San Francisco. It is the right decision for both of us.

As far as he knows, Jeff Campbell still holds the world record for fastest back-country camping trip in Denali National Park, Alaska, at 35 minutes, 15 seconds. The mosquitoes won.

PREVIOUS: Runners have to overcome dust, cramps and vertigo as they negotiate the treacherously steep descent during the 5.6km Mt Marathon Race.

OPPOSITE: With Mt Marathon in the background, the historic city of Seward forms an aptly picturesque gateway to the Alaskan Interior and Kenai Fjords National Park.

Knee-Deep in Powder-like Snow

Karl Bushby

**Tuesday 22 December and Wednesday
23 December 2004**
65°15.085′ N, 148°43.959′ W

Tuesday was much of the same until I reached a large open lake. It's here I had lost the trail, never to see it again. I made camp feeling pretty much beaten and lacking in morale, which forced me to sit and have a rethink. Today has been brutal. I'd lost the track and tried to make some headway, but I just did not have the strength. I'd wasted most of the day looking for the yellow-tape trail markers and not finding any had consequently exhausted all my options. At this rate, I'm not going to make it to the hot springs before this leg's rations run out, and you don't want to get caught out here with no calorie intake. In three days I've moved about 1.5km and I'm damned if I can keep this up.

I chose this cross-country route because it cut a good deal off the road distance between Fairbanks and Manley Hot Springs. My route took me in a more direct line, while the road formed the other two sides of a triangle. However, this awful route has taken far longer than the road. The idea had been to follow in the wake of the snow machines that had used the winter trails, and compressed the snow as they progressed. Unfortunately, it had been so cold recently that very few people were coming out at all and so much snow had fallen that it quickly buried any tracks. Consequently I'm left knee-deep in powder-like snow. My ski shoes are of little use and both my sled and I simply flounder.

I use the satellite phone to call Ramey in Fairbanks and let him know that I'm having a spot of trouble.

'I might try ditching the sled and making for the hot springs in light order. If someone could maybe come out from the Manley direction and meet me on the road at the hot springs and we could then maybe use the machine to form a trail.'

Ramey sets about working on the problem. I sit tight on Wednesday to give Ramey a chance to sort things out before I move on.

Thursday 24 December 2004
65°16.291′ N, 148°51.097′ W

Late Wednesday night, Ramey had confirmed that Dick will try to get out on Sunday with the snow machines. This morning I have one last bash at moving the sled, getting it a short distance before calling time. I really do not want to leave it like this but feel I have little choice. I have to reach the hot springs to meet Dick or I will miss the opportunity to get out of here. It is now -40°C and bitching cold. I stumble around pulling things from my sled that I might need. In these conditions I don't know how long it will take me to get to the hot springs on a compass bearing. There's no trail, and I have to find three log cabins that are only 8.8km away as the crow flies. However, that distance can be deceiving and I don't want to get caught out tonight in this temperature. I'll need my sleeping bags for sure, my flask of hot chocolate, my satellite phone, my warm coat

and my laptop (I'd rather die than leave that to the wolves). I take two days' supply of food and a tank of gas, to get a wood fire going if I need to. I throw all these items into a large waterproof bag then use two nylon straps and karabiners to attach it to my harness. I set off at best speed, which in these conditions is still very slow. It's just one foot in front of the other and keep going. I can see the hills clearly in front of me so it isn't a problem as far as direction goes. Once I'm close to the hot springs I'll use the GPS to home in.

After only 90m my breathing is pretty heavy, it's hard going for sure off trail. Then the terrain starts to get nasty. These flats are crisscrossed with small ridges and rivers that have steep banks. Once in these, it's hard to get out. There is then an open area of fallen trees that is covered with snow. This part is definitely the worst. There might be only about 15m of fallen trees, but it's one hell of a job. These areas seem to be coming in strips. I'd get about 30m of forest and then another 15m of felled timber that is completely covered with deep snow. Although looking flat initially, beneath the snow lies a tangled minefield of all sorts of traps. I struggle and fall for what seems a frustrating eternity, traversing

these areas with the speed of a fly crossing fly-paper. By the time I start climbing into the hills it's already getting dark. The brush and trees at times are thickly entwined, making short work of my now less than waterproof bag.

I lose track of time, deep in my own thoughts, or rather my self-pity. At last I stumble across a firm piece of snow. I look up to find myself staring at a piece of tape…a track! About a mile from the hot springs I have come across a track that leads all the way in. A much better track then I'd had before, with clear indentations that had been left by a snow machine. It's also well-marked with orange tape (not that it matters in the dark). By 7.30pm I come across a cabin. The -45°C. Heat… All I can think about is heat. There's a small wood stove, a pile of cut wood and some matches. Within the hour I'm sitting stripped to my wet but warm long johns, bathed in a bright orange glow and steaming nicely. My kit and clothing dry above a roaring wood stove.

Karl Bushby, an ex-paratrooper in his 30s, is attempting to become the first person to complete an unbroken round-the-world walk. He is now halfway through the 57,972km trek and is due to complete it in 2011.

PREVIOUS: The sun is brightest during winter but appears dimmer in the north because it hangs lower in the sky and its rays must pass through more layers of the atmosphere.

OPPOSITE: An ancient Inuit legend describes the northern lights, or aurora borealis, as flaming torches carried by departed souls guiding travellers to the afterlife.

61°N 144°W
ALASKA, USA

The Alaska Factor

David Waag

Alaska is in a league of its own when it comes to wilderness and the Chugach Range is no exception. Rising from sea level to over 4000m, the Chugach sponges moisture from the Gulf of Alaska and is home to massive glaciers that spill down to the sea and reach into the Alaskan wilderness in all directions. Dramatic snow- and ice-covered peaks rise out of the glaciers like cliffs out of the sea. However, my two ski partners and I have been in Alaska for a week now and have yet to see a clear day, or any high peaks for that matter. Locals tell us that the mountains received more snow in March and April than they did most of the winter. The latest squall leaves snow on the peaks surrounding us and the Chugach Range has yet to reveal itself from behind the sea of clouds.

The unsettled weather grounds us at the pilot's airstrip as he cannot fly into the region without good visibility. Our plan, to explore the range on skis, requires a short flight into the Nelchina Glacier for access and will end as we ski out of the range and into Valdez. Only about 160km as the crow flies, the route could be covered in a matter of days, but we have a full month to explore the rugged and remote reaches of the range. Given the current weather scenario, we bide our time while camped at the airstrip, reviewing maps, playing cards and sorting supplies.

Even at the airstrip, the scale of the landscape around us is massive. The 'Alaska Factor', as I call it, makes it difficult to gauge distance and scale. The landscape here is misleading; everything is on a scale several magnitudes larger than anything I have experienced before. A few hundred metres becomes a kilometre. Backcountry travel is measured in days, not actual distance. And the weather, everyone talks about the weather, and how it must be taken seriously.

Following several slow days spent waiting for the weather to settle, our pilot arrives and declares the weather good enough for our flight into the glacier. In classic Alaskan style, we do not begin flying until almost 9pm. There is no danger of it getting dark any time soon, as we are north of 60 degrees latitude. The lingering evening light just adds to the atmosphere. As the pilot predicted, mixed weather at the airstrip yields to blue sky above the Nelchina Glacier. The snow and ice glow under the evening sky as I step from the plane and haul my gear clear of the plane's path. Surrounded by the terrain we have been dreaming about for months, we watch the plane fly off down the glacier and leave us to establish our first camp as the sun dips towards the horizon.

The Chugach is synonymous with a steep, rugged landscape and records more than 1500cm of precipitation each year, much of which falls as snow. Dwarfed by the landscape, we are apprehensive about the massive faces that rise off the glacier all around us. We choose small peaks and bowls to familiarise ourselves with the terrain and seek solace in our small camp each night. Our daily routine takes on a new significance as we busy ourselves between

26

explorations with the mundane tasks of melting snow for water and preparing meals.

Nearly two weeks into our adventure we continue to climb and ski our way through the mountains, in awe of the terrain. Moving camp becomes our most difficult task, but once a new camp is established we are rewarded with a new set of peaks, ridges and skiable terrain. The 'Alaska Factor' takes its toll on us as we set our sites on peaks that appear within our daily range, only to return exhausted or unsuccessful.

The good-weather window we have enjoyed thus far closes as we move camp over a small pass. What began as ridge-top winds and high clouds in the morning now reduces visibility to 30m and forces us to trade our sunglasses for goggles. We set camp early. Uncertain of our proximity to the large faces that surround us, we make the best estimation we can and dig in.

Wind slams our tent like an angry grizzly and the walls sag like potbellies under the weight of wind-packed snow. Our living space shrinks at the hand of the storm. We hunker down inside, thinly veiled behind the walls of our tent. We alternate the responsibility of digging out the tent every few hours and listen apprehensively to snow slides releasing from nearby faces. Day bleeds into night and the confines of our tent remind us of our insignificance in the larger landscape. By the third day, we are ready for a break from the tents. Venturing into the storm, however, serves little purpose, as travel is out of the question in the current conditions. Stories of 10- and 14-day storm cycles fill our heads while cribbage and gin rummy fill our time.

Finally, on the fourth day of the cycle the wind recedes overnight. Following a fitful rest, the morning silence wakes me. Peering from the tent, I am greeted by a foggy but calm morning. The fog is sure to burn off with time and I press through the door flaps to enjoy the stillness of the day. From what I can see around me, the storm has left an impressive paint job on the landscape. I work to fire up the stove and make a long desired cup of coffee. Much to my surprise a small songbird flitters in out of the fog and lands on our tent. Noticeably disoriented, the bird is the first outside sign of life I have seen since waving goodbye to our pilot some 20-odd days earlier. Unfazed by our presence, the bird stays close by flitting between the tent and our various skis for a perch as the morning fog begins to clear. The analogy of the bird blown in by the storm and lost in the fog is not lost on us. The storm cycle is a good dose of reality in an otherwise rather alien landscape. As the morning haze burns away, the sun begins to warm the cold air and the bird takes to its wings, no doubt in search of a more hospitable landscape. Understanding that a second storm could easily stop us in our tracks once more, we pack our camp and decide it is time that we too continue our adventure in search of a more hospitable landscape.

David Waag is an Oregon-based writer with a passion for mountains and skiing. His travels have taken him to remote mountain ranges in India, Alaska, China, South America, Iceland and Canada.

PREVIOUS: Every year these ephemeral sculptures attract a dedicated group of climbers who brave the elements to tackle the unique and hard-core ascents.

OPPOSITE: The constant threat of falling through a thin layer of snow or ice into a hidden crevasse makes glacier travel one of the most dangerous ways to explore the wilderness.

Floating on the Ocean, Firmly Fixed on Land

Celeste Brash

As I boarded the tiny plane to Manihi, I reflected that perhaps I'd gone mad. I didn't want to go to Manihi and I hardly knew where the Tuamotu archipelago was on the map. Yet I had agreed to meet my boyfriend (who was travelling by sail boat) on the little-known atoll of Ahe, in the middle of the South Pacific.

I'd recently come to learn that Ahe had no airstrip and was serviced by one cargo ship per month, which I'd missed. So I was heading for the next best thing, Manihi, the island next door where I hoped I could find some sort of transportation to take me across approximately 30km of open ocean.

By an amazing stroke of chance, I sat next to the only person on the plane who was going to Ahe. Through a mix of exaggerated sign language and a few phrases of leftover high-school French, I managed to communicate with this friendly old Chinese man that I too was trying to get to Ahe. When the plane landed in Manihi, my new friend took me under his arm and led us directly to a dilapidated speedboat piloted by two weathered young Frenchmen.

It was only then that my surroundings hit me. An atoll is, well, not an island at all. I'd learned about Darwin's theory of atoll formation (coral reef forms around high islands eventually forming small islets – the island itself slowly sinks until all that is left is the ring of coral) but nothing had prepared me for the real thing. As far as I was concerned, the vast translucent blue of the lagoon, the graceful, sweeping beaches of the islets, the breezy palms, were akin to one of the natural wonders of the world. This place could easily be put in the same category as the Grand Canyon or the northern lights. Being on an atoll is like floating on the ocean and being firmly fixed on land at the same time. The amazing part was the thought that there are hundreds of atolls scattered throughout the world's oceans like sparkling confetti, lost and forgotten to the rest of the mountainous world.

My companions and I hopped into our little boat, and off we went. We swept past empty islets of bleached coral and spiny shrubs, past Manihi's flower-filled village of Paeua and out the lagoon's pass towards the open Pacific. There was just a wisp of a breeze, a few smoky clouds in the sky and a marginal swell, so we were able to go full speed towards what looked like an empty space beyond the horizon.

Within 10 minutes, Manihi was disconcertedly far away and I had an in-the-moment revelation that I was with three strange men in an unreliable boat heading towards what looked like the middle of nowhere. Before I could get too nervous, one of the Frenchmen pointed to the horizon. If I squinted my eyes I could just barely make out what looked like a line of black dots hovering above the edge of the earth. Within minutes the dots became lines, and then, visibly, the tops of coconut palms and our first view of Ahe. Manihi was disappearing behind us, and within an hour we were nearing our destination.

As we skirted the exterior reef of the atoll on our way towards the pass, dolphins played in the wake from our boat and I wondered if any

moment in my life would ever be more simple and perfect. The outer crust of Ahe was sienna red, the ocean an inky blue and the waves crashed clear over the reef, bringing the contrasting colours together. We reached the pass, which was wider than Manihi's, and there was a soft scent of flowers blowing through the white, palm-ruffled curves of the entry to the lagoon.

We jetted through the pass and into the lagoon where I could see nearly the entire circle of the low-lying, frond-covered islets that comprised Ahe's entire landmass. This lagoon felt different from the busy one we'd just left in Manihi. There was something delicate, sensual and homey, as if this atoll was an exotic, peaceful nest in the midst of the ocean's vastness.

It took us about half an hour to reach the village from the pass, and there it was: the sail boat with my very pleased and surprised boyfriend waiting on board. We didn't know it yet, but he would later come to live here with his father and I would join him a few years later. I would spend over five years living on Ahe, which had only begun to charm me, but that is another story…

Celeste Brash raised her two babies on remote Ahe atoll with no plumbing, doctors or anything resembling civilisation. Her adventures in motherhood continue to teach her that children, more than anyone, really enjoy off-the-beaten-track travel.

PREVIOUS: The highest point on Manihi, like the other 75 coral islands and atolls that make up the Tuamotu chain, is only about 3m above sea level.

OPPOSITE: Even among local Tahitians Ahe was practically unknown until the discovery of rare black pearls growing in the protected lagoon that is almost completely encircled by impenetrable coral.

Invisible Stars

Janet Brunckhorst

Even in autumn, the California desert is a heat haze. Towns too small to pollute the sky with light squat between grey-blue mesas. Coyotes lope around at dusk, and tortoises move faster than you'd expect – faster than you could move in this heat. I've been photographing star trails in the desert night and pointing the lens into flowering Joshua trees and the lonely sky by day. It's empty here, and silent, and it feels old. We've been in the desert a couple of days, and it's time to move on. As we pull out onto the highway, we realise we haven't planned a route beyond Joshua Tree.

America's highways are the stuff of cinematic legend. Ours is the only car on the road in an *Easy Rider* landscape. Miles are punctuated by billboards and little else. This is a road trip, the way road trips were meant to be.

We drive fast and aimlessly, but soon, inevitably there's a choice to be made. We have to pick a destination. My boyfriend and local guide gives me two options: San Diego or Las Vegas. San Diego has a zoo, and I've heard that the sun always shines, and of course we could go down to Mexico. And I've never been interested in going to Vegas. It doesn't appeal to my sense of adventure, my love of open spaces, my (let's face it) slightly pretentious hankering for cultural experiences. But out on the long, flat highway, it seems like the only logical destination.

I need to see the city that could grow out of this.

We pass the first casino at the border. Gambling's illegal in most of California, but you don't have to get all the way to Sin City to indulge your passion. A couple of yards into Nevada is a sad-looking establishment for those who just can't wait. We press on towards the real thing. And an hour or so later, there it is. Vegas just kind of appears in front of you, rising up out of the desert like a cartoon mirage. Not a mere shimmer of sun on sand, but the whole shebang – palm trees, fountains, nomads' tents, dancing girls. Only this mirage doesn't vanish as you approach. Vegas is solid alright. Whether it's real is another question.

Compared with Australia's sprawling cities, Vegas is a shock as you approach along the highway. One minute you're cruising in the rolling desert; the next, you're on the Strip. No urban sprawl, no ordinary family homes with kids and dogs playing in the yard. Just Vegas, like you always imagined it. We're tourists, so the first thing we do is cruise the Strip, wondering where we'll stay. It's the middle of a searing desert day, and every light in town is burning. This place sucks electricity like nowhere else on earth. You can see its glare from the moon. From street level, it's nothing short of hilarious. Jean Baudrillard once likened Las Vegas to a theme park – just like Disneyland, only people live there, I think he said. My first five minutes in Vegas are spent doubled over with laughter at this spectacle trying to pass itself off as a city. Or many cities – we're driving through the world's greatest hits, crammed into a mile of highway. Shall we stay in Paris or New York? A view of the pyramids might be nice.

You can't do a U-turn on the Strip, and we've passed the last grand edifice. We turn off the Strip in order to head back. And here it is – the other Las Vegas, the backstage area. You'll never see a photograph of this place, and if you did, you wouldn't know it was Vegas. It doesn't even look ordinary – it's as though all the colour has been used up on the Strip and the rest of the town has to express itself in 256 shades of grey. Grey prefab houses with grey, limp laundry. Casinos that have grown up ugly and stunted, as though their seeds fell among rocks. We cruise around trying to find our way back to the highway, feeling both privileged and a little awkward to have glimpsed this gritty reality. Like a showgirl who covers her dark circles and stretch marks for the show, Vegas doesn't really want you to see this.

Back on the Strip, every uniformed waiter, doorman, dealer, clerk, usher and concierge wears a badge bearing their name and home town. Most badges sport US cities – New York, Los Angeles, Chicago, Wichita, Detroit – and the occasional foreign land is in the mix (Fiji, Eritrea). But the clerk who checks us in at the hotel has the most curious badge of all: David, Las Vegas. He's *from* here. From *here,* from the theme park city. He looks like an ordinary guy. He has the same polished, impersonal smile as everyone else who works here. Maybe it comes more naturally when you've been around it all your life. Maybe he was born here – somewhere

off the Strip is a hospital where people can be born. There are schools where children can learn, and supermarkets where parents can buy groceries, and even malls and driving schools and sports stadiums and parks with barbecues and all kinds of other trappings of ordinary life. Maybe there is a real Vegas, but I don't want to see it after all. Now that I'm back on the set, I'm taken with its gaudy excess. I enjoy David's seamless performance. I'm happy to believe the lie of unblemished skin.

I spend a desert night taking pictures of car trails and casino lights; the light pollution renders the stars invisible. Walking back to the hotel after a Cirque du Soleil spectacular, I spot them. On the lawn in front of the Luxor pyramid, a family of ducklings has found a vent to spend the night on. Bills in, bums out, they form a fluffy yellow circle on the grass; the epitome of family-friendly Vegas. It's as charming as it is bizarre. We walk back to our huge room full of mirrors, ready to believe anything.

The next day, we head back out of Vegas and into the desert, which was there all along. Driving north towards San Francisco, it's already hard to believe that we were really there.

Janet Brunckhorst likes to mix a little pampering into her adventure travel (or is it the other way around?). She recently spent two subzero nights in a tent at the Grand Canyon, and later described the experience as 'fun'.

PREVIOUS: In the Death Valley National Park, about 150km from Las Vegas, the city's blazing neon lights are the dominant cause of light pollution.

OPPOSITE: Las Vegas is touted as one of the fastest-growing, most liveable cities in America and away from the Strip, Vegas suburbia is as regimented and humdrum as anywhere.

The Loneliest National Park in America

Andrew Bain

I'm leaving Las Vegas, just as the movie suggested. For 500km I drive north through the grey, mountain-ribbed desert, with sagebrush as my only company. For these desert-encased hours there are just three flyspeck towns and a gash in the earth known as Cathedral Gorge. Lightning strikes snap at the earth from a cloudless sky. Finally, I turn east at US50, the highway dubbed the 'loneliest road in America', in an area described by explorer John Fremont in the 19th century as 'contents almost unknown', and enter Great Basin National Park.

What draws me so far from the bells and yells of Vegas is as much the distance as the natural curiosities bundled together inside Nevada's only national park: a 4000m mountain far removed from any of North America's major ranges, visible 180km before I reach it; the oldest trees in the world; and a glacier where none rightly belongs, at the heart of the US' largest desert. This, not Vegas, is my Nevada, its riches far exceeding those that spew from, and are swallowed by, the Strip.

Fremont's phrase has never really gone out of date. Great Basin remains one of the least visited national parks in the country, receiving around 80,000 people a year (the Great Smoky Mountains National Park gets around nine million). It's near to nothing and close to nobody. Even the town that bills itself as the park gateway is 170km away in Utah. Like the highway, Great Basin may be the loneliest national park in America.

I drive to the end of the main park road, high on 3982m Wheeler Peak, where I must continue my journey on foot, choosing between trails to the Wheeler Peak summit or the glacier beneath. I begin with the mountain.

For a time, as I amble through the grasslands around Stella Lake, it's just me and a few grazing deer. Then, on the quartzite summit ridge, it's just me and the pains of altitude. Two days ago I was at sea level in Los Angeles, now I'm less than 500m below the highest point in the lower 48 states, gripped by headache, nausea and wilting muscles.

As compensation I have a godlike view: the Great Basin desert stretching to an indescribably wide horizon, its sands so pale they resemble clouds seen from above. That I share this desert with the likes of Vegas, Reno and Nevada's infamous 'ranches' seems improbable.

The next morning, through dawn's deceptive desert chill, I set out on the path to the glacier, the darkened spruce and the junkyard of boulders that hide the earth creating the effect of an enchanted forest. Squirrels flee my approach and woodpeckers tap out a rhythm like a morning alarm.

The desert sun follows me onto the mountain, into the cirque and up to the nose of the glacier. In the brewing heat this glacial refugee seems an icy absurdity, a practical joke of nature, not unlike finding a sand dune in a rainforest. It's easy to believe I might still be here when the glacier isn't – maybe it will melt in the time that I stand here – but my feelings of immortality are quickly

shattered, for just a few hundred metres away stands a reminder that I am but a blink on the face of the earth. Among the scree stands a grove of bristlecone pines, the world's oldest trees.

These trees, twisted and polished by millennia of snow, wind and ice, are often described as having a grotesque beauty – Jack Nicholson in wood – but as I stand among them, with their smooth grains as orange as sandstone, I realise that 'beauty' alone will suffice.

There are four bristlecone pine groves clinging to the tree line of the Snake Range, which forms the spine of the national park, and this is the most accessible. The oldest known bristlecone (and hence the world's oldest living tree), at 4950 years, once grew here but was cut down in 1964, 22 years before the creation of the national park. Remaining pines have been dated to 3500 years, making them botanical babies when compared against a 4600-year-old bristlecone pine in California's White Mountains. Even the needles on a bristlecone pine might survive for 40 years; they could have been here since before I was born.

When Jesus and, 500 years before him, Buddha walked the earth, these trees were already mature. Billions of people have lived and died in the time that a bristlecone pine has grown just a few feet. Suddenly, I feel about as temporary as the snow that's beginning to march in over Wheeler Peak. Perhaps the glacier will outlast me, after all.

Andrew Bain is a Melbourne-based writer who has cycled around Australia – a journey that became the book Headwinds *– and trekked and paddled his way through various bits of five continents.*

PREVIOUS: The UN declared 2006 the International Year of Deserts in response to threats posed to delicate desert ecosystems such as the Sand Mountain Dunes in the Great Basin.

OPPOSITE: The origins of the bristlecone pine stretch back 100 million years. It has adapted to some of the earth's toughest environments where, without competition from other plants, it has flourished.

OVERLEAF: High evaporation rates and scarce rainfall mean the Great Basin will never support extensive human settlement, leaving the region's pines, geysers and mineral pools to astound the few explorers passing through.

The Unsocial Desert

Jeff Campbell

The Arizona Strip is the name for the bit of desolation that straddles the Utah-Arizona state line. It's just one small portion of the immense geological marvel that is the USA's Southwest Desert. Modern-day travellers mostly avoid it, since compared with surrounding high-profile wonders like the Grand Canyon to the south, Zion and Bryce Canyons to the north, and Lake Powell to the east, it is every inch the dry, unyielding, rattlesnake-infested wasteland promised in Zane Grey novels and old Hollywood Westerns. It remains a place where, as Wallace Stegner wrote over 60 years ago, it's 'fairly easy to be unsocial or anti-social'.

Notable mainly for what it lacks – water, shade, arable soil, a way across – the land has one thing in abundance: solitude. America's pioneers cursed it – and its cartographers ignored it, mapping this region last of all others in the USA – but there have always been those who have treasured the Strip precisely for its uninviting qualities.

The most notorious have been Mormon fundamentalists, an unsanctioned splinter sect of the Mormon religion that considers polygamy one of God's holiest doctrines. Polygamists make up the majority of Colorado City and Big Water, two of the largest towns on the Strip; for the most part, residents stick to themselves, happy to let the desert shield them from public morality and inconvenient state laws banning plural marriage. Lacking any other good excuse to make trouble, the government usually leaves them alone too.

Others who have taken to this 'unsocial' desert include 19th-century outlaws, who thwarted capture by hiding among its crumbled mesas and tortured canyons. One of the most famous was also a lapsed (or Jack) Mormon: Butch Cassidy, leader of the Wild Bunch. No doubt, outlaws still find this a good place to elude authorities.

Native Americans have always lived here. The Kaibab Paiute survived in isolated peace and what they considered prosperity for over 600 years – until Father Silvestre Escalante encountered them in 1776. Even then, nothing but the white man's diseases really bothered them for another century. Only the industrious Mormons ever competed with the Paiutes to try and make something of this dry parcel, and compared with their successes elsewhere, they failed miserably.

Solitary poets and artists have also found abundant spiritual inspiration here. Everett Ruess is one of the most well-known only because he loved this desert so completely he succeeded in literally vanishing into it (just north of the Strip, along the Escalante River), never to be seen again. Most people who visit today have his same goal in mind – to lose themselves, if not scour their souls clean, in this harsh landscape – just without Ruess' level of commitment. A refreshing day or two, even a few hours, and the quiet tourist hubbub of Kanab or Page can suddenly seem ever-so-welcome.

But invariably, when that antisocial mood strikes, and the question narrows to only where one should go, not whether, the Arizona Strip

44

blossoms into a horn of plenty: for myself, I prefer the slot canyons of the Paria Canyon– Vermillion Cliffs Wilderness Area.

The wilderness area is just across Hwy 89 from Big Water and downriver from a re-created Western movie set (the actual movie set and the town it was based on both having been washed away by flash floods). I like Paria Canyon for three reasons. One, it is relatively easy to get to. Two, its slot canyons have only a few junctions, so it's hard to become actually lost. And three, it's 61km long, so I can get as far away from people as my heart desires and my preparations allow.

When you're within slot canyons, the immense vistas that are the hallmark of the Southwest – where great, empty sagebrush plains roll into tattered mesas and high plateaus; where geology appears exactly as it is, as an unforgiving, heaving tempest – are hidden. Instead, my relationship with the land becomes intensely intimate; in Paria Canyon's Wire Pass, for instance, the walls are at times barely wide enough for your body, and the endless sky is reduced to a neon slash of blue.

Forced to focus on the intricacies of erosion, not the whole of it, I am always amazed at what a surprisingly sensual place the desert actually is. Dry, yes, but water has written everywhere. Raging flash floods cut through ancient hardened seas, leaving behind sandstone trenches of such soft and delicate beauty they seem carved for cathedrals. I find I walk with the same reverent footsteps I use when visiting Paris' Sacre Coeur. Nothing in the Southwest's constantly surreal terrain seems more incredible and graced with divinity than the perfectly sculpted hollows and rounded bowls of a slot canyon's walls, particularly as the wind whispers and the falling light paints the red rock in hues of ever-shifting brilliance.

In the end, I am always grateful for my map and the unseen river's guidance, for it is indeed all-too-easy to forget yourself inside the banded earth, with only embodied, unfolding eternity for a companion.

Jeff Campbell is a San Francisco–based writer who could happily explore no further than the granite mountains and sandstone deserts of the American West to the end of his days.

PREVIOUS: Access to the swirling sculpted sandstone of Coyote Buttes, in the Paria Canyon–Vermillion Cliffs Wilderness Area, is controlled to prevent damage caused by humans.

OPPOSITE: The routes through the mesmerising slot canyons carved out by the Paria River are usually unmarked, but adventurous hikers navigate by following the river's course.

The Wildest Slice of the Wild West

Andrew Dean Nystrom

Born a mile high in Colorado's Rocky Mountains, I have always gravitated towards extreme landscapes: Antarctica, Death Valley, Tierra del Fuego, the vast Patagonian steppe.

In Bolivia alone, I bicycled the 'World's Most Dangerous Road', skied the world's highest developed slope, navigated the world's highest motorable pass, tasted wine at the world's loftiest vineyard, recovered in some of the planet's highest soakable hot springs, and traversed some of the bleakest yet most riveting terrain on earth around the world's largest and highest salt flat, the otherworldly Salar de Uyuni.

After spending a summer conducting scientific field research, surveying the microbial diversity of Yellowstone National Park's myriad hydrothermal areas, I can confirm that none of these superlatives, however, can compare to the sheer wildness of the world's first national park.

Three million people a year visit Yellowstone. Only a small fraction, however, venture beyond the 9000-sq-km park's famous roadside attractions. Even fewer realise that a rewarding two-day hike leads into the heart of the wildest remaining slice of America's mythic Wild West, ending up at the most remote inhabited outpost in the lower 48 United States.

Yellowstone's Thorofare Patrol Cabin is the stuff of legends, the sort of place countless intrepid ramblers have heard about but few have seen first-hand. The remoteness of the seasonal ranger station is trumped only by the fly-in homesteads in the Alaskan Bush and Inuit villages north of the Arctic Circle.

Despite what the region's name connotes, the Thorofare is hardly the high road to anywhere. Quite the contrary, it is a detour leading smack-dab to the middle of nowhere...unless you happen to be an elk poacher, park ranger, rogue outfitter, trophy hunter, trail crew worker, solitude seeker or member of the wide-ranging Delta wolf pack.

Forty-eight kilometres from the nearest road, a lucky ranger lives here in a rustic, two-room log cabin erected in 1915. From July through September, he (there's never been a she, yet) is visited by only a handful of hearty backpackers. Telltale grizzly-bear claw marks furrow the face of the 40-sq-metre cabin. After dark, rangers joke, it is best to knock on the *inside* of the cabin's thick wooden door before making a beeline for the outhouse.

What, I wondered, besides its sheer remoteness, makes this wide-open toss of raw back country so alluring? I found it to be the vital challenge of establishing a rapport with the charismatic menagerie – recently reintroduced grey wolves, wayward wallowing moose, ravenous grizzly bears – and catch-and-release fly-casting for native, blue-ribbon cutthroat trout in gin-clear spawning streams.

Camping in designated sites overlooking the Yellowstone River's meandering upper reaches meant trespassing on the stunning domain of soaring bald eagles and endangered grizzly bears, and falling asleep to a primeval, frisson-

inducing chorus of 'h-o-o-o-o-o-o-o-o-wling' wolves. In autumn, omnivorous grizzlies entered a frenzied state called hyperphagia, when they stuff themselves on whatever they can get their supersize mitts on – moths, pine nuts, roots, berries, ants, grubs, tubers, trout – in preparation for six months of hibernation.

The Thorofare's weather can get treacherous any time of the year: snow has been recorded somewhere in the ecosystem every day of the year. Browse a US weather map on any given day and there is a good chance that Yellowstone will register the nation's lowest temperature.

As for the hike in, it is a flat, dusty two- to four-day slog along the eastern shore of Yellowstone Lake, one of the world's most expansive alpine lakes. In July, the lack of views during the initial stretch is more than made up for by expansive wildflower meadows that burst with colour. Before reaching the patrol cabin, more burned stands of lodgepole pine forest, marshy meadows and challenging stream crossings await.

Just before the first major snowstorm, as the lone ranger and I departed for the civilised comforts of the front country, I pondered the future of this generous slice of unfettered nature. For many, the rapid encroachment of development in the region's fragile buffer zones symbolises the trampling of America's natural heritage brought on by the hell-for-leather race for progress.

Happily, the park remains a psychological and geographical refuge of wilderness (literally 'where the wild beasts roam'). Yet perversely, once such a remote, pristine place is pinpointed on a map, it becomes threatened by everyone wanting to experience it. It remains to be seen if the Greater Yellowstone ecosystem will become an island of ever-decreasing genetic diversity, or if it can persist as a model preserve where humans beneficially coexist with the abundant wildlife.

Andrew Dean Nystrom's Top Trails Yellowstone & Grand Tetons National Parks *hiking guidebook won the 2005 National Outdoor Book Award. He's now seeking enlightenment via a pilgrimage to the world's highest soakable hot springs.*

PREVIOUS: Beneath the 352-sq-km Yellowstone Lake lie the same geysers, hot springs and deep canyons for which the rest of the park is famous.

OPPOSITE: In the 19th century, French trappers interpreted the name bestowed upon the region by Sioux Native Americans as *Roche Jaune* and *Pierre Jaune*, meaning 'Yellow Rock' and 'Yellow Stone'.

Solitary Walking Through Prime Bear Habitat

Gareth McCormack

Sometimes wilderness trekking isn't just about admiring the view. When the wildlife can kill you it adds a whole new dimension to the experience.

I've just left the trailhead in the remote northwest corner of Glacier National Park, Montana, heading for Waterton in Canada. Ahead lies Boulder Pass and three days of the finest alpine scenery in the contiguous USA. Despite the challenge and its natural reward, the ranger's warning rings clear in my mind. 'Listen man, I really recommend you carry bear spray if you're going into that area alone.'

I have no bear spray but after six weeks in the Rockies without a single sighting, I reckon the chances of meeting a grizzly are pretty slim. I'm also $50 better off. I try to concentrate on my surroundings as I pass between the placid waters of Kintla Lake and the great twisted pyramid of Kintla Peak. Yet the nagging doubt persists.

By evening a warm sun lights Gardener Point, and I watch mesmerised as a bald eagle sweeps along the lakeshore. I reach my designated camp site and throw together a hot meal in the little light left. Then I carefully clean up and hoist my food, stove and the clothes I cooked in to the top of the bear pole. Bears are olfactory geniuses and will investigate any interesting smell. I feel exposed enough in my bivvy bag without advertising my presence any further.

Dawn comes with a blanket of fog spread out across the lake. I wait for the sun to rise and have breakfast in its early light, watching the mist burn away in drifting golden wreaths. The goal for my second day is Boulder Pass, some 900m above me. I follow the trail as it winds steadily up through mixed forests until I meet a couple from Florida, the first humans I've encountered on the route so far. We pause for a chat and I can't help notice their rather businesslike holsters containing bear spray aerosols.

The modern take on grizzlies is that they aren't the malevolent man-eaters of popular belief. Under wild conditions the average grizzly will avoid humans and continue rooting around for grubs and berries, so long as we don't sneak up behind them, threaten their cubs, or sit down to dine at a carcass they're scavenging. The thinking on bear spray is not as clear. The aerosols contain the same essential ingredients as mace sprays used by police forces around the world, only much more powerful. But anecdotal evidence suggests that angry bears can virtually ignore it.

Either way I'm more than a little envious as I press on up the trail alone. But the sun is high in a crystalline sky and the day is warming nicely even at this altitude. Fragrant meadows have colonised the open spaces and every so often I cross a meltwater spring and cool off before resuming the long ascent, reaching the camp site in the early afternoon. I use the final hours of daylight to explore Boulder Pass. Great slabs of carved rock cradle networks of dark pools, while brilliant green mosses and patches of wildflowers complete the alpine garden.

I return to camp as the chill draws in and the stars begin to advance across the peaks. I'm woken suddenly in the night – the moon has gone and I can't see anything except stars and faint silhouettes of pines above me. Something large disturbs the branches close by and I freeze. The noise isn't repeated but it's an age before my body relaxes enough to allow me to drift back to sleep.

The final day of the trek dawns bright and clear and the previous night's disturbance seems like a bad dream. I have breakfast in the warm sun and pack up. I climb gently onto clearer slopes around Boulder Pass, then take out my camera to frame a photo of wildflowers.

I hear the bear before I see it – a huffing noise like a muffled bark. I look up to see a silver-grey grizzly charging fast along the trail towards me, head lowered, eyes fixed on me, muscles and fur rippling as it tears across a bank of snow less than 60m away. Its jaws are mashing together in a typical ursine display of agitation.

I try to look away and avoid eye contact, but otherwise I'm struggling for options. I'm wearing a heavy pack and anyway grizzlies can run at least twice as fast as humans. There are no trees to climb, I have no pepper spray and in the absence of the usual explanatory factors for a bear charge, it appears I'll have to take what's coming.

But the bear stops short about 25m away, sits up on its hind legs and thrusts its nose into the air. For a moment we both stand there locked into the confrontation like two gunslingers, waiting for the next move. Then I see the cubs.

Perched on a rock ledge just above the trail, two tiny dark cubs watch their mother, now placed between them and the threat. I must have walked right past them. My mind scrambles for the right thing to do. I crouch, bow my head and try to appear submissive, watching out of the corner of my eye, waiting for the bear to make up its mind. A few tense moments pass before she drops to the ground and starts moving again. For a second I think she's going to attack, but instead she turns and heads for the cubs, rounds them up, and with a final backward glance at me, shepherds them off in the opposite direction.

My legs are shaking uncontrollably as I turn and walk as fast as I dare towards Boulder Pass, shouting expletives as I go. As mortal danger subsides to fear I begin making loud noises every 30 seconds – the recommended way to warn bears of your approach. Normally you feel silly, so you don't really do it. I don't feel silly any more.

My senses are honed to a sharpness I've rarely experienced. Terrified and exhilarated, I realise I've just had one of my life's most memorable experiences. And I still have a day of solitary walking through prime bear habitat ahead of me.

Gareth McCormack has travelled, walked and climbed his way across Asia, Australia, New Zealand and North America. He spends a great deal of every year photographing wild and beautiful parts of the world.

PREVIOUS: To ensure its conservation for future generations campaigners have been lobbying Congress to designate Montana's remaining pristine natural places as wilderness.

OPPOSITE: A bear's sense of smell is seven times greater than a bloodhound's, which is one reason you should never cook food at your camp – another is those claws.

27°S 109°W
EASTER ISLAND,
CHILE

At the Feet of the Stone Giants

Gregor Clark

Easter Island defines isolation like no place on earth. Its closest inhabited neighbour is Pitcairn Island, 2000km to the west; Antarctica lies 6000km south; Chile and the Galápagos, 3500km east and north.

This mysterious speck of land in the middle of the Pacific captured my imagination from an early age. I remember gazing at maps, spinning the globe through a full quarter-turn of uninterrupted blue, wondering how people ever made it there.

Modern-day visitors congregate in Hanga Roa, the island's only settlement, 2km from the airport. I wanted a more solitary experience, beyond the well-known tourist sites. I planned to circumnavigate the coastline on foot, camping each night at the feet of the *moai* (the Polynesian name for Easter Island's famous statues). The explorer in me was irresistibly drawn to the island's less-charted extremities – the wild northwestern coast, where a faint dotted line sketched an apparent footpath, and the eastern Poike Peninsula, depicted only as a blank space on my map.

I set off for Rano Raraku, the ancient quarry 18km east of town. For centuries, stone giants weighing several tonnes were carved in place here on the volcano's edge, then transported to the coast by some still unknown process – using nothing fancier than stones, logs and rope. On the shore just beyond Rano Raraku stood an example of this handiwork, a row of *moai* 8m tall, imposingly resurrected on a rock pedestal backed by a stark headland. The hundreds of carvings still littering the quarry were remnants, left behind when the statue-building culture came to its mysterious halt.

I set up camp, then zigzagged up a little trail past dozens of stone heads. Occasionally a tour group would appear, but for the most part the guys with the big noses had us outnumbered. At the top of the quarry, inside the volcano's crater, wild horses drank at a reed-filled lake ringed with faces protruding at random angles, some falling, some fallen, some buried up to their noses in dirt and grass, some still embedded in the stone from which they had been shaped.

From up here I could see my tent, a little blue dot in a eucalyptus grove at the mountain's base. Beyond it, the entire west side of the island spread out to the ocean: open grasslands and extinct volcanoes bathed in distinct rays of cloud-filtered late-afternoon sun. As I descended towards camp, dozens of horses suddenly came thundering down from the mouth of the crater, their backs gleaming in the waning light.

Back at my camp site, nightfall brought soft South Pacific breezes, the smell of dried grasses and ocean salt, and the constant rustling of leaves overhead. I was alone. Under the stony gaze of hundreds of *moai,* their pockmarked faces illuminated in moonlight, I couldn't escape the eerie feeling of being surrounded by beings who, according to legend, might start walking at any time.

The second afternoon I headed east into the *terra incognita* that had so intrigued me on the map. I crossed a depression called the Poike Trench, reputedly the site of a final battle

between Easter Island's two warring cultures, the Long Ears and the Short Ears. Here the land felt even wilder, without roads or trails. Aside from a small hut there were only immense fields stretching towards the blue horizon, the huge sloping flank of a volcano glimmering green and yellow in the ever-changing light. Dotting the hillside before me were free-roaming horses and big scary cows with horns. Dried lupine seed-pods at my feet rattled like snakes ready to strike. I nearly stumbled over the sun-bleached corpse of a cow draped across the field.

A two-hour walk brought me to the island's easternmost point. Standing here, the volcanic cone at my back cut off any view to the west and huge cliffs dropped in all other directions to the unbroken sweep of Pacific below. I felt like the last man on earth.

As I retraced my steps, passing the hut perched on the trench's edge, two men greeted me in Spanish. They had long, black hair and were dressed in jeans, work shirts and bandanas – cowboys whose jobs took them to this remote part of the island to keep an eye on the wandering, un-fenced herds of livestock. We chatted briefly about the beauty of the afternoon, and before I knew it they were inviting me in for coffee. The inside of their hut was simple: hard-earth floors with only a picnic table and a wood-burning stove for furniture. Coffee quickly became dinner – homegrown boiled beef, sweet potatoes and rolls with marmalade squeezed from a plastic bag. We talked till dusk, drinking cups of Nescafé poured from an enormous metal teapot.

I spent the next two days completing my island circuit. The first evening I slept at Anakena, a sandy cove on the north coast where centuries ago the original Easter Islanders came ashore with their leader Hotu Matu'a after ca-noeing thousands of kilometres across the Pacific. Where did they come from? What were they looking for? How did they survive such a journey? Nobody knows. I drifted off to sleep, contemplating these questions, then woke at 2am to a brilliant sky full of stars and a half moon shining over the sea, the same sky Hotu Matu'a would have navigated by.

I continued west along the wild north coast, sandwiched between the sea and the green- and black-streaked cliff face of Mounga Teravaka. Near the island's northwest corner, the otherworldly sound of sea water crashing up through blowholes distracted me, and I tripped over a pile of rocks half buried in weeds. Looking down, I was amazed to find myself staring at two long-ago-toppled *moai* never returned to their pedestal.

I arrived back in Hanga Roa sunbaked but happy. Coming from where I had been, this sleepy town of a few thousand felt like a metropolis. Roosters crowed, salsa and Polynesian music blared from doorways, the bright pink and orange of hibiscus flowers seemed strangely jarring.

The next morning I bumped into one of the cowboys, who surprised me with a souvenir Easter Island statue. In return I said I'd send him some bandanas from the US. His address was startlingly simple:

Leo Riroroko

Correo

Rapa Nui (Chile)

Just his name, the Spanish word for post office and the Polynesian word for Easter Island.

I loved the idea that these three simple lines could reach a place so remote. A few days later, I sent the bandanas. Somewhere on the Poike Peninsula, I hope they're still flying wild in the wind.

Gregor Clark's insatiable love of foreign languages and wild places has sent him exploring 'what's around the next bend' in 50 countries, including remote spots such as Easter Island, Greenland and the Galápagos.

PREVIOUS: The island's famous eastward-looking *moai* statues were carved out of a volcanic rock called tuff using basalt tools. The last of the *moai* is believed to have been carved as late as 1868.

OPPOSITE: Easter Island was once a densely forested island paradise thought to contain as many as 16 million palms, supporting a rich biodiversity that sustained its isolated Polynesian settlers for 15 centuries.

Alone in the Middle of the Tundra

Etain O'Carroll

It's 20°C below and a thick ice fog has settled in over Edmonton airport. I'm going nowhere today. It's another two days before the fog lifts and I can board the plane. I watch in awe as ice is brushed off the wings as we prepare for takeoff. I'm hopelessly out of depth. I'm a greenhorn from rural Ireland, it's my first trip 'up north' and I'm still 1800km south of my destination.

After a brief stopover in Yellowknife I squeeze in between hardened Arctic miners, government reps and the local Inuit travelling home after a trip 'out'. I'm heading for Cambridge Bay on Victoria Island, about 200km north of the Arctic Circle. To the Inuit it is Ikaluktutiak, or Fair Fishing Place, and with 1300 inhabitants it's the largest town for miles around. In fact there's nothing else for miles around, hundreds of miles around.

Flying across the high Canadian Arctic, the land seems infinite, the blinding, flat whiteness broken only every few hours by a tiny fly-in community. There are no roads out here and the only way in or out is by air. As I leave the plane the cold, raw air makes me cough, and I have to bend double against the wind just to make my way to the tiny terminal building. Outside I burn my hand on the door handle of a local taxi. I really have no idea what I'm getting into.

Cambridge Bay isn't high on the list of places to visit before you die. It's not a romanticised world of dog teams and igloos, but a much more real and confused place where life is a hybrid of the old times and the new. Musk ox heads sit on doorsteps, while inside women clean caribou skins as they watch *American Idol* or *Oprah*.

Government workers fly in here reluctantly and get out again as fast as they can, but I can't help but feel they're missing the point of being here. It's not the town that is important but the desolate, inhospitable expanse of windswept ice and snow that surrounds it. Spend any time at all on the tundra and you'll soon realise just why this seemingly barren land is so precious to the Inuit.

I'm going ice fishing with Sandra, my new housemate, and we head out of town on her snowmobile. It's a glorious sunny day, a balmy 20°C below with endless, pure blue skies. We're heading for Kitiga Lake, 18km from town and a good place to catch Arctic char.

There's something deeply moving about travelling across the tundra. There's just nothing there. Nothing, not even a tree, in any direction and it's difficult to describe how that isolation makes you feel. It's flat, frozen and barren, snow and ice stretch as far as the eye can see and it is truly mesmerising.

Having unloaded an auger off the snowmobile we attack the ice but even with an added extension all we do is create a shimmering, glassy hole – with a solid bottom. Sandra heads back to town to borrow a second extension. She waves goodbye and I'm left alone, the sound of the snowmobile retreating into the distance. Soon the silence engulfs me. My breath, the squeaky sound of the snow beneath my feet and the swish of rubbing fabric are the loudest things around.

The silence is profound and incredibly power-ful. I feel like I'm being observed from above, a tiny black dot in a vast expanse of white. The tundra stretches in undulating white waves, not a single manmade object in sight. Suddenly I'm very aware of who and what I am, and how vul-nerable I am in this position. I'm a tiny blip on the landscape, thousands of miles from home, protected only by my anti-gravity insulation boots and an ultra-hi-tech parka.

I'm fully aware that this is no defence against nature. All sense of control over my life has evaporated and I am at the mercy of the elements. How deliciously frightening it is and how won-derfully liberating. My very existence is only a hiccup in this vast universe. I feel hyper-aware of my surroundings, and my thought process. I'm not usually given to profound musings on my place in the grand scheme of things but this sudden and utter vulnerability forces me into deep contemplation. I'm very much alive, more alive than I've ever felt before and tripping over myself just trying to take it all in.

The ice occasionally lets out echoing cracks and groans as I study the stunning angular shapes of snow sculpted by the wind. This truly is *Nunassiaq* – the beautiful land. It is haunting, powerful and unforgiving. There are blue skies now but I know that Arctic weather is extremely unpredictable and storms can blow up out of nowhere, without any notice, at any time of year. It is this ultimate defencelessness that thrills me. I feel extremely lucky to be here.

A distant rumble becomes the unmistakable sound of a snowmobile and soon I'm attacking the ice again, up and down with the auger, my former sense of elation marred by the physical effort and the sound of the motor. We try in three different places and eventually give up; the ice is over 2m deep and we never make it through. But it doesn't matter in the slightest. I've never really liked fishing anyway. Being left there alone in the middle of the tundra was a far greater prize than any Arctic char.

Etain O'Carroll is a travel writer and photog-rapher smitten by extremes and strangely attracted to the discomforts of epic bus jour-neys, hellish roads, unrecognisable foods and ridiculously low temperatures.

PREVIOUS: The Inuit have been creating *inuksuit* rock sculptures for centuries and have used them to mark trails and fishing sites, as well as doors to alternate realms of reality.

OPPOSITE: Inuit languages use multiple suffixes to derive words, meaning that the number of words for different types of snow is only limited by the speaker's imagination.

0°S 78°W
COTOPAXI VOLCANO, ECUADOR

The Perfect Mountain

Carolyn McCarthy

Cotopaxi's night air prickled. The snow crunched beneath my crampons like sugared cereal and moonlight tinted the glacier's serrated edges blue. I turned off my head lamp and picked my way up, ice tool firm in hand. Looking down on Latacunga's bright pinpricks marking the valley floor, I wondered if a soul down there was awake. It seemed like another planet.

At 5897m, Cotopaxi is Ecuador's second-highest peak, a barely technical climb whose altitude and weather provide challenge enough for a dilettante. The western hemisphere's highest equatorial point, this middle ground connects sky to molten earth and jungle to high plain. It divides known from unknown, what I'd done and what I might yet be able to do.

Heading up mountains is not my obsession, but rather, a periodic reminder to embrace my scrappy life. When my climbing partner had backed out at the last minute I was pressed to find a guide. Outfitters of ill repute abounded. With rusted crampons and rental windbreakers, one even boasted *'llevamos hasta niños y muertos'*, meaning they could summit even with children and the dead. I hoped for a more thoughtful experience. Finally, I met Eduardo, a veteran climber who sewed fleece layers on a '50s Singer in his shop, and I decided he was the one.

We approached via the lesser-used southern route. The previous evening we had turned in before eight but I had slept lightly, curled tight against the cold. Winds bullied the tent and my thoughts had churned. When I finally awoke I had overslept a precious hour. We readied in the dark; under thick layers my stomach percolated a combination of anticipation and dread.

We stepped out into a bath of stars. As soon as I began the uphill climb I warmed up. With the moment of action at hand came relief. It wouldn't be time to wonder anymore. I fell into an easy rhythm of step upon step. Though mist hovered low and the wind slapped my side I was energised, compelled by an expansive feeling that I couldn't contain.

Everything simplified on the mountain. There was the task at hand, repetitive, combined with the motor of my breath, and the occasional thought that bloomed in the long spaces between nothing, in the cadence of steps: one, two, one, two. We hiked at a quick clip but slowed as we gained altitude. I began to pause longer between each step. I admired the wind-crusted patterns of ripples and pockmarks, the ethereal shades of blue in the underbelly of snow shapes. When the sun climbed higher and burned hotter, Eduardo cracked the whip.

'What happened to you? We were making such good time.'

I had to move. *Soroche*, or altitude sickness, was twirling my insides, warping time, magnifying both my doubt and wonder. Thoughts easily distracted me. I drifted through them, searching for wisdom, inspiration, something to grab onto. I tried concentrating on the mountain but halving my normal supply of oxygen had handicapped me.

My head throbbed. My mind clouded. Oxygen slowly squeezed into the narrow corridors of my head. We had been moving for hours without rest. As close as I was now, I had trouble feeling urgency. I was content to stand there, cocked on the steep angle of a volcano, studying my deterioration. Time slipped by.

'*Vamos*,' Eduardo pressed.

I begged for one deep breath first. But it just wasn't possible.

A rope was the umbilical cord between us. Should one of us fall, the other could anchor into the snow with the ice tool. However, the rope never even became taut. Eduardo led, tirelessly pushing on whenever I had almost caught up. I considered telling him off but remembered he was paid for this efficiency.

Under the equatorial sun, snow quickly disintegrates. We needed to reach the summit while our route was shaded. By midmorning the snow's firm surface would soften, leaving us to wade in hip-deep slush. Worse, we would risk snow slides. Eduardo didn't have to remind me of the dangers. Breathless and short-tempered, I determined to grind through the burgeoning stupor.

Mittens drenched, I took the last pitch much like a baby making a risky amble to the coffee table. Snow-melt gushed beneath me, soaking my front when I rested. I used my hands to pull up on frozen knobs of snow, resting my tender, shaky feet.

At 9.37am I slid onto the rim. The crater spanned before me, a beautiful marshmallow puff of snow with smoke trilling from its lip.

Eduardo congratulated me and grabbed my camera to snap a photo. This is it, I smiled. I felt…ill. Across the football field–sized crater indistinct figures of climbers made their approach towards a small crest, the official summit. They could have it.

It seemed that the perfect mountain made me an incohesive, gasping jumble. In the end, Cotopaxi made less sense than the idea of it.

'Whenever you're ready,' Eduardo said, meaning now. My three minutes were up. I had thought I'd feel whole and wax poetic, but somewhere in the journey my intellect had shut off. I took half a ham sandwich stiff with ice crystals from my pocket and nibbled.

I had come all this way, only to find the landscape turned interior. I wished for more. Looking outward, I saw that Cotopaxi accounted for a small space. The earth flowed beyond, its ends rumpled like a fluffed tablecloth. My curiosity bent towards the numerous villages and towns etched into the shadows. What human dramas did they host? I crumpled the greasy sandwich wrapper back into my pocket before it dared take flight. As for these airless steeps, they were but fantasy and madness.

Carolyn McCarthy guides treks through northern Patagonia during writing lulls. She holds a Master's degree in creative writing and an ice-climbing certificate from a now-defunct Andean institute. Her expertise in roadless Chile comes from the time-tried practice of getting lost.

PREVIOUS: Cotopaxi (which means 'neck of the moon' in Quechua) is easily one of the world's most photogenic volcanoes but it's also one of the most dangerous to climb.

OPPOSITE: When German geologist Wilhelm Reiss and Colombian Ángel Escobar made the first ascent of Cotopaxi in 1872 they climbed an ice-free trail up a recent lava flow.

In the Swamp, Surrounded

Karl Bushby

Monday 5 February 2001
07°41′ N, 77°10′ W

The day begins with 'What the hell do I do now?' The mangroves to my front are so thick and deep I can't see through them. I'm out of the river, back into dry mode and I sit for a while, thinking. I don't know, maybe it's half a kilometre to the hill; I can just make it out. There is no way I can force myself through this stuff, certainly not with my kit on. The good news, however, is that mangrove cuts very easily, and the thick stems are felled almost effortlessly with a single blow. The only trouble is, this goes on for so long I begin to tire, left gasping and soaked in sweat. I make some progress but the ground beneath me begins to lose its firmness and becomes increasingly wet and boggy. I'm soon forced to turn back and try a different direction, all my previous effort wasted. The mosquitoes have decided to hang around today, a cloud of them keeping up the continuous assault. I hardly seem to be making any forward movement at all, and yet I'm burning out. I didn't eat this morning and my food for some time has been very thin on the ground, leaving me permanently hungry. Now that the workload has suddenly increased, I am feeling this very rapidly.

For hours the grind continues and I feel I'm getting nowhere. I am still in the swamp, surrounded by thick vegetation. Not only mangrove but dense palms, vines and mud... Oh so much mud. Continually forced to retreat back towards the east, it's a real hand-to-hand fight. I keep losing my way back out and also my orientation. It's just so overwhelming. I am growing weaker and beginning to wonder if this route is even possible. Yet I do make a few good turns and find firm ground that begins to rise. It's working... It's working! By the end of the day I've made possibly 2km to 3km and I feel exhausted. But look! I'm in. There, more high ground to my front. Maybe tomorrow. What a day, may your god help me.

Darest thou now, O soul
Walk out with me toward the unknown region,
Where neither ground is for the feet nor any path to follow?
—'Leaves of Grass', Walt Whitman

Tuesday 6 February 2001
07°45′ N, 77°11′ W

Mosquitoes, mosquitoes, mosquitoes... Oh Lord! I now begin to climb and the forest changes in nature, to different vegetation. It's a little easier at times, yet overall still 'in-your-face' hand-to-hand combat, machete blow after machete blow, step for step. It's thick, with vines that seem to have a mind of their own, wrapping themselves around my legs, neck and arms, gripping my rucksack and holding me back as I try to move forward. Every movement to progress takes intense effort. The mosquitoes are everywhere and I'm sucking them in, choking as I gasp for breath. I'm soaked through all the time, forced to take a rest every 10 minutes. I climb for a short distance then the ground drops,

before climbing for yet another short distance, and so it goes. I keep moving, but it's hard, so hard!

There's no real top canopy, so most of the sunlight makes it through to the forest floor, fostering plant growth. This is secondary jungle, a real bitch. I only have one glove, having lost the other one before Riosucio, so I use an old bandage wrapped around my left hand to keep the mosquitoes off. I am also forced to use my head net as I'm being driven insane, although by now I've grown used to the mosquito bites. My face no longer itches, although I still feel the bites, but I can't stand them all over me. I keep pushing and pushing. I'm making little progress, but at least it is progress.

I feel pretty safe out here, as I'm in the middle of nowhere and it's highly unlikely I'll find a soul. 'Don't cut your way through the jungle. Manoeuvre through, saving energy.' So the wisdom goes, yet I cannot move a metre without cutting. It's like being anchored by nylon cord and trying to run. I grow weaker as the day progresses, and the strength goes from my machete blows. Sometimes I stand there hitting the vines and nothing happens... Then I just fall on my arse... Somebody give me strength! I start to get worried; I'm scared I might not be able to make it through this lot before my rations run out. There's so little progress, and so far to go. Tracks, I need tracks. They could be dangerous, yet if I don't find them...

Bugger... How will I cope?

Karl Bushby, an ex-paratrooper in his 30s, is attempting to become the first person to complete an unbroken, round-the-world walk. Having started in 1998, he is now halfway through the 57,972km trek and is due to complete it in 2011. Giant Steps, *an account of his great trek to date, offers further insight into his adventure.*

PREVIOUS: The British Army have a saying that goes 'if you can soldier in the jungle, you can soldier anywhere'. Negotiating a path through the Darien Gap would test even the steeliest resolve.

OPPOSITE: Mangroves produce aerial roots that become embedded in the mud, propping up the tree and forming a base for the deposit of silt and other material carried by the tides.

Nothing to Do but Hope & Walk

Karl Bushby

Saturday 27 January 2001

I push on until reaching Bajira. From here I will find the track heading west to Riosucio. I arrive weak, tired and fit to drop. The sun had taken a lot out of me. Again I find myself surrounded by people and I'm pleased to find the army here in strength. The local AUC find me in the crowd and pull me out for a talk. Again I'm told it will be a grave mistake to try to walk the track. The guerrillas here are the most ferocious of all I'm told, and I will be left for dead. I'd heard in Medellin about the FARC in this area being the most feared. Called the 'Dragons of Uraba', they are fearsome beasts by all accounts, and I have seen graffiti on walls and houses proclaiming this. Hell's teeth, am I really going to have to do this. Listening to these people I'm left scared out of my wits. These people live here. They know the area. Who am I to walk in from the other side of the world and tell them they're wrong? I pace around a little in deep thought. Well, this would appear to be it. The time to make the decision. When it came to the crunch, I'd always said I would be prepared to put my life on the line, but oh my, now it is time it really isn't so easy. I am still hopeful that they are wrong. I still believe that if caught I'll live through it, but I can't avoid my hope being riddled with doubt. Can I get away with this? In any sort of contact the best I can expect is to lose all my equipment…and what then? A deep and palpable fear comes over me. At no point on my journey, or in fact at any time in my life,

have I been so scared, or really thought about dying, until now. I stand alone on the dusty track, motionless, staring at my feet. The crowd standing nearby, equally motionless, watch and wait for me to make up my mind…

Why am I even thinking about it? Of course I'm going down that track. I was always going to go down that track, and if I survive this there will be other tracks like it in my life. I nod to the men, who look at each other with raised eyebrows. The crowd follows as they lead me to see 'the boss'. He stands in the town plaza, having just finished a meeting of some kind. I explain my reason and route, to which this very sober, strait-laced man says little, except that it is my choice. He says it's not a problem for him and orders one of his men to show me where the track picks up again outside of the village. Once there, my instructions consist of 'follow the track, always remain straight ahead, don't veer left or right'. Wishing me the best of luck, the man shakes my hand and I'm left to get on with it.

It's now getting late and my first concern is to find somewhere to sleep. Lord, I need sleep. Food, I need that too. I come across the troops encamped on the outskirts. I'm stopped and questioned.

'Going where?' Am I insane? I obviously am. The young soldiers get a little excited and make me stay put until they get word to their officer. He obviously wants to speak to me, so I'm taken to meet him. The lieutenant is sitting with his radio operator on the porch of a house they occupy. After the usual questions and answers

are done I'm fed a mess tin of rice and meat, and invited to spend the night here. There is the usual persuasion to change my route if possible, but my mind is set. It doesn't seem to matter what could happen any more. My dice are rolling.

Sunday 28 January 2001

It's fair to say that last night I had the best sleep I've had in a long time. I wake early, pack my kit, and then sit on the porch watching the sunrise. The world has taken a turn for the surreal and feels very strange. An odd calm has come over me, or maybe I just don't know how to react to a day like this. The troops give me a canteen of warm chocolate and a flat, fried *arepa* (corn pancake). Not really a meal, but a damn sight better than nothing. The lieutenant appears with his first sergeant and the pair attempt to change my mind about the journey. However, once they see I'm steadfast in my resolve, there is little more they can do. The lieutenant takes a Dictaphone from his pocket, saying they will have to get my decision recorded so that they won't suffer any comebacks when I'm eventually found dead. The sergeant now sets out the dangers facing me on the track in a clear, loud voice. He gives a brief rundown on the political situation here in Colombia. Because of 'Plan Colombia', a major US backing and funding for the Colombian government, I would now be regarded as an enemy by the FARC.

'You understand all I've just said?'

'Yes.'

'It's very clear?'

'Yes.'

'We have given you all the information we can and it is your choice?'

'Yep! I understand completely!'

'OK.'

The lieutenant then writes out an official note, stating the time, date, place, unit and people involved. It gives official sanction to the tape recording we'd just made and also stated that the decision to continue is mine, absolving them of responsibility. The lieutenant signs it, the sergeant adds his signature as a witness, and then I sign. Meanwhile a soldier had been dispatched to get a photocopy of my passport. By now I am feeling almost sick with fear. Can you imagine going through such a process. It's like an official execution. What if this is the last day of my life? I'd written a short letter to be sent to Catty, explaining my situation on this date, at this time and location, so that she could pass it on. I give it to the lieutenant, explaining that this could be my last letter home and could he post it when possible. Of course, he says, and a carbon copy of the official document would be sent with it.

The young soldiers stand and watch, dumbstruck. After lots of handshaking and 'best wishes', I set off. A radio message is sent to the troops in Riosucio explaining that I'm en route. As I pass through the last defensive positions I try to convince myself that this is not as bad as it might seem. Just move and keep moving. I was frightened, yet I could do nothing now but hope and walk. Fortune favours the brave, my father had written in his last email to me in Medellin, ending it with 'Who dares, wins'. Nice quotes, but a bulletproof vest or something a little more physical would be nice right now. Somewhere out there is 'The Dragon'...will it find me?

Karl Bushby, an ex-paratrooper in his 30s, is attempting to become the first person to complete an unbroken, round-the-world walk. Having started in 1998, he is now halfway through the 57,972km trek and is due to complete it in 2011. Giant Steps, *an account of his great trek to date, offers further insight into his adventure.*

PREVIOUS: In 1972 the dense Colombian jungle yielded La Ciudad Perdida (The Lost City). With armed conflict preventing further exploration it's possible secrets still lie hidden in the undergrowth.

OPPOSITE: FARC guerillas and government troops have been fighting for over 40 years in a war that has displaced every one of the region's indigenous inhabitants.

14°S 76°W
MIDDLE OF THE COASTAL DESERT, PERU

The Coastal Desert

Ben Kozel

Dregs from water bottle number three lightly scald the back of my throat. As cracked lips struggle to form a seal around the opening, my view of the ridge top ahead is distorted through the curve of plastic. It's an image that writhes seductively. I know a church will be visible in the gully on the far side. The map also shows a road. This will likely be little more than a couple of wheel ruts, but a road nonetheless. And all roads lead somewhere.

Atop the ridge, a light breeze peels away the layer of still air trapping heat against our skins. But this moment of welcome relief goes by almost unnoticed. In the gully below there is no church, and there is no road. In fact, the gully bears scant resemblance whatsoever to the array of contour lines representing it on paper.

Murmurs of doubt had arisen several hours earlier – a routine check of compass bearings revealed a slight discrepancy in the positioning of a craggy hill. It had been dismissed, at the time, as a glitch. Yet there is nothing 'slight' about the most recent discrepancy. And in the circumstances, even an admission that our maps are 'slightly out' would have no ring of inconsequence about it. We are in the middle of Peru's coastal desert, and I have no fourth water bottle.

The coastal desert of South America sweeps down more than half the western edge of the continent. It is an arid strip separating the High Andes from the Pacific, produced by the cold-water upwelling from abyssal ocean depths.

Chilled by the sea surface, moisture-laden air does not rise to the heights needed for it to condense and fall as rain. Just across Peru's border with Chile is the driest desert on Earth – the Atacama. In some parts of the Atacama rainfall has never been recorded.

For two days we have tracked up the valley of an ephemeral tributary of the Majes River. At first the setting had seemed otherworldly, a rock-strewn Mars-scape, copper- and sepia-hued, devoid of water and life. Nearer the valley head, tall cacti punch through the baked earth. They stand straight as sentinels, all-knowing custodians of this lonely place, yet keeping mute as we argue over which way to head now.

Convention suddenly seems as shrouded in haze as this desiccated land. How can something like this be happening at the very cusp of the 21st century? Maps are one of travel's fundamental pillars. They've evolved to be rocks of certainty, mainstays of reliability. If your map betrays you, what remains left to trust?

The maps are the most detailed available for the region. Yet like most of the other valleys that feed little but dust into the Majes, this one does not have a name. That, in itself, speaks volumes. Place names are a reminder that you are within the known world, a comforting confirmation of the fact that at least one other intrepid soul has gone this way before you, and survived long enough to commemorate their king, their mother, or their favourite cat.

A great swath of the coastal desert, however, is a landscape of coordinates only, where

contour lines identify individual features like fingerprints. But how precise are they in this instance? Topographic drawing that does not match with the observable reality smacks of guesswork, or at best, some wilful hurriedness on the part of either surveyor or cartographer. Perhaps it highlights a truth that, despite the relatively close proximity of several towns, nobody ever has reason to come this way. Herein lies a paradox of the Andes. As the crow flies you are never far from civilisation. And yet, for the wingless, the severity of this mighty mountain range can resign one to the notion that a neighbouring valley might as well lie on the other side of the planet.

We traverse the gully, reddening eyes fixed in hope on a second ridge. But the view from this one too is heartbreaking. Thirst has slowed the passage of time. Or else time is distended within this 'uncharted' void. Trekking up the nameless valley was supposed to be a shortcut. Our backpacks are so heavy. I am convinced mine will ultimately cripple me for life. Carrying them any further than is absolutely necessary had seemed, therefore, like madness. And yet, the longer option of continuing to follow the Majes River had merely been adjudged the maddest pick of what is, in all honesty, a rather nutty bunch. Essentially, the safe negotiation of the valley without a name is reliant on one hefty assumption – that the natural spring marked on the map, the one drawn right alongside the church, is still flowing. Cartographic errors aside, it's reasonable to think that since the date of the map's publication, the spring has simply dried up.

British Army troops are said to drink their own urine when access to water is scarce. But two days of strict water rationing has combined with the relentless heat to turn ours the colour of dark ale. Suggestions that the cacti may provide deliverance wither just as quickly. One sip of the juice dripping from their cut flesh is enough to twist the face into a mask of pure repulsion, and confirm the prospect of a death even worse than dehydration.

Hope instead arrives as a line of powdered earth, a haphazard ribbon of ground where the ubiquitous stones are not. Without doubt they have been kicked away or crushed under the hooves of livestock. However, the dry-preserved nature of this place means animals may not have walked the trail for decades. The coastal desert is a realm of forever, a land deep in slumber.

We follow the stock trail up a third ridge. At the top stands a 3m-high cross. My heart quickens. From somewhere my body finds the moisture needed to make my hands go clammy. The cross's timbers are like old bones, drained completely of the life they had once known. But at the base of the gully over which they cast their benevolence, lush, spring-fed greenery beats back the savage brown hills and their prickly henchmen.

In more ways than one, it feels good to step back onto the map.

Ben Kozel is lured by the remote and the wild. He prefers the slower journey – rowing an old boat, or leading camels – giving people and place time to get under his skin.

PREVIOUS: For 3500km the deserts of coastal Peru and northern Chile form a continuous belt along the western escarpment of the Andean Cordillera, encompassing some of the world's driest terrain.

OPPOSITE: Crescentic sand dunes are mounds that are generally wider than they are long and are the most common dune form on both Earth and Mars.

41°S 72°W
PUELO VALLEY, CHILE

Beyond Road's End

Carolyn McCarthy

Puelo Valley is Patagonia's living frontier – a nowhere land boxed in by turquoise rivers and mountains snarled with vegetation, cut off from modern Chile by its improbable and breathtaking design. A century ago adventurers left their villages and the great estancias of Argentina to carve a home for themselves in these distant hills. They came on foot or horseback, scrabbled with hunger and seclusion, and dared to stay.

To understand this hinterland is to wander the narrow horse paths, the sloping meadows and dim corridors of southern beech that lead to solitary, slanted homes whose chimneys sigh constant furls of smoke. Homesteaders are anchored to the landscape. They mind the sheep, tend the fields and wait for winter's bursting rivers to retreat.

While this valley is by no means virgin – cow pastures have replaced swaths of old-growth forest and the once-abundant *huemul* (Andean deer) have retreated to the ridge tops – isolation has held it still in time. The prospect of a road may change all that, as it plows up valley, gobbling the ox trail and promising unknown expediency. For locals it is both blessing and curse: a welcome bridge to goods and medicine, but a sure sign that Puelo's cowboy era will come to pass.

But not just yet.

A visit to the region is still steeped in uncertainty and inconvenience, the soakings and strandings that mark this blistered slow dance with the past. I arrive at the village on a dark April morning to find sheep grazing the damp schoolhouse lawn and muddy Wellingtons lined up on the stoop. The kids, who board in spare bunkrooms and commute weekly by horseback, press up to the window to glimpse the stranger. They call you aunt or uncle. Few outsiders turn up here. Those who do get anything ranging from bristled stares to the hospitality we learned in Bible lessons but have nearly never experienced.

Over the next two days my hike up valley follows a worn path trail through musky wood and rosehips, past teal finger lakes and sagging barns. Mist binds the mountaintops, releasing spurts of rain that cast the forest in a deeper, slicker sheen. A rider passes, tugging a packhorse over loose boulders, the horse's sagging load snapping twigs and branches. The rider props ups the shifting sacks and nods good day before spurring past.

Far from any house or village, these wordless encounters are the norm, part of the economy of solitude. The frugality of these exchanges first bothered me, but with time they come to make sense in this realm of woods, rocks and rivers. It seems apt to travel like one more silent creature that slips past your gaze and disappears.

The final leg of my journey takes me across the wobbly footbridge spanning the Puelo River's pale, gem-coloured waters, where the dark shapes of salmon flicker back and forth. I fork into a remote offshoot where the trail narrows. The rain, a near-constant companion, begins lashing out in torrents. It soaks through

my clothes and skin, getting in my nostrils and eyelashes. Keeping trail is a matter of following the thin strip of mud through the green and making feeble progress over the vast trunks felled across the crashing brooks. It's enough to consider giving up, if there were a retreat.

I persist with one good reason. In the far corners of the valley, where no-one ever happens by, a visit can be a celebration. Stories are exchanged until the candles puddle to raw floorboards. Daily life takes on high drama in a place where wild boars court domestic sows and a trip to the store means riding waist-deep across glacier-fed rivers. Likewise, news of the outside is cherished. Yellowed newspapers and flyers for hardware store sales are stacked and stored to be reread on rainy days. A visitor can hope, if the weather clears, to explore the trail-less territory that leads to distant glaciers and rippling views of the Andean divide. And after a long day's journey, there is the contentment of resting under the leaden weight of sheepskins and raw wool covers. The nearer I get, the more my anticipation grows.

'By God woman,' scolds Bernardita, 'Get in before you drown.'

Soon my socks and layers are festooned above the great iron stove, droplets spattering the hot surface and beading off. The kettle is filled. When the water is almost boiling, my hostess pours and we take turns passing an old scratchy gourd filled with *yerba maté,* a bitter tea sipped through a long metal straw. I begin to thaw.

Leaving is as difficult as arriving. In the morning when I prepare my pack and put on my boots, my host shakes her head. The streams have flooded. There's no crossing, even on a horse. She knows as one who has lived her life according to the rain, who can measure its accumulation with an ear tuned to its patter. A delay is a common occurrence, not worthy of disappointment. I could be stuck a day or a week, no matter. Company is relished. Bernardita hums and feeds a couple of split logs to the stove.

For a traveller addicted to the rush of movement, the fleeting encounter and lush landscapes rushing past, it is a whole other lesson to sit still while the cold seeps through the gaps between the planks. This is nowhere. Travel becomes about finding humanity in isolation: the welcoming of strangers, slow talk punctuated by a roiling teakettle. Puelo Valley is a raw, rough-edged postcard whose beauty is defined by patience and companionship.

Carolyn McCarthy guides treks through northern Patagonia during writing lulls. She holds a Master's degree in creative writing and an ice-climbing certificate from a now-defunct Andean institute. Her expertise in roadless Chile comes from the time-tried practice of getting lost.

PREVIOUS: Patagonia is one of three major centres where palaeontologists go in search of the fossilised remains of the fearsome dinosaur predator Tyrannosaurus Rex and its larger cousins.

OPPOSITE: In describing the remote and sparsely populated Patagonian wilderness, legendary author Paul Theroux starkly stated that 'nowhere is a place'.

Alone in the Ruins of Machu Picchu

Gregor Clark

My guidebook said you could visit the ruins at night. As I watched the sun set over Machu Picchu, this thought tantalised me. Ten hours of exploring had only left me hungry for more.

All day long I had been rubbing shoulders with the tourist throngs, people who like me were mesmerised by the beauty of the ruins and their setting, and ecstatic to have reached this most famous of South American destinations. Not that I begrudged anybody else the experience, but the crowds were overwhelming. Since daybreak, tour buses had been snaking up and down the hairpin switchbacks connecting the mountaintop to the Urubamba valley far below. I kept remembering those words from my guidebook, wondering if the crowds might disperse after nightfall, permitting a more tranquil visit.

In a way it's wonderful that Machu Picchu can nowadays be visited on a day trip from Cuzco. Everyone probably *should* have a chance to see this remarkable place, and hundreds of thousands of lives are enriched by the experience every year. But how ironic that a spot chosen by the Incas for its solitary majesty, as the lofty and unattainable mountaintop refuge of nobles or priests, should have become a poster child for the tourist industry.

Until the last century, Machu Picchu truly was the middle of nowhere, unknown to anybody except its Inca builders and local residents. Invisible and nearly inaccessible from the valley below, it slipped – following Inca abandonment – into three centuries of vine- and jungle-covered oblivion, ending in 1911 when American explorer Hiram Bingham catapulted it into universal consciousness. Bingham's account of his first cliffhanging ascent to the ruins provides a riveting portrayal of how unanticipated his discovery really was.

Like many modern-day travellers I hoped to get a taste of Machu Picchu's original 'lost in the clouds' atmosphere by approaching the ruins the slow way – on foot, via the Inca Trail. I joined the obligatory tour group in Cuzco, then spent the next four days surrounded by others making the classic pilgrimage. Along the way, we crossed several breathtaking (literally and figuratively) Andean passes, treading on original Inca paving stones, and passing several other fine ruins.

Our last overnight stop was at an exquisitely beautiful site called Huinay Huayna, where dozens of impossibly steep terraces cascaded into a deep green gorge backed by a high waterfall. My newfound travelling companions included five Argentines who shared my interest in exploring Huinay Huayna by moonlight. The only problem was a slight difference in styles. Mine was more along the lines of silent and meditative contemplation; theirs involved a ritualistic circle chant, led by the charismatic lone male in the group, who I thereafter nicknamed the Warlock. Absenting myself from the circle that night, I made a mental note to keep my distance from them the next day at Machu Picchu.

Before dawn the following morning we climbed to the mountaintop Gateway of the Sun,

hoping for the classic panoramic view of Machu Picchu before the tour buses arrived. Unfortunately, the weather did not cooperate. With dozens of other disappointed trekkers, I shivered on the hilltop in chilly fog for two hours, waiting for a sunrise that never came, then trudged down the hill to Machu Picchu itself. As I descended, the clouds started lifting, revealing the place to be every bit as spectacular as I could have hoped. By day's end, my tour group had dispersed, apparently having seen enough of the ruins and preferring a hot bath. I, however, felt I was just scratching the surface.

Inquiring about 'night visit' tickets, I was directed to a counter near the entrance gate. I fully expected to encounter a small army of other nocturnal adventurers. After waiting patiently while the last daytime visitors filtered from the site, I was startled to suddenly find myself alone with the night watchman, who was asking me how long I'd like to 'stay in there'. Uncertain of his meaning, I sputtered, 'Uh, I don't know, maybe an hour or two.' He explained that he was leaving for his dinner break, so he'd simply lock me in and return when I was ready.

So began my unexpectedly intimate encounter with one of the world's most overrun tourist destinations. The last traces of daylight were disappearing as I heard the heavy gate clank shut behind me. Insects and birds chirped loudly. Inca stone walls plunged headlong towards the dizzyingly deep gorge of the Urubamba River hundreds of metres below. Knife-edged green mountains rose up on all sides, their peaks obscured by a dense layer of cottony clouds turned bluish-grey by the vanishing sun. Before me great stone steps descended through a trapezoidal door into the complex of temples, houses, terraces and fountains that the Incas built half a millennium ago. The moon was now almost directly overhead, casting enough light to walk by, moving in and out of the clouds, and there I was, completely alone in the ruins of Machu Picchu.

In the moonlit plaza below me stood a solitary tree, which I had grown fond of during my daytime visit. I descended to take in the whole scene from beneath its arching branches. By daylight Machu Picchu's beauty was surreal enough, an almost perfect melding of human and natural design. By night it was utterly spellbinding.

Sitting there in the moonlight, it was impossible to avoid an eerie fascination with the question of whether there might be ghosts roaming about. The night chill began to come on, and I shivered involuntarily. Suddenly I felt with distinct certainty that I was not alone. Two mysterious living presences were moving in the shadows. From behind me came a sudden snort, then heavy breathing only inches from my neck. I nearly jumped out of my skin, then, screwing up all my courage to face my pursuer, I turned. There stood two huge, furry llamas who had come down to share the evening with me!

The llamas squeaked, I laughed at myself, and then we wandered our separate ways into the night.

Gregor Clark's insatiable love of foreign languages and wild places has sent him exploring 'what's around the next bend' in 50 countries, including remote spots such as Easter Island, Greenland and the Galápagos.

PREVIOUS: When archaeologist Hiram Bingham rediscovered the ruins of Machu Picchu in 1911 he is alleged to have speculated whether anyone would believe what he had found.

OPPOSITE: In a feat of uncanny mathematics and precision engineering Inca masons were able to fit the huge stones together in such a way that the buildings would be earthquake-proof.

OVERLEAF: The ruins of Machu Picchu are perched on a high saddle between two peaks and are made up of 18 sq km of terraced stonework linked by over 3000 steps.

Suddenly Rendered Immobile

Karl Bushby

**3 February 1999. 19:28 hours. 20°C.
43°14′ S, 70°51′ W**

Slept well. This morning's very cold due to the strong wind. On the road at 9.45am, setting off into the hard wind, but at least it's downhill. I have been travelling generally downhill for nearly two days now, dropping deeper into the valleys. The sun soon comes up and I begin to feel a touch warmer. Despite the wind I make good progress. It's good being in the valleys, where everything is so much greener, with plenty of trees and places to sleep. Today I pass my first wheat fields, running along the valley floor. There are also plenty of cattle here. I continue to be amazed by the number of birds of prey I see. The sky seems full of them: falcons, buzzards and some very large birds that must be eagles. It's odd to see them hanging around in groups in the fields, maybe up to seven or eight birds. Possibly they are after insects.

I am having a good day until approximately 3pm, when one arm of the towing yoke of the 'beast' (my trailer) snaps clean off, and I'm suddenly rendered immobile. I pull off the road and once again sit face to face with an ugly problem, while being hammered by wind and dust. I first try replacing the arm with a bungee, to get mobile and find somewhere to get out of the wind, but this doesn't work. I find the 'beast' almost impossible to pull on one yoke, and trying to replace the missing yoke with a bungee is useless. I pull off the road a few yards on and pace up and down looking at my problem, thinking. Wood and wire is no good. I trawl the roadsides – nothing but the odd tin can or plastic bottle. Nearby is an old earthworks, used perhaps when constructing the road, and it's here I find a piece of thick black plastic piping. This seems just the ticket, and a plan begins to formulate. I pull it out of the ground, cut the piping to length, and then squash one end of the tube before bending it to match the angle of the broken piece. The plastic is very hard and once lashed to the frame will prove rigid. I take out my Leatherman tool and use the blade to begin cutting a hole for the small piece of bungee that will attach the piping to my rucksack. As I whittle away, the blade slips off and skewers straight into my left wrist. I flinch, draw back and as I do a bright-red jet of blood shoots for a metre across the ground. Wide-eyed, I slam my thumb down onto the cut.

'SHIT. SHIT. SHIT.'

I sit in stunned silence for a while, and then slowly release my thumb to check again. Blood spurts out again, and back goes the thumb. All of a sudden things don't seem to be going very well. I sit cross-legged in a cloud of dust kicked up by the wind.

'Stay calm, stay calm,' I tell myself. 'If the worst comes to the worst I'm on a road (albeit there doesn't seem to be anything on it) and I'll get a lift to Esquel.' It appears I have done one of two things: I've severed an artery or I've nicked an artery. If it's the former I could be in for an interesting time. If I've just nicked it my chances are substantially improved. By now I

feel a little queasy, which is to be expected, as it's not every day you see your own blood jetting from your wrist. I lie back and look skywards.

'Relax, just relax. I'll give it a few minutes of pressure and have another look. If I can't arrest the bleeding I'll have to get help.' I break into a nervous laughter. 'This is alright, sitting here in a sandstorm, amongst the debris of my trailer with a slit wrist. All I need to do now is to poke myself in the eye and stagger onto some long-forgotten landmine.'

I sit up, the queasiness fading. What now? I begin to release the pressure on my thumb, then raise it slowly. There's a clean 1cm puncture wound that seems to be held closed by blood clots. I move my wrist slightly and the wound opens, with bright-red blood bubbling out. I replace my thumb.

'This is good,' I tell myself. 'We can cope with this.'

The wound is very deep, however, and I'll need to suture it. I dig out my alcohol and medical kit, then sit huddled by the broken trailer attempting to shield myself from the wind. Rooting through my kit I find a 22mm needle, thread and some gauze pads. I wash the wound carefully with alcohol, but it's still bleeding quite badly. Dust and dirt kicked up by the wind stick to the blood and it's all quite messy. I try desperately to keep that area out of the wind, infection being foremost in my mind. After a lot of fumbling around and swabbing, I manage to get a stitch into the centre of the wound, but trying to tie knots in these conditions is a real pain, and a very fiddly job with one hand. On my third and final stitch, I pull too hard and the skin tears, so I have to put a fourth wider and deeper stitch in place. Bright-red blood still wells out between the stitches, but after a minute or so it begins to clot quite nicely. 'The job's a good 'un!'

I dress the wound with gauze pads and crepe bandage, happy now that I have it under control. Then back to the trailer, where I strap and bungee the pipe into place before attaching it to my rucksack. Bingo! We're in business, and back on the road. I push on for a last 45 minutes then stop in an area of trees where the valley narrows. Finding a good spot to pitch tent, I relax. I have still managed to do the day's anticipated distance, and despite life's little problems, I'm happy. I've won the day.

Karl Bushby, an ex-paratrooper in his 30s, is attempting to become the first person to complete an unbroken, round-the-world walk. Having started in 1998, he is now halfway through the 57,972km trek and is due to complete it in 2011. Giant Steps, *an account of his great trek to date, offers further insight into his adventure.*

PREVIOUS: From the south all the way north to the Sierra Nevada stretch rolling waves of glistening tussock grass, perfectly adapted to growing in the windswept Patagonian badlands.

OPPOSITE: Patagonia is dominated by the Andes, the world's longest mountain range, which runs the length of South America from Colombia to the Strait of Magellan and across to Tierra del Fuego.

The Jungle Came Alive Around Me

David Lukas

In 1988 I journeyed to Manu National Park in the Peruvian Amazon to work on a research project recording the mating behaviour of a small understorey bird. My job there was simple: sit on a stool deep in the forest for nine hours a day and take notes on bird behaviour. To reach the site we had made a hellacious 12-hour drive in the back of a pick-up over the Andes from the ancient city of Cuzco, then travelled in motorised canoes for three or four days into the heart of the park, arriving at an extremely remote research station in a vast region that is off limits to tourists.

For the uninitiated, Manu National Park exists on a scale that is difficult to comprehend. Its 20,000 sq km have never been hunted, exploited or explored, and at the time of my visit uncontacted tribes still lived in the area. It is the richest and most pristine remaining piece of the Amazonian rainforest and the staggering diversity and abundance of its plants and animals is scarcely matched anywhere else in the world. For example, 15% of the world's bird species are found in the park, and extremely rare creatures such as jaguars, giant otters, tapirs and harpy eagles are still readily seen here.

This is probably the most exciting place in the world to explore the prodigious vitality of life that our ancestors took for granted, and here I was stuck sitting on a stool for my entire three-month stay. It was just my luck that the lead researcher had miscalculated the breeding season of our bird study and the birds weren't doing anything of interest. I ended up spending three months sitting on a stool with nothing to do except remain as motionless as possible and watch the jungle come alive around me. It was the most incredible experience in my life.

Like a good scientist, my field notebooks started out full of detailed observations and lists of plants and animals. I was blown away by the paradise tanagers, screaming pihas, pale-tailed barbthroats and hundreds of other birds. The air throbbed with the ceaseless din of countless insects. Tapirs walked by in the forest gloom and spider monkeys would come sit with their elbows on their knees and watch me or lie on their backs and relax in happy, chattering groups. The animals had absolutely no fear and it made me realise how much it hurts the human spirit that animals flee from us everywhere we walk. There is something profoundly moving about being accepted by the community of life and it seems we have lost touch with this.

One day I sat musing about the challenge that a coworker had posed: to come up with the three most perfect adjectives to describe the rainforest. 'Gossamer' and 'messy' occurred to me within minutes but after two months I was still struggling to find my third choice. On this day, like every other, I had been watching the fantastic play of light as tiny piercing rays of sunlight shot down from the canopy and pulsated like radiant pillars in the moist haze. Every leaf oozed fine mists, hundreds of backlit insects darted in and out of the shafts of light, spider webs glistened like jewelled nets – and I realised that my third adjective would be 'translucent'.

There isn't much else to think about in a job like I had and this was a major breakthrough, so I started writing furiously in my notebook. But then I heard a soft crinkle and turned in time to see an ocelot step through a golden sunbeam and walk right up to me. It paused and glanced up as it passed by, but was utterly unconcerned. Everything in my psyche melted down at that moment, and translucent changed from being an abstract label for the rainforest into a word for the threshold I crossed in my relationship with the natural world.

I understood then that Amazon rainforest was not a novelty for tourists, or a collection of objects for scientists to study, it was a place where lines blurred and we could experience the wholeness of intact ecosystems. Here in the Amazon, the heartbeat of this immensely productive forest pumped a ceaseless column of rich nutrients and gases like a smoke signal into the atmosphere, where it swirled outward to bring life to the entire planet. In some small way, we all hope and pray that this vital heart of our planet is still alive. On that thrumming day of light and myth, I was lucky enough to touch it.

David Lukas is a lifelong student of the natural world, whether travelling far and wide or studying the wildlife of his backyard wilderness in California.

PREVIOUS: The Manu River provides refuge for species of caiman (predators similar to the alligator), which over the past century have been hunted to the brink of extinction.

OPPOSITE: Boat travel is central to jungle life with the Manu River acting as a thoroughfare through the 20,000-sq-km national park, linking the entire northern domain.

A Flat, White Expanse of Salt

Etain O'Carroll

It's the train ride from hell that gets me to Uyuni, a small mining town in Bolivia's remotest highland. I stumble into a guesthouse at 5am for two hours' kip before being woken by the blinding light and my own shivering. It's midwinter at 3653m and bloody cold.

I've come to see Uyuni's fabled salt pan, the largest in the world, stretching for an unfathomable 9000 sq km and surrounded by desert. The salt flats are one of Bolivia's biggest tourist attractions but in low season they're deserted. I buddy up with the other stray gringos in town and we decide to share a jeep to take us across the *salar* (salt pan), through the Atacama desert and on to the border with Chile.

We set off on a rutted, pockmarked excuse of a road, mountains rising abruptly from the scorched desert and heat shimmering across the sand. The trail soon disappears and we lurch out onto the *salar*, an immense blanket of white that extends as far as the eye can see.

The air is exceptionally clear and the sky stretches in an extraordinary expanse above us while a chain of snowcapped peaks floats majestically on the horizon. We're soon surrounded in all directions and it's mesmerising. The glare is almost unbearable and despite my mountain specific sunglasses I fight back the urge to close my eyes and relieve the tortuous squint that has settled across my entire face.

Our first stop is the Hotel Playa Blanca, a tourist trap constructed entirely from salt. That's salt walls, beds, tables, chairs and even tacky souvenirs made from salt. It's deserted.

There are no customers out here, no inhabitants, and only a trickle of tourists at this time of year. But it's as close to commercial tourism as you get and our driver seems proud of it.

Driving on across the *salar* we arrive at Isla de Pescadores, a rocky volcanic outcrop covered in giant cacti up to 400 years old. Vicuñas, a smaller relative of the llama, graze languidly between them. We tumble out of the jeep and walk through the scrub to the summit. I'm breathless by the time I make the top but the view is hypnotic. Light glimmers everywhere, cacti are silhouetted against the glaring sun, jagged peaks and snowcapped volcanoes glimmer on the horizon and in between, in every direction, a flat, white expanse of salt stretches to the edge of the earth.

We load back into the jeep but we're soon bogged down in brine. The driver slows to a snail's pace and we can all feel the wheels sinking into the slushy surface. Silently we sink deeper and deeper into the water but somehow our driver manages to keep moving. It's several hours later before we eventually lurch onto the sand of the Atacama and heave a collective sigh of relief.

The Atacama is the driest desert in the world and on average only sees 1cm of moisture a year, most of it from fog. Some parts have never recorded a rainfall. As we drive across the sandy plain, herds of llamas and vicuñas race alongside the jeep and in the distance a dust storm weaves its way across the desert.

Eight hours after leaving Uyuni we finally pull into the tiny adobe village of San Juan. It too

There isn't much else to think about in a job like I had and this was a major breakthrough, so I started writing furiously in my notebook. But then I heard a soft crinkle and turned in time to see an ocelot step through a golden sunbeam and walk right up to me. It paused and glanced up as it passed by, but was utterly unconcerned. Everything in my psyche melted down at that moment, and translucent changed from being an abstract label for the rainforest into a word for the threshold I crossed in my relationship with the natural world.

I understood then that Amazon rainforest was not a novelty for tourists, or a collection of objects for scientists to study, it was a place where lines blurred and we could experience the wholeness of intact ecosystems. Here in the Amazon, the heartbeat of this immensely productive forest pumped a ceaseless column of rich nutrients and gases like a smoke signal into the atmosphere, where it swirled outward to bring life to the entire planet. In some small way, we all hope and pray that this vital heart of our planet is still alive. On that thrumming day of light and myth, I was lucky enough to touch it.

David Lukas is a lifelong student of the natural world, whether travelling far and wide or studying the wildlife of his backyard wilderness in California.

A Flat, White Expanse of Salt

Etain O'Carroll

It's the train ride from hell that gets me to Uyuni, a small mining town in Bolivia's remotest highland. I stumble into a guesthouse at 5am for two hours' kip before being woken by the blinding light and my own shivering. It's midwinter at 3653m and bloody cold.

I've come to see Uyuni's fabled salt pan, the largest in the world, stretching for an unfathomable 9000 sq km and surrounded by desert. The salt flats are one of Bolivia's biggest tourist attractions but in low season they're deserted. I buddy up with the other stray gringos in town and we decide to share a jeep to take us across the *salar* (salt pan), through the Atacama desert and on to the border with Chile.

We set off on a rutted, pockmarked excuse of a road, mountains rising abruptly from the scorched desert and heat shimmering across the sand. The trail soon disappears and we lurch out onto the *salar,* an immense blanket of white that extends as far as the eye can see.

The air is exceptionally clear and the sky stretches in an extraordinary expanse above us while a chain of snowcapped peaks floats majestically on the horizon. We're soon surrounded in all directions and it's mesmerising. The glare is almost unbearable and despite my mountain-specific sunglasses I fight back the urge to close my eyes and relieve the tortuous squint that has settled across my entire face.

Our first stop is the Hotel Playa Blanca, a tourist trap constructed entirely from salt. That's salt walls, beds, tables, chairs and even tacky souvenirs made from salt. It's deserted.

There are no customers out here, no inhabitants, and only a trickle of tourists at this time of year. But it's as close to commercial tourism as you get and our driver seems proud of it.

Driving on across the *salar* we arrive at Isla de Pescadores, a rocky volcanic outcrop covered in giant cacti up to 400 years old. Vicuñas, a smaller relative of the llama, graze languidly between them. We tumble out of the jeep and walk through the scrub to the summit. I'm breathless by the time I make the top but the view is hypnotic. Light glimmers everywhere, cacti are silhouetted against the glaring sun, jagged peaks and snowcapped volcanoes glimmer on the horizon and in between, in every direction, a flat, white expanse of salt stretches to the edge of the earth.

We load back into the jeep but we're soon bogged down in brine. The driver slows to a snail's pace and we can feel the wheels sinking into the slushy surface. Silently we sink deeper and deeper into the water but somehow our driver manages to keep moving. It's several hours later before we eventually lurch onto the sand of the Atacama and heave a collective sigh of relief.

The Atacama is the driest desert in the world and on average only sees 1cm of moisture a year, most of it from fog. Some parts have never recorded a rainfall. As we drive across the sandy plain, herds of llamas and vicuñas race alongside the jeep and in the distance a dust storm weaves its way across the desert.

Eight hours after leaving Uyuni we finally pull into the tiny adobe village of San Juan. It too

PREVIOUS: The Manu River provides refuge for species of caiman (predators similar to the alligator), which over the past century have been hunted to the brink of extinction.

OPPOSITE: Boat travel is central to jungle life with the Manu River acting as a thoroughfare through the 20,000-sq-km national park, linking the entire northern domain.

seems deserted save for a few goats wandering down the streets. We bed down in a basic guesthouse and by morning the desert has sucked all moisture from my skin. I feel like I've had a face-lift and my legs look like snakeskin.

San Juan vanishes in a cloud of dust as we leave and we spend the day gaining elevation, going further and further into the desert and away from settlement of any kind. This is a harsh, desolate landscape flanked by spectacular mountain ranges and totally devoid of life. Bacteria don't even survive out here.

The scenery is otherworldly though, jagged peaks and sweeping dunes cradle the crystal-clear turquoise water of Laguna Chiguana, temporary home to a group of rare James' flamingos which have gathered for the winter breeding season. They seem totally out of place in the lunar landscape. Further on ferocious winds have carved out surreal, freestanding rock forms in the high-altitude valley at Pampa Siloli. The jagged edges and stunning curves of the Arbol de Piedra, the Stone Tree, are magnificent, an 8m Dali-esque figure balancing on an elegant trunk and sculpted by nature into a tortured form.

The fiery red waters of Laguna Colorada are bizarre too. Surrounded by white dunes of borax and coloured by algae growing in the mineral-rich water, the lake looks highly toxic and foreboding. Jagged black peaks rise abruptly behind it into the immense blue sky but at this altitude I find it tiring just walking to the rustic shelter where we'll stay for the night. We're at an elevation of 4800m, it's bitterly cold and I'm breathless and lethargic. No-one is hungry and no-one can sleep. It's still dark when we set off on the last day of the trip and head for Sol de Mañana, a geyser basin perched at 5000m. We arrive just as the sun begins to rise over the mountain peaks, steam hisses as it rises straight up out of the fumaroles, and the earth splutters and boils, billowing clouds of vapour into the sky. Apart from the whiff of sulphur hanging in the air it could be the set of a cheap sci-fi movie.

Our last stop is Laguna Verde at the foot of majestic Volcán Licacábur. The lake is renowned for its changing colour, and I sit enthralled as it transforms from its stony blue to an iridescent green, right before my eyes. This corner of Bolivia is simply awe-inspiring, home to some of the most spectacular and extreme landscapes on earth and yet completely undeveloped. I feel humbled by it and privileged to have seen it.

Etain O'Carroll is a travel writer and photographer smitten by extremes and strangely attracted to the discomforts of epic bus journeys, hellish roads, unrecognisable foods and ridiculously low temperatures.

PREVIOUS: How times change: the Uyuni Salt Pan is all that remains of a massive prehistoric lake that is now surrounded by the world's driest desert.

OPPOSITE: From 1924 until their rediscovery over 30 years later James' flamingos, which only live in the high altitude regions of the Andes, were thought to be extinct.

A Continent with No Road Signs

Andrew Stevenson

'Hate to see someone sick,' Vidar, one of the crewmen, says, explaining why he has been sitting in the bar for the second night in a row while his erstwhile shipmate hunkers down in their cabin. He hastily grabs his beer as the *Polar Star,* a Swedish icebreaker, rises and then lurches into a prolonged roll as it tumbles down the side of an ocean crest. The captain describes this as a 'calm' crossing of the Drake 'Lake', but the peculiar features of an icebreaker's rounded hull make it anything but calm.

In my vague schoolboy recollection of British-rendered history, I thought it was Scott who achieved the honour of reaching the South Pole first, in 1911. In fact, it was Roald Amundsen, 'cheating' with a team of dogs, who left a Norwegian flag and what must have been a heartbreaking note for Captain Robert F Scott. It seems remarkable on a continent with no road signs, covered in an expanse of ice, in the days before handheld GPS, that Scott could have contrived to have arrived a month later, at exactly the same spot that Amundsen had left his devastating note. If I'd been Scott, I would have lied. 'What note?' I'd say later, claiming I'd never seen the wretched missive because I'd been there first.

Remarkably, no-one else reached the South Pole again until 1956.

I soon realised the most comfortable place on the ship was my cabin midships, at the bottom of the pendulum, just above the water line. Velcro pyjamas and bed sheets would have been a further distinct advantage.

Two days after I had set off with so much blithe enthusiasm, I woke up in a perfectly darkened cabin, heavy deadlights still bolted securely over the portholes. My instinctive reaction was to grab the mattress, but I wasn't rolling or pitching any longer and the sound of the engines was a rhythmic hum rather than the intermittent thudding crash of reinforced steel hull against tonnes of water.

I shuffled to the stern where I unbolted the bank-vault door and stepped out into bright sunshine and the view of an orange ball of light ricocheting off a perfectly glassy-smooth ocean. At four in the morning the only other person awake was Sergey, the Russian second officer at the helm, and a Filipino crewman diligently washing the salt spray off the bridge windows.

The icebreaker's electrically powered engines were a benign purr, and we seemed to be motionless, apart from chunks of ice sliding past us at nine knots as we cruised down the Neumayer Channel through a spectacular landscape of pristine, snow-covered mountains and glaciers bathed in the delicate first blush of morning.

The awesome sense of peacefulness, of emptiness, of something still untouched by mankind, is pervasive here. This seventh continent, where there is no permanent community, has a magical allure. It's a sad reflection on civilisation that the concept of a continent where humans don't live has such a profound appeal. Proving the point, a pair of Minke whales breached several times in succession against a backdrop of a snow-clad mountain.

At the British Antarctic Survey base of Port Lockroy I cadged a ride for shore, bouncing on the side of a rubber Zodiac getting a wet bum whilst being whisked to one of the most isolated outposts of the human race. This is an easier entrée to an elite club of 'adventurers' and 'explorers' than climbing Everest, notwithstanding the fact that bouncing out of the Zodiac into the water would be akin to falling into a vat of acid.

I placed a foot on one the few stretches of shoreline accessible on the Antarctic continent, eager to make friends with a bunch of Gentoo penguins. With no predators on land and unable to fly away, the Gentoo penguins waddled about clumsily, as penguins do. A polar bear, if he ever did manage to catch a lift on a huge iceberg and migrate from the North Pole, would have died very fat and happy down here.

There hadn't been a cloud in the sky when we had disembarked, but within a short time the wind picked up and the sky became overcast. What had seemed an enchanting, enticing snowscape suddenly seemed formidable and inhospitable. My passport hastily stamped 'British Antarctic Territory, Port Lockroy', I returned with the crew back to the icebreaker through a snow squall. Three penguins fleeing a leopard seal popped out of the water like fleas into the middle of our tiny Zodiac. Having successfully escaped the pursuing leopard seal, they waddled wide-eyed to the stern and skipped over the transom. But back on the icebreaker, trying to get through the Penola Channel to another research station where three Ukrainian scientists were eagerly awaiting our arrival to help celebrate the New Year, we became locked in the pack ice.

A cross, mounted on a small exposure of rock outside an abandoned research hut on our starboard side was a reminder of how dangerous the ice can be. Three of the previous inhabitants of the hut had gone out on the pack ice when it cracked, detached and became an ice floe drifting out to sea. They were never seen again. How awful it must have been when they realised their predicament, and their likely fate. The cross was a constant reminder of their misadventure as, for the next seven hours, the captain attempted to turn the *Polar Star* around so that we could head back out through the ice we had cut through earlier. The lonely Ukrainian trio must have been fit to be tied as they saw us retreat, just a couple of hours before midnight on New Year's Eve.

A fortnight later, heading back through the Drake's Passage, hunkered down in my cabin with my toes and fingers wedged between the gyrating mattress and the wooden sideboards, I had two pressing questions remaining. How *did* Scott find the *exact* spot where Amundsen left his taunting letter in the middle of that vast ice continent? And if you stood there, at the precise point of the Geographical South Pole, would you get dizzy seeing the world spin around you?

Andrew Stevenson has travelled extensively throughout his life. Trained as an economist, the topics of his travelogues, photographic books and films include the Himalayas, New Zealand, Australia and Norway.

PREVIOUS: 'Ice-strengthened' Antarctic supply ships have a double hull so that if an iceberg punctures the outer hull the inner one will, hopefully, remain intact.

OPPOSITE: The waters surrounding Antarctica contain over 90% of the world's icebergs. Small ones are the size of a piano, whilst the biggest recorded was larger than Luxembourg.

A Perfect, Glassy Swell

Craig Scutt

Halfway to the beach Dave slams on the brakes. Dust billows up from the unsealed road. 'Get out,' he chirps, 'You want to see where we're going, right?'

I climb out of the jeep and join him at the edge of a low cliff looking out over the Atlantic. 'Out there,' he points, 'Can you see it?' I look in the direction his finger's pointing and can just make out a tiny speck of white water bubbling on the ocean about a kilometre offshore. 'It's going to be epic, man,' he says, slinging his brown arm over my shoulder, 'I can feel it.'

Because the reef is so far out it's impossible to tell exactly how good the waves are without actually being there. But just to be able to see the white water means something is going on. The problem is getting out there.

Far below, creamy beaches stretch away to the north and south, like a soft, thin carpet wrapping round the island. A heavy shore-break churns up the sand close in. Further out over the shallows the water is that beautiful shade of turquoise you see in picture postcards of Caribbean Islands. Nearer the reef, the ledge of rock forming the landmass drops away, and the water changes to a deep, dark shade of blue. 'Come on,' says Dave, already back behind the wheel, 'We're wasting time.'

Surfing secret spots with a local is like getting VIP treatment at your favourite nightclub. You suddenly have access to rooms, a bar and a DJ that you never knew existed. Without warning Dave pulls up on a verge at the start of an unmarked path leading down to the beach. We pull our boards from the back and head straight for the surf.

I follow him as he picks a path over the black rocks making up the point. He then launches himself onto the back of a receding wave. Swells mass angrily over the point, frothing up the water. I manage to time my own entry right and avoid being dumped painfully back onto the rocks. It's a long way to the reef but we paddle hard, amped with adrenaline and excitement about what's in store.

After 20 minutes Dave stops paddling and sits on his board, facing the shore. As the ground-swell moves in he is lifted up and down like a kid bobbing on a seesaw. 'Isn't it beautiful?' he beams. I turn to see the lush green island rising above pristine white beaches and the midnight shadows of the rocks. Wisps of cloud streak the sky. The sun burns bright overhead.

Two metres away, without warning, something dark and shiny flaps out the water. My heart launches out of my mouth, making me fall off my board sideways. 'What the fuck was that?' I half screech at Dave as I pull myself back onto the board. 'Just a little fishy,' he grins. 'You should have seen your face, man,' he says as he starts paddling, 'I wish I had a camera.'

We are only halfway to the reef and an urge to head back to shore surges over me like a tide. I have surfed in many places but this is easily the furthest I've had to paddle out. Maybe it's because I've been living in a city too long but lying on the water, so far from land, I feel hopelessly out of my depth. This is the ocean. I am

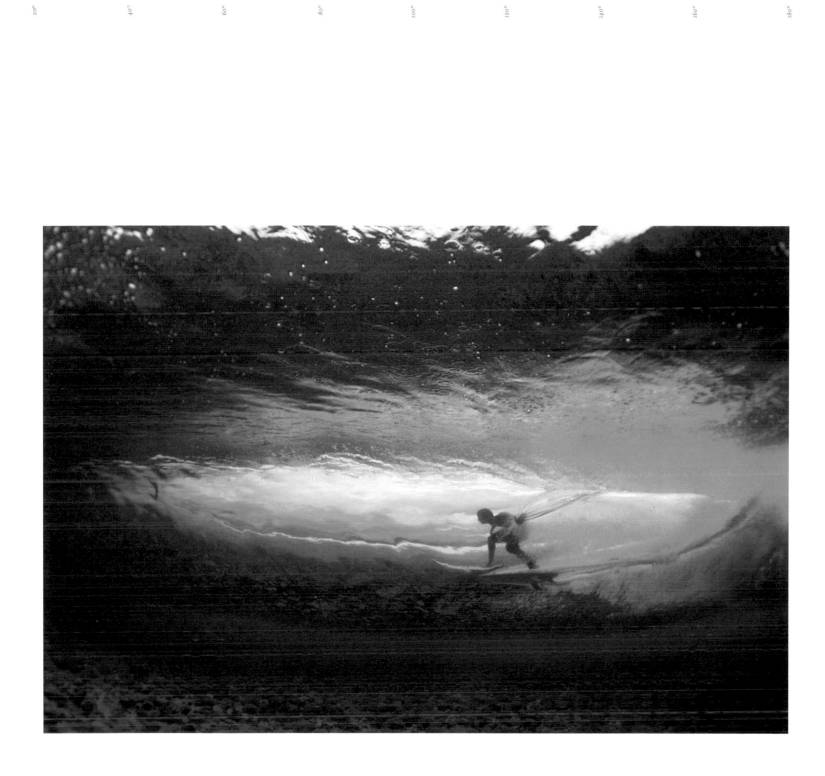

not a fish. But I could be food for a fish. Usually when a little one jumps out the water it means something bigger, with sharp teeth, is chasing it. A creeping fear rises from the sea, paralysing me. 'Come on, man,' shouts Dave, as if he had been reading my mind, 'Not far to go.'

I reign in my imagination. I will never have the chance to be out here again. Besides, I tell myself, what doesn't kill you makes you stronger. I catch up with Dave and we press on side by side, our arms breaking the water in unison. My shoulders start to burn. The physical exertion gives me strength and I begin to feel more relaxed. Then the water turns cold.

We have passed over the ledge I could see from the track, where the ocean became a dark, threatening blue. I look down. I can see shadows moving below the surface, slow, black and ominous. It must be the clouds. Anxiety reaches up, touching my fingertips as they move through the inky water, propelling me further into the deep.

The ocean spreads out, broad as night, in every direction. I picture myself from the sea floor, flapping pathetically, inefficiently on the surface. I am krill to a whale, a grain of sand to a beach, an insignificant speck of cosmic dust floating in the void. How incomprehensible the immensity of the ocean! Here, in the midst of its great presence I finally realise the profundity of the phrase 'a drop in the ocean'. More than two thirds of the surface of the earth, itself barely a pinprick into the fabric of the universe, is covered by water. I have never felt smaller and, knowing my true scale in the world, more at peace.

Soon the sound of waves thundering into the reef sharpens my senses. The break is truly epic, like Dave promised. Thick, mean, hollow barrels exploding smoothly down the line onto the rock shelf. Sun glints off the face of every wave before the lip wraps over to form a perfect, glassy tubular swell.

Far from the empty shore we catch wave after perfect wave. Whether we think it or not, we are alone and vulnerable. If anything goes wrong, like I misjudge the takeoff and slam into the reef, or Dave is held under by a wave and runs out of breath, then there is every chance the event will go unrecorded.

Dave catches a wave and disappears over the ledge. Anxiously I watch the back of the wave until I see him pop over the shoulder and begin paddling towards me. Relaxed, I swivel round and sit on my board facing the horizon. It seems eerily close. We are so far out that it would only take a storm or a strong current to push us out into the endless deep. Somewhere lays an unseen line. If we cross it, the ocean will claim us.

Craig Scutt has lived on three continents and thinks everywhere's a good home. He hopes to come back as a Lonely Planet photographers' camera lens.

PREVIOUS: Coral reefs are among the oldest and most delicate ecosystems on the planet, and are estimated to host over a million distinct species of fish, invertebrates and algae.

OPPOSITE: The earliest settlements discovered on the island date back to around the fourth millennium BC, during which time St Maartens was a secluded, peaceful island paradise.

Amid the Icy Vastness

Mark Elliott

We're stuck. It happened about two hours ago. Or was it two centuries? Time itself has stopped.

I'm in a tiny, open motorboat, trapped in coalescing sea ice off the South Greenland coast. We're five hours' ride from the nearest village, so forget rescue parties. That village, outrageously beautiful Aappilattoq, is one of the world's most remote villages, with only 160 souls and no helicopter. Anyway, how would the villagers know where to look? Mobile phones don't work – the seals don't need them, after all. Skipper Anton's radio should do better. But we can't even reach the other boat that we had been travelling with. Not that they could help anyway. Hunter Adolf, strange name for an Inuit, could fire off his gun. But if anyone heard, they'd assume he was shooting seals.

The ice continues to press itself together. And the boat, so minuscule amid the icy vastness, is now being squeezed out of the water entirely. As I write it has popped up onto a near-flat plate of frozen ocean. Next stop mid-Atlantic.

I love life. I love to live. Without really thinking about it, I'd always assumed that if the grim reaper started flailing death's scythe in my direction, I'd be diving for cover, parrying the blows, fighting to keep going.

So what on earth am I doing here, sitting passively in the cold clutches of icy doom? Death is hanging over me, yet, to my amazement, all I can do is gawp at the extraordinary beauty around me. More colours of white than can be described. A cubist sea painted in glacier chunks and walrus duvets. It all looks so perfect. It all seems so still. Yet all that ice is powerfully, inexorably, in motion. All around. Crushing and isolating us. Death and beauty kissing one another in white, heart-stopping passion.

The thinking side of my brain contemplates panic. So I keep it busy flicking through memories of heroic Arctic survivals. Of those who survived years trapped in the Arctic ice. But I'm not Shackleton. We don't have a galleon with masts and furniture we can burn to keep warm. And I'm not Nansen, happy to see where in the Atlantic I might emerge in a year or two's time. We don't have a spare year's supplies. In fact, we don't have anything to eat beyond a pack of fisherman's dry biscuits. I don't even have properly warm clothes for a night at sea. I had thought we were going for a brief potter round the fjord, not out hunting seals in the treacherous coastal ice floes.

When the sun sulks, it's already freezing cold. But fear is somehow so pointless. And the other side of my mind reminds me once more to relish the beauty while I can.

So, haunted by fear's spectre, I stare with even greater awe. The fabulous rocky bluffs of the coastal fjords rise like mirages on the horizon, reappearing and disappearing in the wreaths of fog that are preparing to mark our graves when we decide to freeze. The sun is getting low, the fog is returning. 'No!' I tell myself yet again, as my mind goes back to fishing for strands of miracle or superhuman plans. No! I'm not in a movie. Even if I were strong and agile enough to

110

iceberg hop towards the shore, there'd be stretches of open water to cross. And even if I made it to land? So what? There'd be no roads, no villages, no human habitation, not even a tree or bush for shelter on the glacier-scratched rocks. For hundreds of kilometres of coastline, the only *Homo sapiens* are tucked up in a single radio-flight-control station guiding planes overhead from Europe to Canada. I could look for the aerial! Yeah? OK then, off you go. I sat still.

For two hours I'd said much more to myself than to my fellow boatmen. To some extent I wanted to quietly assume that Anton and Adolf had everything under control. After all, these were their waters. This was their daily life. Did this happen regularly? Not speaking a word of Greenlandic, I couldn't ask them. Anyway, Inuits aren't a talkative bunch. Most communication is nonverbal. Perhaps they were they just waiting for the tide to turn? Letting nature unravel the icy jigsaw in which it had playfully trapped us.

But after two hours, their smiles have taken on an ever more forced look. In Eskimo face-code I suspect that this means 'We're a teeny bit frightened.' OK, so my smile reading is as elementary as my Inuit. But it's time to overcome blissed-out resignation and try to do something. Let's move that icy jigsaw.

The boat, a mere wooden frame with outboard motor, offers no shelter. But at least that makes it relatively light to carry. Well, if not carry then drag – with three men working together it's just possible to heave it a foot or two at a time. The trouble is we're not really sure which direction to move it. What we need is to find a lead, an area of water between ice blocks. Even a few centimetres of deep water would allow us to use the outboard motor to help the ice-pushing.

Fortunately, most of the ice is flat sheets of sea-freeze rather than the dauntingly huge mountains that are real icebergs. We strike out and on a second attempt get lucky, coaxing the spine of the boat into a few centimetres of deeper water. Using the boat as a giant butter knife, we attempt to force blocks apart. I lie on the prow, my feet pressing with maximum force on the ice block to my right, Adolf doing the same to the left while Anton revs the outboard to drive us forward. Perhaps 30cm. Perhaps only 20cm. Is this progress? How long can this go on? I suddenly understand for the first time the old saying 'to work like one's life depended on it'.

The effort combines a curious mixture of brute force and balletic grace. The dance has just one step – a back-flip fall into the boat once the craft suddenly lurches forward. There's no learning time. One mistake would be fatal. Leaving the pirouette too late and falling in the frozen water means certain death, given my total lack of dry clothes, blankets or cover. But there's no other way. And separating these giant blocks requires all my strength. Plus a little puzzle solving to unlock looser groups of ice-blocks to make it all easier.

Two hours have passed. We've made barely 250m and the sun is setting. But suddenly, miraculously, we're through. The blocks start to part with less effort. And then – bliss! Open water. The next five hours are still fraught. There are ice fragments to dodge and the boat has no lights. There's no moon either. But – another miracle – tonight's aurora, the magical northern lights, have come to our salvation. They're the strongest I've ever seen. Astonishing bright columns of electric lime-green swirl in majestic arcs, occasionally tinged with red. And churned by our outboard motor, agitated phytoplankton create a dancing silver thread through the deep, dark wake.

Half frozen, yet euphoric with survival and such indescribable beauty, I float on the edge of consciousness all the way back to Aappilattoq, a bed and warmth.

Mark Elliott perversely writes guidebooks to the world's least-touristed areas, a financially idiotic occupation bringing many KGB suspicions of spying, and hair-tearing get-me-out-of-here adventures, but most of all a great faith in humanity.

PREVIOUS: Around 10,000 to 15,000 icebergs are calved each year by the vast glaciers of West Greenland. They are then masterfully sculpted by the forces of the sun, waves, wind and rain.

OPPOSITE: The brightly painted houses in Greenlandic villages reflect the days when a building's purpose was defined by its colour, such as yellow for hospitals, red for government offices and blue for utilities.

Gazing Out Towards the Vast Greenland Icecap

Grant Dixon

We fly low above a grey sea. Less than an hour out of Iceland's northwest outpost of Isafjörður, sea ice appears below, and the sea is completely frozen long before we cross the Greenland coast. Snowy bluffs of the summer coastline soon give way to steep-sided peaks and ridges separated by broad glaciers as we continue 60km inland. We are soon flying level with or below the surrounding summits, before a bumpy glacier landing in the heart of the Watkins Bjerge (mountains), a cluster of the highest peaks north of the Arctic Circle.

A ski-equipped Twin Otter flight from Iceland is an easy way to access remotest Greenland, but flying for a couple of hours over icy sea and massive glaciers, then listening to the fading drone of the departing plane, rather emphasises our distance from sensible, settled people. To what end, to stand atop basalt layer-cake peaks capped by snow and gaze out towards the vast Greenland icecap?

We sit amongst our pile of gear, a windless day with a clear blue sky, and it is so quiet. Occasionally the odd seabird may fly or be blown inland, but in general nothing lives here. The colours of the area are basic and elemental – white, blue and brown – and our bright clothing, tents and skis emphasise our foreignness. We are here for a brief flirtation with this apparently lifeless land.

It's May, with 24-hour daylight here in the far north. The light and excitement make sleep fitful this first night. Lying awake at 1am, I admire the pastel colours of sky and snow from the relative warmth of my tent, as the sun dips towards the northern horizon. It's a hint of what the Norwegian Arctic explorer and scientist Fridtjof Nansen (1861–1930) was alluding to when he wrote:

Nothing more wonderfully beautiful can exist than the Arctic night. It is dreamland, painted in the imagination's most delicate tints; it is colour etheralised. One shade melts into the other, so that you cannot tell where one ends and the other begins, and yet they are all there.

We head first to Gunnbjørns Fjeld, the highest peak in Greenland. Distances are greater than they appear in the clear Arctic air, and it is a long haul to the base of the final ice wall below the summit. Inland, beyond the huge Christian IV Glacier, 15km wide, the Greenland icecap forms a white horizon. The icecap is 2500km long, up to 3000m thick and covers 85% of this 2.4-million-sq-km island. Tiredness is temporarily forgotten as we don skis for the 1500m descent back to camp, exhilarating runs punctuated with cautious weaving between crevasses. Sleep comes easily in my cosy tent that night, despite the light.

We move camp several times over the subsequent weeks, towing small sleds laden with food and survival gear up to camp on the névés of various glaciers, then climbing the surrounding peaks. Such glacier travel is a slog at times, sled hauling through softening snow, and balancing burning thigh muscles with the grip limit of our skis' climbing skins on steeper gradients. If the

114

glacier surface isn't smooth, at day's end tender hips are often the price for jerking the laden sleds over ice ribs and sastrugi. However, the views are always worth the effort – striated walls of rock and snow, castellated ridges, tottering séracs perched on steep slopes, ice fields with rocky ridges and nunataks fading into the distant haze, and, to the far east, flat sea ice glistening in low sun beyond the ranges.

Glacier life has its quirks and rituals. In camp, the roar of our stove often disturbs the stillness, but melting snow for water is an essential multi-hour daily chore. Ironically, staying cool when moving is sometimes more difficult than keeping warm, and can involve repeated clothing tweaks. Radiant heat on clear and sunny days can be considerable, despite low air temperatures, and sweat-damp clothes are worth avoiding as they may later freeze.

We leave camp at 5am for our final climb, the air frigid and snow frozen hard, but still we are soon sweating with effort. Cloud fills the valleys today, but we rise above it. Hours later, by the time we lunch atop another summit, the cloud has thickened and now forms an unbroken mass from coast to icecap, the surrounding peaks and ranges protruding islands. Our ski descent changes character as we enter the rising cloud layer; the light is flat and dull, and even when I can see some distance ahead, there is no depth perception. We creep downwards, my companions mere ghostly outlines in the mist, snowploughing slowly and trying to discern our upward tracks to plot a safe route amongst the crevasses.

We scan a sky bisected by the vapour trail of an intercontinental jet, a reminder we aren't alone, and eventually a small moving dot appears above the distant mountains, the engine sound reaching us a little later. It's time to rejoin the other world.

Grant Dixon is chronically attracted to cool-climate landscapes and undertakes regular forays seeking white and icy places around the planet, on foot, ski and by sea.

PREVIOUS: In the 10th century Eric the Red headed west after he was banished from his native Iceland. In AD 982 he discovered Greenland – so named to encourage wary settlers to go there.

OPPOSITE: The peaks of East Greenland represents a final frozen frontier to mountaineers. Many are yet to be climbed, or even visited, due to the extreme remoteness of their location.

The Edge of the Map

Sarah Andrews

The wind-blasted juniper trees here at the western edge of El Hierro have been warped and twisted into shapes that seem almost human. Squinting my eyes, I can make out the graceful arch of a dancer and the bent back of an old woman. I'm convinced that if I turn my back the shapes will break out of position and come to life.

Eerie though it may be, this cluster of wild juniper trees fits the atmosphere of El Hierro. A tiny volcanic island flung off the western coast of Africa, El Hierro is the smallest and most forgotten of Spain's Canary Islands archipelago. It sits less than 80km from the hedonistic chaos on the island of Tenerife, where I was lounging on the beach just yesterday, but it feels a world away. An oftentimes harsh volcanic landscape, a climate of ferocious wind and thick fog, and a sparse population of fewer than 10,000 hardy souls cloak the island in a mysterious air that couldn't be further from Tenerife's carefree golden beaches.

The awe-inspiring physical realities of El Hierro – its jagged rocks, fearsome wind and remote location – are part of what drew me here. But even more alluring is the island's past. During most of modern history, this out-of-the-way spot of land was the end of the known world. It's a concept that my airplane-hopping, Internet-surfing generation can't quite grasp, but I was intrigued by the idea of standing in a place that was once on the edge of the map, at the very end of the Earth. So here I am, one ferry ride and a rental car later, looking out beyond El Hierro's western shore into the great expanse of the Atlantic, trying to imagine that I don't know what lies beyond it.

In AD 150 Ptolemy drew a meridian line through this spot and marked it as the world's end. Until new lands were discovered in the 1400s, Europeans believed that El Hierro was literally the last place on Earth. Although I have a slightly better grasp of geography than those earlier explorers, at least when it comes to the islands and continents further west, I can't shake the feeling that El Hierro marks the end of something. That maybe it would be possible after all to walk off its shore and simply drop off the Earth.

The solitude associated with this place is palpable, not only in the juniper grove that stands as mute testament to the dominance of the elements, but everywhere. The island is a harsh place in so many ways; I feel as though it's daring me to come closer. Such severity seems fitting for a place so long considered to be at the edge of the world.

If you approach El Hierro from the ocean on ferry, as I did, it's easy to see that the rocky coast is all but inaccessible from the water. The shore is lined with sharp volcanic rocks, pounding waves and cliffs plunging 900m or more into the churning Atlantic. Looking out from the ferry's deck, it comes as a surprise when the boat steers itself towards the rock walls and somehow finds a small harbour to slip into.

The land doesn't offer much comfort either. Just 50,000 years ago, a blink of an eye geologically

speaking, a tremor caused a third of the island to break off and slide into the Atlantic, creating a tsunami so enormous that it was probably felt on the shores of America. Now, a whopping 800 volcanoes litter the 277 sq km that are left of El Hierro, and the lava they've spit out has rendered much of the island barren. There hasn't been an eruption for two centuries or so, but the threat of one lingers in the air.

Even the wildlife here is peculiar. The nearly extinct lizard of Salmor is an enormous reptile that's become something of a symbol for the island. A greyish-brown creature that can grow to be as large as a house cat, the lizard is disturbing in appearance but supposedly harmless.

Impenetrable cliffs, volcano-strewn landscapes and native wildlife worthy of a science fiction movie. Simply put, El Hierro is not to be trifled with.

Yet for all this, I can't help but be fascinated by El Hierro, the old meridian zero, the ultimate frontier land. The sense of otherworldly isolation that penetrates the island and its history is exactly what draws me to it. I'm in awe of the strange volcanic landscapes, where rocks can look either like smooth, twisted taffy or like painfully sharp beds of knives, and where only a few brave shrubs dare to lift their heads among the black rock formations that stand like monuments to the power of nature. It is beautiful in its silence.

When I finally get around to exploring the interior of the island, I'm surprised to find that there is more to El Hierro than harsh terrain and tearing winds. Every now and again the fog recedes, revealing views of green hillsides dotted with farmhouses, and of pineapple groves dug into the volcanic soil. Yet those more ordinary attractions simply don't have the same pull and power over me as El Hierro's outer reaches, where stark volcanic panoramas reign.

In all honesty, El Hierro is not the sort of place I'd like to live in (an island without a single stoplight or elevator is great for escapism, but not for everyday life), but it is the sort of place that calls to me long after I've left. When I'm back home amid chaos and stress, I will close my eyes and imagine myself back at the western edge of the world, driving through its lunar-like badlands and dormant volcanoes. I'll imagine myself stopping at the shore to stand atop a cliff and stare down into the crashing waves below. And I'll take comfort in the permanence of the juniper trees, contorted and twisted, sculpted by the hand of the wind.

North Carolinian Sarah Andrews first discovered the badlands of El Hierro while writing Lonely Planet's Canary Islands *guide. Though her work as a freelance travel writer has taken her to plenty of other shores since, she still hasn't found a spot that can rival eerie, isolated El Hierro.*

PREVIOUS: *Las Sabinas* (creeping junipers) are possibly the most famous trees on earth – their tortured shapes are a result of being twisted by the trade winds that screech across the island.

OPPOSITE: The entire coastline of El Hierro is dominated by brooding, inaccessible volcanic cliffs rising up to 1000m high, within which are nestled wonderful natural rock pools and sheltered coves.

A Speck in the Sahara

Sam Benson

As the driver swept us off the broken-down bus like stray chickens, I began to suspect that this was finally the end of the line.

A rollicking ferry from the southern coast of Spain, a filthy train from Tangiers to Fès and a bumpy, all-night bus over the bone-chilling Atlas Mountains had unceremoniously dropped me in the dusty kasbah town of Rissani, at the northern edge of the Sahara Desert.

Towering dunes arose like waves behind the resort hotel in nearby Merzouga; French tourists languidly smoked cigarettes. Our guide squatted in the hazy heat next to the camels, gesticulating with his buddies. I sat and waited, wondering when we would leave. I had come to the Sahara looking for the ultimate escape – from life, from broken love, from responsibilities. I imagined a Zen landscape of nothingness, an ocean of red sands broken only by palm oases.

What I hadn't counted on was the ornery personality of my camel. Nothing breaks the meditative silence of the great Sahara like a huge glob of spit being hurled at you by a pissed-off mount. It was my fault, I admit. To begin with, I'd sat on the camel incorrectly, forcing her nearly to buckle as she unfolded to stand like origami in reverse. Ever since then, this camel had it in for me. She knew I wasn't her master. Every step the camel took across the rolling desert, I slipped a bit further down her back. Too quickly, the sun began to sink over the dunes. As darkness floated down like a blanket, my camel succeeded in her scheme to ditch me completely. I fell on the sand with a thud.

My guide hadn't noticed in his rush to push onward and set up camp. So there I was, alone and lost in the dunes, holding a flimsy pair of reins and begging my camel not to bolt. 'Sugar?' I offered the camel. 'You want some sugar when we get to camp? How about a nice leg of mutton?' She only eyed me suspiciously.

Between moments of sheer panic, though, I realised I'd made it. At last, here I was in the middle of nowhere. There was no-one else, at least not that I could see, anywhere on this city-less horizon. Nothing moved in the coolness of the desert night. It was so quiet I imagined I could hear the stars rustle. This is what infinity must feel like: immeasurable, ecstatic and scary. A speck in the Sahara was all I was.

Of course, the desert only feels empty to those who don't live in it. Later, by the campfire, as we waited for the tea water to boil, I heard what sounded like a gunshot. Then another, and another.

The noises weren't weapons. They were tribal drums, sending messages across the expanse. Salutations? Warnings? Camel jokes? Whatever they said, it was proof we weren't alone. What I'd mistaken for the middle of nowhere was in fact the centre of a web of nomadic cultures that had existed for centuries.

We woke early the next day with the sun beating down on our tents. Yawning, I shuffled away from camp and scrambled up the biggest dune I could find. In the soft light, the designs drawn by the wind in the rippling sand were still geometrically perfect, undisturbed except by my own haphazard footprints. Even atop the dune, I still couldn't see another living being anywhere. But after last night, I knew they were there.

My camel snorted loudly. I looked back towards camp to see her stubbornly hobbling over the next dune. Running away alone in the Sahara could be deadly, though. As I slid down the sands and ran over to rope her back, I knew it was time for me to stop running away and to go home, too.

When she's not guarding her backpack from smelly chickens on rickety buses headed for the world's most strange and remote borderlands, Sam Benson calls California home.

OPPOSITE: Much of the Sahara consists of enormous, shifting sand dunes, or ergs (some over 200m high), made of fine loose sand that can be extremely difficult to cross.

OVERLEAF: Only with the introduction of camels around AD 200 did long-distance merchant travel across the Sahara become possible or profitable.

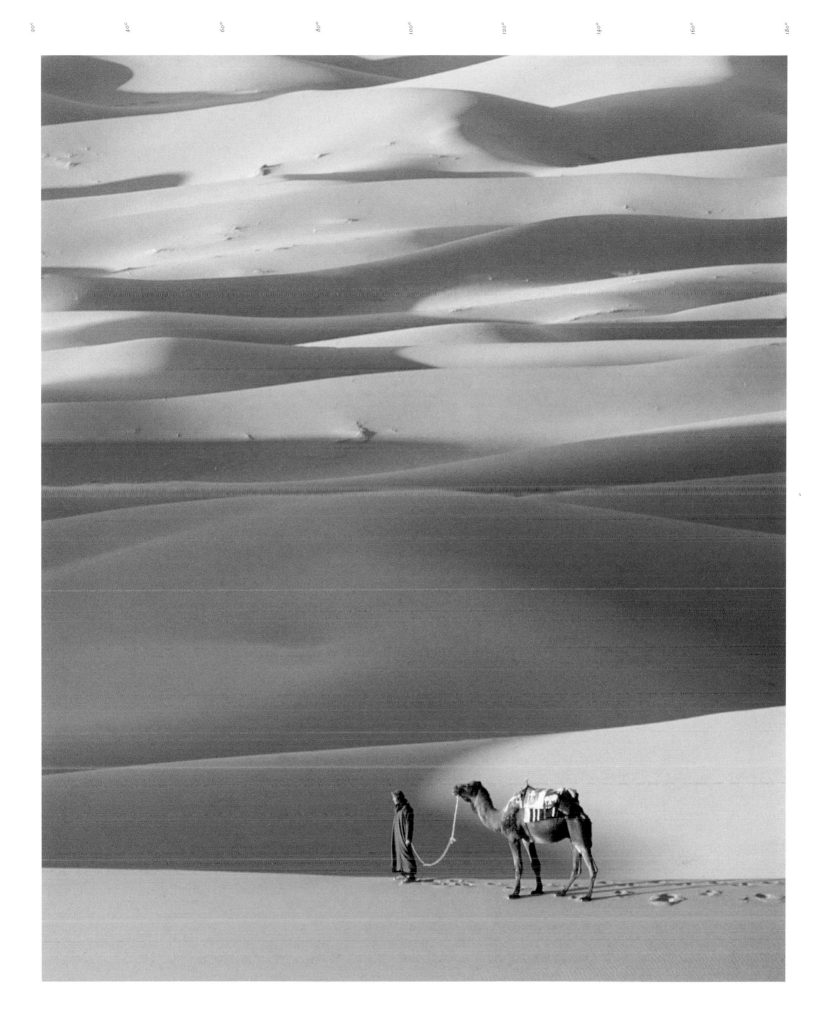

A Glorious Illusion

Des Hannigan

The mountain wilderness of Wester Ross in northwest Scotland may seem modest when measured against the Himalaya. The main peaks are just over 1000m high and as far as wilderness goes you are rarely more than 20km from a road. But a Scottish wilderness is a wilderness to die for. You do not go lightly into these hard hills.

Once, I wandered for weeks on end through Wester Ross. I slept under rocks or in a tiny bivouac tent and each day I moved deeper and deeper into the wilderness. Eventually, I settled for a time beside a broad pool of water called Fuar Loch-mor (the Big Cold Loch), which lies cupped beneath the fabulous mountain of A' Mhaighdean (the Maiden). From the Maiden's shapely summit a great cliff of silvery-white quartzite spills like a bridal veil straight into the icy, glittering water of the loch. The adjoining sandstone peak of Ruadh Stac-mor (the Big Red Peak) is oxblood in colour. A painter could not make more savage or more beautiful brush strokes than these.

It was late May. A miraculous heat wave had taken hold of that usually rain-sodden land. I tramped for miles through the mountains, scrambled along airy ridges and clawed my way up damp, gloomy gullies. I saw no other human being. My food supplies were frugal; I drank sparkling water wherever it bubbled from the ground; I talked to myself in strange tongues. Occasionally, the weather broke and rain deluged the mountains. Then the heat wave took hold once more.

Fuar Loch lies at about 700m. From its southern edge, vast cliffs tumble down to a smaller lake and then plunge into the broad Fionn Loch valley, whose lakes, pools and bogs send silver streams shimmering towards the distant sea. In the evenings I sat at the edge of the cliffs surveying my kingdom. One glorious evening, the cloud layer was about 200m below me. The valley was stuffed with pillows of fleecy white. The sky above was crystal clear and the tops of the mountains rose like islands from the cloud sea. Streamers of mist and thin sheets of cloud smoked up the face of the cliffs and dissolved in the clear air above. The declining sun blazed in the western sky.

I stood up at one point and as I did so a figure appeared suddenly on a projecting spur of rock about 30m below and 100m away. It was silhouetted against hazy cloud and was surrounded by a halo of golden light that was edged with rainbow colours. I waved and the figure waved back. I raised both arms from my sides and the figure did the same. I waggled my arms and the figure waggled back.

Nothing had changed. This was not some fellow orphan of the hills come to break the spell of solitude. I knew from the first moment of seeing the apparition that I was looking at myself, or at a projected image of myself. It was a sort of 'vision' certainly; a glorious illusion, a trick of the light known as a 'Glory', caused by the sun projecting my shape onto the filmy sheet of cloud below. The Glory is so rare, and so enchanting, that given the right frame of mind

126

there are those who might be convinced by seeing a Glory that they had experienced a true 'visitation'. It makes you wonder about all those pious young shepherds and village 'saints' who have been transfixed by alleged supernatural visions among hills and brilliantly lit landscapes. We see what we want to see.

I gave up on visions at an early age, when my parents told me, rather brusquely, that Santa Claus and Tooth Fairies no longer existed, but that God was non-negotiable. Soon after, I negotiated my way out of Godliness as well. I don't do drugs either; but I can get quite high on thin air and here, below A' Mhaighdean, by the Fuar Loch, I was definitely in the mood for visions. Mountain air, daily physical exertion, plenty of pure water, minimal food, and the pleasure of being in a much-loved place, cranked up the elation that was triggered by seeing the Glory. I wandered the hills for the next couple of days in a state of euphoria. Soon, however, my food ran out and, with huge storm clouds grumbling in the west as warning of breaking weather, I headed south through the mountains to reach a road that led eventually to the tiny settlement of Torridon.

It takes time to adjust to other people after prolonged solitude. I was sitting by the path a short distance from the road when three walkers strode by. They were the first human beings I had seen in a long time. I said hello and remarked on what a beautiful day it was. They barely grunted in return and then increased their pace. A day or so later we met by chance in a bar in Torridon and after a few friendly drinks they told me that they had been fairly alarmed by my appearance.

'You looked completely crazy,' they said. 'Your clothes and gear were in rags and your hair and beard were all tangled up. There was a totally mad look in your eyes. And when you spoke! Hell! Out came this weird croaking sound. Complete gibberish! We took off…'

They must have thought they were seeing things…

Des Hannigan spent his youth amid the mountains of his native Scotland, beset by visions. Then he went to sea for a very long time. When he came back, the mountains were still there.

PREVIOUS: The Scottish Highlands are the most ancient mountains in Europe and are the roots of a once much larger mountain range that was formed more than 400 million years ago.

OPPOSITE: These mountains would once have stood higher than the Himalayas, but millions of years of weathering and glacial erosion have shaved the mighty peaks to under 2000m.

Resting Through the Hollow Hours

Ethan Gelber

We knew we would step off the bus in the wee-est hours of the morning, a long dark spell before the first sun-up taxi *baché* (pick-up truck) would take us the 30km to meet the first ferry across the Niger River to Djenné. We had been reassured that we would have no trouble resting through those hollow hours. Of course, we had envisioned such untroubled rest in beds surrounded by four walls and a roof securing us and our belongings from the chill night and wayward hands. How naïve!

Mali, a landlocked Sahelian country, spills south out of the Sahara's empty southern periphery and into the broad plains bordering the Niger River, Africa's third-longest waterway. My friend and I, brought to neighbouring Senegal by work, had impulsively decided to spend five days (not nearly enough time) on a rash scramble through some of the highlights of this land fabled as the home of Timbuktu. We knew we wouldn't get to Timbuktu itself; however, with no time to dawdle, upon arrival in Bamako, the capital city, we accepted the services of the first guide who found us (someone always does), an amiable and able young man known as Camille le Magnifique.

At first, Camille balked at our proposed programme, claiming rightly that it was too ambitious. But we were ambitious people and insisted. Since we were on a tight budget and would have to rely on local transport, he warned us about the discomfort of sometimes travelling late into the evening or even at night. Again, we were not to be swayed. Our backpacks were light, our spirits unencumbered, our mettle undented. What could a few long bus rides deep into a dark African night do to an indomitable gusto for adventure, right?

And so we followed Camille as he finessed a bewildering transport system and secured seats on a late-afternoon bus headed east to the town of Mopti. We would alight several hours before the bus reached Mopti, at a road junction approximately 500km from Bamako. Our objective was a daybreak arrival at the historic city of Djenné, site of Mali's most famous mosque and market.

The bus ride was a test of pluck and patience, so often the case in Africa. A short time into the trip, the sun disappeared, and with it went the idle distraction of the land around us, melting into the deepening rural gloaming. Seated near the front of the vehicle, as the tunnel of darkness and crush of passengers pressed in tight, we stared through the windshield and felt like expiated souls plummeting into a forgotten lightless purgatory. The horizon, a smudged mauve outline dappled with rare, bare light bulbs or fires, was soon lost in pitch-black. The mesmerising faded road lines eventually vanished entirely. The bus was an isolated vessel, agitated by unseen forces, charging headlong into sensorial emptiness.

We must have dozed. Camille woke us with the hard edge of his voice. The bus had stopped. The door was open. There was nothing to be seen outside in the void. But he was adamant: this is where we must get off. We grabbed our

130

packs and stumbled out into a bracing nip. Apparently, we were at our crossroads. Our sleep-addled brains were too dull to grasp anything immediately.

However, as the bus rumbled away, down its ribbon of night, people and a place took shape in the shadows. A moonless sky thick with unfamiliar constellations. A tumble of small shacks, some caged in thin bars of light radiating from between irregular vertical wallboards. Clusters of shrouded figures tending to low ember-orange glows. Two shapes broke away from the nearest huddle and shuffled towards us. Camille swiftly intercepted and in a hushed mumble – the better not to further unquiet the stillness – seemed to be making arrangements. We assumed he was asking about one of the shacks, a temporary shelter for us until this deracinated nowhere became somewhere again.

When Camille returned, he was dragging several large pieces of cardboard. Helping him, we moved a short distance down the road, away from the huts and dim circles of light to a slight embankment, where we discovered a neat row of more spooled cardboard. He gestured to the ground before us. Here, he whispered. We should bundle ourselves in corrugated paper blankets, just as the others had done. It was then we realised that the other cardboard rolls were actually other people, Malians, enjoying untroubled rest, awaiting, like us, the first morning rides. According to Camille, most arrivals at this road junction avoid the shanty sanctuaries, where

the noise, light and drinking hold no promise of either repose or safe refuge. We too would join one rank of cardboard cannolis, securely self-patrolled by a changing watch.

It took a moment to get not-uncomfortable. We donned extra layers and tried to pad our limbs with sheets of newspaper. We experimented with wrapping techniques, resignedly reconciling ourselves to the roll-in like those around us. We turned away from the gleam of the shacks and the high beams of the rare night traffic. Lying on the light incline, settled, we contemplated our view: a colourless and contourless continuum, a monolithic nothingness, coated ink upon ink. Neither of us, both well travelled, had ever felt so far from home, from anywhere, from everywhere.

Dawn took the whole of the sky. In an instant the full bowl above slipped free of its veil. Crooked baobab tree outlines, frozen in place, hung with odd weight. The eerie early clamour of nature found new volume. An engine revved and Camille urged us into sad compressed seats in a shivering steel shell. We slowly revived, returned to our senses, and, once the gritty jalopy jolted into motion and gathered speed, found ourselves sluicing through sand like a sleigh through snow, back on the road to somewhere.

Ethan Gelber, never unhappily lost, has rolled on two wheels in 40 countries on five continents, including a circumnavigation of the Mediterranean Sea by bike.

PREVIOUS: The Great Mosque of Djenné is greatly revered and every year the whole town comes together to replaster its weathered walls in a joyous and vital festival of restoration.

OPPOSITE: Although the national highway is often flanked with vegetation close to the Nile, its ochre hue is a constant reminder of the nearby encroaching Sahara.

OVERLEAF: At night the massive walls of the Mosque cool down. Decorative ceramic caps placed over air vents and crafted by the women of the town can be removed to ventilate the interior.

Crawling Across the Vast Frozen Ocean

Ben Saunders

In my experience, people don't often 'get' the North Pole. They sometimes think it's in Finland somewhere, or perhaps tucked away in the frozen forests of Lapland: the red- and white-striped pole in the middle of a clearing, not far from Father Christmas' log cabin.

But it's not. It's in the middle of the sea, for starters, slap bang in the centre of the 14-million-sq-km Arctic Ocean. The Geographic North Pole is where all time zones and all the lines of longitude converge; the axis of the earth's rotation. Ninety degrees north. And because it's in the sea, and the floating crust of ice on the Arctic Ocean is in a constant state of flux, drifting, breaking up and refreezing, there's nothing there. There isn't even a pole at the Pole. Stick a flag there, and it won't stay at the Pole for long; pretty quickly it'll drift off towards Canada or Greenland. That's providing there's even ice there to stick a flag in – in the summer there's a good chance these days it'll be open water.

On 11 May 2004, I was standing alone at the North Pole. I was the only human being in an area 1½ times the size of North America. In the middle of nowhere, and in the middle of everywhere, the entire planet rotating beneath my feet. I'd travelled there alone on foot, from the edge of the pack ice off the north Siberian coastline, pulling all the food and supplies I needed to stay alive for the 10-week journey, the equivalent of 31 marathons back-to-back over the constantly shifting ice pack. More than 2000 people have reached the summit of Everest. Twelve people have stood on the moon. As far as

skiing solo to the North Pole goes, I'm number four. And I think the reason for that is twofold – firstly it's a daft and pointless thing to do, on many levels. There's nothing actually there, it's just a bit of ice like any other. And I'm not skiing along drawing maps – we all know where it is nowadays, there are fantastic satellite photos on the Internet, so I'm not an explorer in the Edwardian sense, smoking a pipe and naming mountain ranges. Secondly, it's a fairly dangerous, and a fairly challenging thing to have a crack at. Reinhold Messner called it '10 times as dangerous as Everest' after his aborted North Pole attempt in the 1990s.

If there was any element of exploration to my 2004 expedition, it was internal, not external. Exploring human limits, not geographical ones. There were days when I'd wake up, forcing myself out of the relative warmth of my iced-up sleeping bag and heading out into temperatures in the minus 40s, when it felt like the Arctic wanted me dead, making me painfully aware of my own speck of warmth, crawling across the vast frozen ocean. Days when just staying alive felt like trying to keep a candle lit in a draughty corridor. Days when part of me would secretly hope that I'd fall over and injure myself badly enough to be able to call for evacuation with my pride intact. Days of white-out, blisters, frozen snot and tears.

But it wasn't all bad. The Arctic is a genuinely awe-inspiring place to be, and I feel incredibly privileged to have experienced the shifting, frozen wastes of the Arctic Ocean at first hand;

this is, after all, an environment under threat. Many experts predict the Arctic Ocean will be largely ice-free in summer by the end of this century.

It took me 68 days to reach the North Pole on foot from the edge of the pack ice off the north coast of Siberia, and there's nothing there. I remember the day vividly. Ninety degrees north. The axis of the earth's rotation. All the lines of longitude and all the time zones converged underneath my feet. The Geographic North Pole.

I'd had 68 days to rehearse a speech, yet when I turned on the video camera and counted down the last few feet on my GPS, I didn't know what to say.

I felt a mixture of emotions – overwhelming joy and happiness, relief, sadness, frustration that I was there too late in the season to reach the Canadian coastline. I thought of the Finnish expeditioner Dominick Arduin, who died that spring trying to reach the same point. And I thought how strange it is that there's nothing there. It's a bit of ice, just like any other.

I knew that all along, of course, but it still seemed so odd that the only proof is a number on the GPS: N90.00.000. I sat down on my sledge and within moments I had drifted away from the spot. It's a cliché, but it's true – the important bit is the journey, not the destination.

And what a journey it had been. I'd had way more than I bargained for – the conditions were worse than ever and I'd had to dig deeper than I ever imagined possible just to keep going. My motivation and my goals changed drastically. At the start, it was about competition. Making a statement. I came to realise, of course, that the only competition was with myself, and that the only thing I was 'conquering' was my own self-doubt. The Arctic changes every year – skiing to the North Pole isn't like running the 100 metres. It's not even like climbing Everest, or skiing to the South Pole, because it's getting tougher and tougher as the ice melts further each year.

I dug out the satellite phone from my sledge, plugged in my jury-rigged battery pack, powered it up, and dialled three numbers: my mum, my girlfriend, and Chris Hyman, the CEO of Serco, my sponsor.

And I got three answer-phones.

Ben Saunders is the youngest person to ski solo to the North Pole. In 2006 he was planning to set out on the longest unsupported polar journey in history.

PREVIOUS: On an unsupported expedition to the North Pole explorers must be completely self-sufficient, dragging more than 130kg of food, fuel and supplies across the frozen wilderness.

OPPOSITE: In 1895 Norwegians Nansen and Johansen abandoned their attempt to reach the Pole after realising the moving ice pack was heading 'backwards' faster than they could move 'forwards'.

138

Dawn at the Summit of Mont Blanc

Helen Fairbairn

Poking my head out of the tent at 2.30am, two things are immediately apparent. First: we'd better get a move on. The head torches of other climbers can already be seen twinkling high on the slope outside. Second: it's bloomin' freezing.

I duck back inside and pull the zip closed to cut out an icy blast of air. All night our tent, dug into its little snow hole, has kept us cosy while the wind howled. Now we have to abandon our warm sleeping bags, locate thermals, gloves and crampons, and head out into the bitter night.

Our goal? Dawn at the summit of Mont Blanc. To gaze out across the continent from the roof of Western Europe. Middle of nowhere, or middle of everywhere? On top of it all is what concerns us.

At 4810m, Mont Blanc is the geological culmination of the sprawling glaciers and rock spires that form the European Alps. It has taken months of planning to arrive at this, our final push for the summit. Several weeks exploring high alpine trails proved our stamina, and we took care to spend the previous two nights at 3800m and 3200m. We know from experience that preparation is everything when dealing with altitude.

The only factor we can't control is the weather. Adverse conditions over the last couple of days have led to the cancellation of most summit attempts. Judging by the activity around us, some parties have decided to stay here, beside the Refuge de L'Aguille de Goûter at 3167m, and wait for the cloud to disperse.

Today's forecast promises clear skies, and the stars above offer hope for improvement. Yet within a couple of hours of setting out many parties are turning back. There's no denying that that the wind is stronger than we would have liked. Still, our small group of two is moving quickly and strongly in comparison with most, and the snow underfoot is firm and crisp.

The lower slopes pass in a blur, with all attention focussed on the small circle of ground illuminated by the head torch. The slow, repetitive steps and the rhythmic crunch of snow become mesmeric. Once an hour or so we pause, and only then do we lift our heads, allow our lungs a short break, and take in the wider scene. The interstellar display overhead is nothing short of spectacular, the stars disappearing behind the outline of jagged ridges at the skyline.

Our breaks seem few and far between as the cold wind forces us to keep moving. By the time we reach the Bosses Ridge the night has brightened to predawn twilight. This is it, the crux of our chosen route. The mountain now narrows before us, forming a knife-edge some 150m long. To either side of the arête, precipitous slopes drop away for thousands of metres. The lights of Chamonix town can be seen twinkling at the base of the slope to the north, four vertical kilometres below. To talk about exposure is to underestimate the situation.

With the ridge staring us in the face, we finally have to admit that conditions are less than ideal. More people are turning back than continuing, and we hunker down in the snow to consider our options. The summit isn't far away on the other side, but it's a question of getting that far.

Winds of 60km/h are buffeting us, and it's clear the ridge allows very little margin for error.

Nonetheless, some parties are continuing, and we make our decision. Nothing is clear-cut, and if we were in the same situation again there would still be no obvious choice. We rope up, double-check our crampons, and ease slowly onto the ridge.

Progress is painstaking and the wind forces us to a complete stop on several occasions. The swirling spindrift blinds us and tiny shards of ice attack our cheeks with ferocity. I venture just one quick peek into the gaping chasms on either side, concentrating all my senses on placing my feet on what I hope is firm ground beneath me. The only other thing I have eyes for is my partner, attached to me by what could prove either a lifeline or a deathline depending on the speed of our reactions.

As the ridge at last expands beneath us, we gather once more into a huddle. Again, to go on or go back? I don't even pause for thought – there's no way I'm re-crossing that thing again so soon.

We arrive at the rounded summit of Mont Blanc just as the sun is rising. With no monument to mark the top and just two other climbers to share the experience with, we feel like we're on an island in a sea of mountains. All around us, as far as the eye can see, angular peaks jut above the blanket of cloud.

It's seven o'clock in the morning and as the adrenaline abates my body finally begins to relax. I know my partner's inane grin is mirrored on my face. Somehow I think we might just take a little time to appreciate the meaning of life before we start the trip back down.

The wild areas of the world hold a particular attraction for Helen, a mountain-lover and dedicated kayaker. She regularly escapes the winter in Ireland to rekindle her relationship with things more exotic.

PREVIOUS: In medieval times the mountain was known as Mont Maudit, the 'Accursed Mountain', and legend has it there was once a Celtic temple on one of its passes.

OPPOSITE: The safety rope trailed by high-altitude climbers is their last hope of survival should an innocuous slip lead to a life-threatening drop off a cliff or into a crevasse.

21°N 13°E
SAHARA DESERT, NIGER

142

Lost in the World's Largest Desert

Tom Parkinson

It's not every day you end up holding a camel hostage. In this case it was more of a security deposit – when you get lost in the middle of the world's largest desert and have to ask a Tuareg nomad to show you the way, it's pretty sensible to hold on to something while he drives off with one of your party to find the piste. Not for the first time, I found myself wondering what exactly I was doing roaming the northern Sahara with six middle-aged Brandenburgers, two Opel Vectras and a Nissan combivan.

To be honest, the whole situation was pretty bizarre from start to finish. I had set out from Tamanrasset in southern Algeria and travelled down the stunning desert route in a packed 4WD vehicle, accompanied by a grizzled Algerian called Hassain who had 'adopted' me during the 24-hour wait. After shivering overnight in our sleeping bags on a restaurant patio in the frontier town of In Guezzam (and getting bitten on the forehead by a mosquito for my pains), we paid for a lift to the well-organised Algerian military border post, then on to the much more chaotic Nigerien post, where we hoped to grab a lift on one of the massive freight trucks that regularly ply the Sahara trail. It was here that I first met the Germans.

More accurately, I met the Nigerien border guard who was haggling over a cube fridge with the Germans. Seeing another European wander in, he decided I must be an impartial expert on consumer electronics and asked me to inspect his purchase to see if he was getting a good deal – of course there was no electricity to test if it actually worked, but surely I could tell just by looking? I assured him that it did indeed seem to be a genuine fridge in good condition and went back outside, where it suddenly occurred to me that hitching a lift with these rather well-equipped fellow travellers could be a quick and pleasant alternative to spending three days perched on top of a cargo lorry.

As luck would have it, the sale of the fridge left just enough room for me to squeeze into the Nissan alongside the 80-gallon water barrel and massed camping paraphernalia (with the luxury of three vehicles to fill, the guys had definitely erred on the side of overpacking). My bar-fluent Berlin German smoothed the way nicely, and my student French skills also proved useful, as I subsequently discovered none of my six companions spoke any at all, quite an oversight in a region where it's the only lingua franca outside Arabic. Blissfully clueless, we piled into the cars and set off, following the trail due south to Arlit, the first real town on the Niger side of the sands. Within a few hours we were hopelessly lost.

That's the problem with negotiating the Sahara under your own steam: the only roads through the endless sweeping sands are the so-called pistes, consisting solely of massed tyre tracks marked out with black barrels every few hundred metres. With absolutely no trees, rocks or other landmarks to navigate by, if you have to take a detour round a shifting dune, or follow the wrong tracks, or decide you want to check out that mirage over there, it's very, very easy to

lose the chain of barrels, and once you've lost it it can be very, very hard to find it again. It's all very well standing atop a sand dune and taking in the relentless, transcendent emptiness, but when you don't know where you are it's quite another story. They say the desert holds many secrets, and becoming one of them is not a tantalising prospect.

Fortunately, just as we were about to backtrack three hours of driving, a Tuareg tribesman appeared from nowhere. These fiercely traditional people are the original desert warriors, still carving out a precarious nomadic existence from the fickle sands, and we couldn't have hoped for a better rescuer, despite the awkward fact that we had absolutely no common language. After 45 minutes of slightly tense waiting with the hapless camel we were back on track again, having paid our 'ransom' in water, the only currency that really matters out here.

I spent the next couple of days with the guys, with plenty more unusual challenges along the way: translating the lyrics to 'A Horse With No Name' into German, explaining to patrolling soldiers what we were doing camped in the middle of the desert, haggling over car prices with Nigerien mobsters, sightseeing in blacked-out brothels, bumping into Bavarians and debating fornication with an overzealous evangelist. It wasn't until I got home, though, that I realised we must have left Algeria right around the time of a series of high-profile kidnappings: 31 travellers, mostly German, had been abducted by Islamist guerrillas in the northern Sahara while driving their own vehicles, and remained captive for six months. Compared with that our own desert troubles seemed pretty insignificant, and in fact we were downright lucky the whole way – though who knows if the camel would agree...

Tom Parkinson has worked for Lonely Planet since 2002, mainly in random corners of Africa, and seems to have a knack for getting lost in remote places. He was last seen in Borneo.

PREVIOUS: The hazards of desert driving include a bewildering inability to focus on nonexistent landmarks, stifling heat, lingering thirst, creeping tiredness, and the constant fear of breaking down and being stranded.

OPPOSTIE: In 2004 a 5000-year-old burial site was discovered 'by accident' among the 160km-long sand dunes of Niger's Ténéré Desert, one of the driest areas of the Sahara.

146

A Rush into Perilous Night

Ethan Gelber

We paused at the edge of the Lendava Tunnel. It would be the longest one, almost 700m end to end. Several of the previous passages had been short enough that we never dipped fully into darkness. But this one had daunting span, a befuddling bend in the middle, and no lights at all, the bulbs and wiring having not been renewed since the cessation of hostilities. A pedal through this monster would be a rush into perilous night. Although traffic was only sporadic, daring it not to rage through the gloom while we were snared and invisible within was too much of a gamble.

It was a rainy spring day in 1998 in Bosnia-Hercegovina and we were cycling down towards the Dalmatian coast, returning from a visit to Sarajevo as part of an educational bicycle expedition. All morning we had coasted through an eerie hush, beneath the cloud-shrouded, weather-rutted, towering and majestic walls of two karst massifs, the Vrsnica and Prenj mountains, split by the unruly Neretva River. The landscape was truly spectacular, serenely at odds with the remnants of the recent human tragedy it had witnessed – ruined cadavers of buildings, rare, battered vehicles (often armoured personnel carriers or military jeeps), occasional tentative signs of the kind of life that could one day return (shuttered roadside grilled-lamb restaurants, dented food kiosks at abandoned panoramic rest areas).

We had already been travelling, mostly on two wheels, for more than six months, tracing the shores of the Mediterranean Sea counter-clockwise from Morocco across parts of North Africa, through the Middle East and Turkey, and into Eastern Europe. We had been through so much: alternately iced and singed by the elements, chastened by winds and fear and despair, touched by generosity and indigence, and buoyed by kindness. But not until that pause before the tunnel mouth on a desolate stretch of war-ravaged Hercegovinian road between Jablanica and Mostar, flanked by the raucous, opaque-turquoise Neretva, did I feel momentarily lost. Not off course, but marooned.

There is nothing uplifting about a war zone, perhaps even less so once a conflict has ended. Roads and bridges scarred by mortars; homes and businesses thrashed and pocked by artillery; lawns uprooted by tank tracks and heavy ordnance; once-colourful scraps of clothing and household goods sundered and muddied; and, more haunting than anything, the vacant faces of the living, pale and pained death masks more unnerving than the shattered features of the dead – everything screams of forced dislocation and destruction.

No, there is nothing cheerful about a war zone. And yet, on more than one occasion, I have found myself gazing through blast holes at shrapnel-strafed walls, trying to imagine the happiness of the innocent family for which the walls had once provided shelter, until caught in crossfire. I have stilled my breathing to wonder at the morbid silence. To the residents of a quiet rural community, the silence had probably been a boon. Now emptiness and loss have turned the

20°   40°   60°   80°   100°   120°   140°   160°   180°

13°E

13°30'

148

silence sinister and hollow. I have sniffed the exploded soil, searching beneath the saltpetre and char for the satisfying and pungent earthy redolence of natural decay.

This is what had happened in the Balkans. In town after town, war had chased ambulant life out of Neretva River valley. Its aftermath left me feeling incongruous. What is to become of a little abandoned village, I asked, after its name has been swept away by the currents of violence, after it is deserted by humanity? A sense of devastation had redoubled as I wandered about and sought out (or had been found by) the survivors – unaffected townsfolk, artisans with calloused hands, farmers and anglers with a crust of bread or drop of whiskey to share, innocently over-inquisitive children. What goes on inside the heads of these victims of the incomprehensible battles brought to them?

A honk snapped me out of my reverie. My attention had been wandering, divided between the grand pageantry of the natural arena and the tiny, tainted traces of the vanished people. I had begun to long for a return to a place where

the juxtaposition was less brutal. Where I, a lonely cyclist, wouldn't feel so absurd. I longed for a place, and for a future to this place, where people's faces would bring just as much grounding radiance to a cloudless afternoon as the light glinting off the water running through it.

Another honk. A bus had eased its pace behind us and was flashing its headlights. The driver, a sallow, disembodied visage blurred between sweeps of ineffective windshield wipers, motioned to the road in front of him. He would usher us through the tunnel, protect us from the pitfalls of obscurity, the threats of being in the wrong place at the wrong time, and our own trapped thoughts.

There really is nothing heartening about a war zone, except the people who show hints of the gentle monotony, the humanity, the peace that will follow.

Ethan Gelber, never unhappily lost, has rolled on two wheels in 40 countries on five continents, including a circumnavigation of the Mediterranean Sea by bike.

PREVIOUS: The Bosnian War ended in 1995 and in many parts of the countryside both the land and the shells of partially destroyed buildings are still littered with landmines.

OPPOSITE: Following the wilful destruction of the Old Bridge of Mostar, the international community rallied to build a replica using stones from the earlier construction.

150

Axle-Deep in Soft Sand

Siona Jenkins

Vast, stark, unforgiving, barren: the desert conjures up more clichés than almost any other landscape. And here I was stuck in the middle of one: the movie sandstorm scene. The world was reduced to a gritty brown howl and my car was axle-deep in soft sand, but there was no Ralph Fiennes or TE Lawrence to keep me company.

It was my own fault. I had wanted to go on a trip through Egypt's Western Desert but couldn't afford to pay the best guide, Amr, for a solo trip. When he heard that I had a jeep he volunteered me to be a driver for a trip he was taking with two other women.

'Can you drive in the sand?' he asked.

'Well, I'm a pretty good driver so I'm sure I'll be able to pick it up,' I replied confidently.

We had spent most of the day driving along a desert highway from Cairo to Al-Kharga Oasis, about 600km to the southwest. Amr had seen through my bravado and drafted in his friend, Mohammed, with a third car, so we formed a small convoy as we made our way through the barren expanse. Close to sunset, at a spot indistinguishable from anywhere else we'd been that day, Amr pulled over and gave me instructions.

'Get into four high and follow me. But don't get your tyres in my tracks and make sure you maintain a distance of 50m. If you feel that you're sinking, move your steering wheel from side to side for extra traction. And *don't* use your brakes. Mohammed will be behind you in case you have a problem. OK?,' he called as he hurried back to his car. The wind was picking up and sand was starting to blow.

'Um, yeah.'

He turned off the road and into the scrubby desert landscape. For about a quarter of an hour I followed him, wondering how far 50m was. It was getting dark and increasingly windy but I was keeping up. When I felt the car slide a bit I tried moving the wheel from side to side and got my grip.

'A doddle,' I thought complacently.

Then the scrub disappeared and we hit soft sand. I fishtailed, applied the brakes and sank. Amr disappeared.

Mohammed almost hit me, veered off to the side and also disappeared. I put my foot on the accelerator but seemed to sink even lower. I then tried to get out and see how far down I'd gone but was hit by a wall of stinging sand. It was almost completely dark and I had no idea where I was. Best to sit tight, I thought, trying not to think of the army of King Cambyses that had been swallowed by a sandstorm in the Western Desert back in 525 BC.

After an eternity a weak light appeared and Mohammed, his face covered with a scarf, knocked on the window. I let him in. 'The camp's just over here,' he said, pointing ahead. 'Let's try and get you out.' I clambered into the back seat and let him have a go. No luck. While amazingly patient and courteous, he was clearly unimpressed by my driving skills and swore lightly in Arabic. I thought it best not to let on that I'm fluent.

Eventually, he gave up. 'We have to dig,' he said resignedly.

So we braved the sand and dug. 'Just think of all those women who pay huge sums for chemical peels,' I told myself. 'And I'm getting an organic one for free.'

A couple of hours later Mohammed finally drove us into our camp, such as it was. It was too windy for a fire so we ate cold food in one of the cars and then retired to bed in our tents, fully clad and covered in sand.

The following morning the wind still howled but the sand was back on the ground and the sun shone brightly. I got out of my tent and saw that we were sheltered by a dune. Beyond it was a huge mudbrick ruin beside a clump of palm trees. It looked impossibly lonely and very beautiful.

'It's a Roman fortress,' said Amr, as he handed me a cup of coffee. 'This was a trade route a couple of thousand years ago. Then the wells dried up. Why don't you take a look?'

I can never get over the sheer volume of ancient monuments in Egypt. Here we were in the middle of the desert looking at a forgotten building that would be a national treasure in any other country. My companions (remarkably polite about my driving skills, all things considered) explored with me, marvelling at how time and sand can erode even the most powerful of empires.

An even more poignant discovery awaited us at the nearby escarpment. Mummy wrappings littered the sand and here and there lay human bones, many bearing traces of mummified flesh and hair. We later found out that they had been hacked out of their rock-cut tombs by modern treasure hunters hoping to find jewellery amid the linen wrapped around the corpses. They had probably been soldiers who had manned this garrison back when it was an outpost of Rome. It can't have been a sought-after assignment. The bodies had been crudely mummified to ensure an afterlife, but now the desecrated bones lay bleaching in the sun. It was a gruesome reminder that greed respects neither death nor a remote location.

Back at the camp, Amr had more surprises in store for us. 'Look what we found under your tent!' he laughed. We peered into a Tupperware container he was waving under our noses. There was a large, very angry scorpion sliding down its sides. 'It must have been blown over here in the wind,' he said. 'Don't forget to shake out your boots in the mornings because sometimes they crawl inside.'

I nodded, trying not to dwell on the fact that for hours only a thin layer of nylon had separated me from death – or at least a vicious bite.

'Now we're going to have a dune driving lesson,' he announced, taking the scorpion over to a clump of vegetation and shaking it out of the box.

I was impressed that he still had any faith in my driving. But we were heading deeper into the desert, so I suppose he had little choice.

'On dunes you need to keep up your speed, but remember that different dune formations have different shapes, so until you've got experience you must follow my tracks as closely as you can, or you could go flying off a sheer drop,' he warned. 'But remember not to go inside my tracks because I'll have broken the surface of the sand and you'll sink. Ready?'

'As I'll ever be,' I answered. Lisa, one of the two women whose safari I'd crashed, decided to take her life in her hands and come with me.

It was close to noon and the wind was blowing the surface sand in swirls, blurring the outline of the dunes. It was like being in an impressionist painting. Amr got into his jeep and drove swiftly up the first dune. I followed, trying to find his tracks before they disappeared. Mohammed brought up the rear, presumably to rescue me again.

As we swerved up and down the dunes I began to feel how the sand affected the steering and started to relax. The speed was exhilarating and soon Lisa and I were whooping like a couple of banshees. We were disappointed when the lesson ended and Amr drove down onto an adjacent area of relatively solid scrub.

'That was great,' he said. 'I think you've got it!'

We chattered about technique and waited for Mohammed. After 10 minutes we started to get worried and drove back beside the dunes looking for him. Soon we spied his gleaming white jeep stuck in the sand and Mohammed wading through its softness towards us. It was hard not to indulge a moment of smug triumph that I'd made it through and he hadn't.

This was wiped away as a pale Mohammed clutched his side and recounted how he had lost my tracks and flown off a dune. When we reached the jeep, we saw that it had nosedived into the sand. Its steering wheel had folded with the impact of Mohammed's body, despite his seat belt. Our dune lesson suddenly seemed a lot more serious.

The jeep would not start, so Amr got us to work moving all food and drink from the back while he removed as many engine components as we could carry, 'so that nobody can steal them'.

'But we're miles from the nearest settlement,' we laughed. 'Who could possibly steal anything out here?'

'You'd be surprised,' he said. 'You saw the mummies.'

We left poor Mohammed, broken ribs bandaged, in a dusty hotel lobby in Al-Kharga. His jeep was later loaded onto a flatbed truck and driven up to Cairo. We headed back into the desert, where I had developed a healthy respect for sand – and for the determination of treasure hunters.

Siona Jenkins worked as a freelance journalist and travel writer in Egypt for 14 years. She recently moved to London, from where she plots ways to get back to the desert.

PREVIOUS: The Western Desert extends from the Nile to the Libyan border and from the Mediterranean Sea south towards Sudan, spanning almost two-thirds of Egypt's territory.

OPPOSITE: It rains about once every five to 10 years in the Western Desert and the first sign of brooding storm clouds always brings with it great hope for much-needed water.

The Engine Roars with Anticipation

Matthew D Firestone

Heading west from Durban, the morning calm is suddenly punctuated by a loud, distinctive *crack* as my two travel companions prepare to savour the sweet amber nectar of the day's first Castle lager. She's wrapped in a palette of majestic purple, drunk on the splendid isolation of the road ahead. He's flashing his trademark grin, a subtle combination of ease and sophistication. I'm staring through the windshield at a mosaic of splattered insects, listening hesitantly to the metallic sounds of clanking rocks.

'We're in for a tough drive,' I confess.

We all nod in silent agreement.

On the horizon, we catch the first glimpse of our destination.

The Drakensberg are believed to have been first settled by San hunter-gatherers around one million years ago. In the 13th century, chiefdoms migrating from the Great Lakes of Central Africa reached uKhahlamba or 'Barrier of Spears', and settled an area destined to become part of the great Zulu nation. Europeans began arriving en masse in 1837 when Boer settlers crossed the mountains on the Great Trek from Cape Colony in search of their 'Promised Land'. Forty years later, the name *Drakensberg*, or 'Dragon Mountains', was coined when a Boer father and son reported that they saw the mythical beast flying over the mountain range. Superstition and lore have always been associated with the Drakensberg, and it is no surprise that JRR Tolkien, who spent his childhood in nearby Bloemfontein, drew inspiration from these mountains when conjuring up images of the Misty Mountains of Middle Earth.

Under the shelter of a gnarled cypress, lunch takes the form of sinewy scraps of *kudu biltong,* washed down with the refreshing tang of fresh lychee juice. In the mountains above, cascading waterfalls carve the basalt peaks with a honed precision, giving life to the mossy cushions beneath us. Time passes, though it is impossible to mark as life on the road has numbed our temporal senses. Shadows begin to lengthen, and soon the valley floor is bathed in soft, pastel light. Gazing out across the daisy-filled grasslands, our eyes slowly trace the steady arc of the sun across the African sky.

We move on.

Hypnotic flashes of countryside race past us on both sides as the road forges ahead with singular purpose. The darkening peaks loom heavily overhead as a constant reminder of our trespass. And then in an instant, the muted *twang* of a steel cable coming undone resonates through the accelerator with a surprising intensity. Panic sets in as the pedal drops to the floorboard and lies there, limp and unresponsive. The engine starts to idle while the rush of the wind slows to a gentle breeze.

We've stopped.

We all have different defence mechanisms for dealing with stress. She's lying down in a grassy field with a wildflower in her hand, allowing the seeping coolness of the bare ground to wash over her without a struggle. He's carefully surveying the situation with calm, collected

movements and calculated precision. I'm lost in a jumble of thoughts, paralysed with inaction. The darkening peaks continue to loom heavily overhead.

We're going nowhere.

Time passes, slowly. Our temporal senses sharpen as the reality of our situation sets in. Everyone remains silent, but the blankness of our expressions cannot hide our thoughts. On the side of a dirt road at the bottom of a valley in the middle of nowhere, we're infinitely alone. In a harsh and unforgiving environment, error is punished cruelly.

We're going nowhere.

Divine intervention.

Mere coincidence.

Dumb luck.

In the distance we spot a truck heading in our direction.

A heavy-set man lets out a huge, rolling belly-laugh when he eyes the state of our car. My baby-blue 1984 Ford Sierra (affectionately dubbed Suzi) and I had been together for the better part of a year now, though I must confess that she had lost her good looks with age. Her front bumper rested in pieces somewhere in the Kalahari. Her right headlight dangled grotesquely from its socket. Her rear-view mirror was strategically placed in the backseat of the car. When the man asks me for her keys so he can listen to the engine, I simply hand him the large, flathead screwdriver I had been holding in my hand.

'You do know this is a 4x4 road, right?' he snickers.

'In her former life, Suzi was a Sherman tank,' I reply with bursting pride.

We're towed to a modest homestead at the base of the mountains where my companions and I are offered a brief glance of African ingenuity. In a matter of minutes, the heavy-set man fashions a new accelerator cable out of copper wire, duct tape and a paperclip, and installs it with a steady hand and a meticulous eye. With a quick turn of the screwdriver and a measured tap on the accelerator, Suzi's engine roars with anticipation of the journey to come. The moon hangs low in the African sky, shedding pale twilight on the road that lies ahead.

Heading northwest towards the Lesotho border, the evening calm is suddenly punctuated by a loud, distinctive *crack* as my two travel companions prepare to savour the sweet amber nectar of the day's last Castle lager.

Matthew D Firestone is a professional couch surfer who has ridden breaks in over 50 countries, including tubular lefts in the Kalahari Desert and gnarly rights in the High Atlas.

PREVIOUS: The fertile valleys and rugged mountains of the Drakensberg were formed not by tectonic upheavals, but by erosion over about 1000 million years.

OPPOSITE: The abundant lakes and rivers in the Drakensberg were a major prize for the warlike Amangwane tribe who drove earlier settlers into the mountains in the 1800s.

158

The Mystical Mountain

Kate Armstrong

Sapitwa Peak, our hiking destination on Malawi's Mulanje Massif, means 'don't go there' in the local language. Of course, we didn't know that at the time. Our hosts, themselves keen hikers and temporary residents, were unable to come with us on our walk, but gave us maps and directions.

Accompanied by our porter-cum-guide, Dickson, my partner and I set off up the base of the Massif, a giant slab of granite rock that soars majestically into the sky from the Phalombe Plain. Covering almost 640 sq km, the Massif forms part of the mountain range that runs down eastern Africa from Ethiopia to South Africa's Eastern Cape region. This awesome sight rises out of the surrounding tea plantations, the crops' bright green carpet is broken only by the vivid red and yellow of the tea pickers' caps and head scarves, which bob up and down as they pick tea leaves. Even more spectacular, the Massif boasts the 3002m Sapitwa Peak, the highest peak in South-Central Africa.

Local people believe that *mizimu* (spirits) live on Sapitwa. They believe that spirits also inhabit the nearby Mt Mchese, and a lower section of the Chapaluka path known as Ziwo La Nkhalamba, or 'the old man's pool', so named because an old man was said to have fallen here, never to be seen again.

The gradient steepens quickly and we climb slowly into the dry scrub and scale the massive granite boulders. Silence soon envelops our ascent. After the colourful bustle of the local village we enter a disarmingly quiet realm; it's an eerie calm in rugged terrain. I ponder on nature and the mystical qualities of remoteness and isolation.

As if sensing my thoughts, Dickson tells us about local beliefs. Sometimes, he says, when you walk on Mt Mulanje you may come across food on the path. You must eat it without looking around you. If you look up, a 'white spirit' will come and take you. Others believe that the spirits will capture you and lock you in a rock before eventually releasing you. At this stage, the only spirit I'm contemplating is that from a hip flask; I am panting too much to ask Dickson to explain further, or to allow my imagination to flirt with my wits. My ears thump, my nose drips, and I watch nothing but the next step.

Finally, several hours later, we reach the top, the Thucila Plateau. Spread before us is a windswept expanse of grassy plain bordered by mountainous peaks, including Sapitwa Peak in the distance. The area is devoid of people. There are no animals. There is no sound, not even of wind. It's like being in an air-locked room – the silence really *is* deafening. Even the air is unperfumed; it's neutralised by its own crispness. Clouds fill the basin and we are above them. Within minutes, they lift and swirl rapidly upwards, like a vortex in reverse. The light alters quickly – there's the pristine clarity that comes with elevation – to a sharp blue sky. It's like watching a nature film on rapid time-lapse. It's bewitching. My goose bumps are not caused by the chilly air.

20°

40°

60°

80°

100°

120°

140°

160°

180°

That night, with Sapitwa looming at a safe distance, my *Mzungu*-style (white person–style) camping routine distracts fanciful thoughts of African ghosts; I unfurl the sleeping mat, take a chilly stroll to the crude toilet and then prepare my dried noodles. I begin to feel uneasy when, as dusk kicks in, my partner has not returned from a bath in a nearby waterhole. When his head eventually appears on the horizon, he laughs at my obvious relief.

This unprecedented sense of altitude and isolation (and, I am gradually admitting to my over-logical self, a mystical atmosphere) continues over our two-day route, in which we travel nature's magical biosphere of contrasting landscapes: lush vegetation and barren terrain, past waterfalls, waterholes, deep gorges and gentle plateaus. We edge around Sapitwa, choosing not to climb her because of our time constraints.

Instead, we tackle our descent. Slowly we make our way to below the cloud line, where we negotiate massive boulders and slippery shale. Two barefooted locals (each with a long plank of woods balanced on their head) appear from nowhere and nimbly pass us at a run. We near

the bottom, and with it comes a sense of normality. As quickly as we've left the Massif behind, we're thrust into a boisterous African routine: women boiling pots of water, shrieking children, smouldering fires. Then, back on a dirt road, we share the journey with Africans on their way to the bustling market.

That night, back in town, we regale our tales to our hosts. They explain why they hadn't accompanied us. We are shocked. They had been holding a commemorative service for a friend who'd disappeared on Mt Mulanje exactly a year before. Her body was never found. Despite intensive searches, from the local witch doctors applying their *juju* (magic), to sophisticated, Westernised search and rescue methods, no-one has come up with a plausible explanation for her disappearance.

Kate Armstrong has trekked, eaten and chatted her way around southern Africa and beyond. Her cultural conquests include learning Spanish in Bolivia, Portuguese in Mozambique and dancing in a Bolivian folkloric dance troupe.

PREVIOUS: The giant slab of coarse-grained igneous granite that makes up the Massif was formed over a million years ago and covers an area of almost 640 sq km.

OPPOSITE: Sapitwa in the Mulanje Massif is the highest peak in South-Central Africa and can be admired at a distance from across the fertile Phalombe Plains.

High & Dry

Tom Parkinson

The Chalbi Desert isn't the remotest spot on earth, but the middle of nowhere seems a lot more like the middle of nowhere when you think you might be stuck there. As we struggled to shovel enough dirt under the wheels to get our vehicle's axle off the wheel rut where it was firmly lodged, sunset drew on in the Kenyan scrub and we started to realise we'd taken a wrong turn somewhere in the last 200km or so. There are no expletives quite pithy enough to describe that particular form of nagging panic.

For those unfamiliar with East Africa's remoter spots, the Chalbi Desert is an expanse of scrub tundra in northern Kenya, occupying much of the space between the Central Highlands and Lake Turkana, the vast soda lake that starts in Ethiopia and extends south down the Great Rift Valley. It's largely made up of arid volcanic plains and dust, punctuated with struggling thorn trees and the occasional dry river bed.

And as we found out, it eats cars for breakfast.

We were on our way from the chaotic frontier town of Maralal to the tiny settlement of Loyangalani on Lake Turkana, negotiating the rough tracks of the Kenyan badlands in a small Maruti 4WD, essentially a tin can with an overpowered engine. It should have been an easy day's drive, even given the road conditions, and we were making good time right up until we left the small valley town of South Horr, 70km shy of our destination. It was only once we'd been driving through the same dusty terrain for well over two hours that we started to realise we really should have come across something recognisable by then. After all, how hard can it be to spot a lake that covers 6400 sq km?

The annoying thing was we had absolutely no idea where we'd gone wrong. The Chalbi is not a large area by African standards, or even compared with the vast wastelands of northeastern Kenya, and while there are no roads or signposts it's not as featureless as the endless sands of a 'classic' desert like the Sahara. As far as we were concerned, the route we were taking was simply a straight road north, and we hadn't taken a single turn off the main track. All around us, the barren plains had given us no indication that we might be going the wrong way as we followed the multiple tyre tracks in front of us.

It was those tracks that got us into trouble. We realised after the first serious jolt that most of the ruts were a lot deeper than they looked – sadly our efforts to avoid them could only last so long, and finally we slammed straight into a set of tracks that was just too high for our poor Maruti's wheel base, bringing us to an abrupt halt. A huge cloud of thick, red dust engulfed the car, leaving us looking like war-painted ginger warriors, and my driver, Sammy, spluttered something I suspect wasn't the Swahili for 'oh bother'. Once we'd finished coughing and laughing at each other's dust-encrusted faces, we got out to inspect the damage and realised that we were high and dry, with the chassis firmly wedged against the ground. With no shovel to hand and no other traffic to help us out, we had

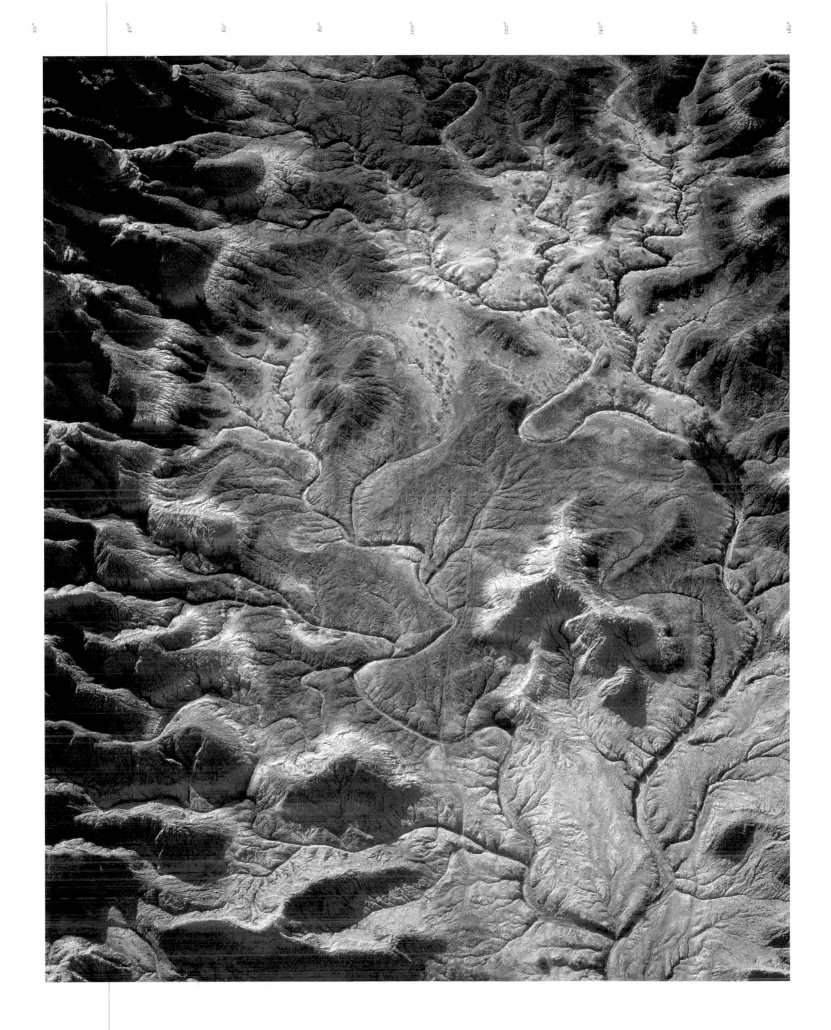

to resort to scooping out the powdery red soil from underneath the car with our feet and trying to pack it tightly enough under the wheels to get some traction. We were almost ready to give up and bed down in the car when it finally came free. I jumped in at a run, Sammy gunned the throttle and we tore off again, not daring to slow down over the ruts or admit that we really didn't know where we were going.

Just as dark fell and we thought we were well and truly stranded, we came across a minor miracle: a village. I have never been so glad to see a collection of straw huts in my life, and the fact that the first people to greet us were a pair of attractive young girls with no tops on was an even more unexpected bonus. Behind the tribal settlement was a small collection of more modern concrete shacks, which turned out to be the town of Kargi, an insignificant outpost and unlikely conference centre halfway between Turkana and the main Ethiopia–Kenya road –

you'll now find it in Lonely Planet *Kenya*, a tribute to its lifesaving presence in our hour of need. Despite the lack of running water, the criminally overpriced meal and the mice scurrying around my head, I've seldom been more thankful for a bed at night.

There is an epilogue to this journey: a colleague of mine did the same trip two years later, having heard my pub rendition of the story, and claimed that as far as he could tell we'd only gone about 95km out of our way, and that actually we hadn't even reached the Chalbi proper. We still disagree on this, of course, but it just goes to show, if you don't know where you are it doesn't really matter which bit of nowhere you're stuck in…

Tom Parkinson has worked for Lonely Planet since 2002, mainly in random corners of Africa, and seems to have a knack for getting lost in remote places. He was last seen in Borneo.

PREVIOUS: Rainfall over the Chalbi Desert is irregular and a constant steady wind dries up the soil and the plants ensuring that vast areas have little or no vegetation.

OPPOSITE: According to the archaeological record our ancestors, the first *Homo sapiens*, were fishing the waters of Lake Turkana around 50,000 years ago.

The Place That Even God Forgot

Tim Cope

I broke my way from the tent into a world entombed by winter. The Betpak Dala, or 'Starving Steppe' as it means in Kazakh, spread out in the gloom of predawn with the gentle crests and falls of a frozen sea. Nomads traditionally migrate onto the Betpak in the summer from the deserts in South Kazakhstan, but now it was empty, the only signs of life some clay nomad graves and the tracks of wolves. Three hours of packing and loading later I kicked Tigon, my Kazakh hunting dog, out of the tent and swung up into the saddle. Then there was just snow exploding into plumes below me with the rush of hooves, and my three horses cutting a line towards an empty horizon.

By afternoon it was dropping into the minus-30s and we rose onto a plateau raked by cutting winds. You could stare into the haze of powdery white and find no sense of scale or end to the world. Usually this emptiness would instil a sense of calm and freedom, but today it brought dread. Overnight my sleeping bag had frozen, the tent had ripped, and now one of the horses was beginning to limp. Today was Christmas Eve, and the thought of being alone made me pine for a family home. My hopes rested on the only dot on my map of the Betpak Dala, the gold-mining village of Akbakai.

As sun set the distant silhouette of mining equipment materialised and I pushed the horses on, intoxicated by visions of hot tea, company and a barn full of hay. It wasn't until I picked my way through metal scraps on the edge of town that I woke from my stupor. I made for the only figure in sight, a man collecting firewood, and pleaded for help.

'Where?! What?!' he screamed over the wind. His look was more one of horror than compassion, but eventually he led me away to a half-built mudbrick shack.

'This is my café. It is still being built. You can put your horses in the billiard room for the night, and sleep here with my workers.'

Horses unpacked and sheltered, Tigon and I leapt inside. A flickering coal stove offered a fragmented picture of two old spring beds, deteriorating mattresses and a cardboard-matted floor. Misha and Grisha, the Russian labourers living here, were too inebriated to speak, but details didn't matter now. I sank into a mattress and felt my body melt into sleep.

Morning brought a sharper reality. Woken by puppies licking my face I pried my eyes open to a panorama of dog poo, ash and dirt. Among this sat a frying pan fused with burnt potato, a chipped teacup and empty vodka bottles. Two bodies lay on the other bed under a pile of rags, dead to the world but alive with the stench of cigarette smoke and compost. Grisha had a dirt-polished scalp, scant patches of hair and a wild moustache. Misha, on the other hand, had gums as toothless and blackened as the coal stove. They were finally stirred by their own snoring and came to with a sense of excitement.

'So Tim, Australian! We understand that today is your Christmas. By all means we will have a celebration tonight. A treat!'

My thoughts were already with the horses. On the steppe they could roam and graze, even dig up the snow to find grass if necessary. Here I had to find them fodder before I could think about celebrating Christmas.

While Misha and Grisha lay a trap for street pigeons I left the hut and picked my way through deserted streets littered with frozen rubbish and bunker-type homes. The only sign of life was the belching and groaning of the gold mine on the edge of town.

Eventually I met Serek, a local Kazakh who split his time between sifting contraband gold and working as the local hunting inspector. Despite being gruff and unwilling to step outside his front door, he was forthcoming.

'OK then! I will sell you one round bale of hay. But you can only keep your horses here for two days, and you must clean out the shit!'

With that he slammed the door.

By the time I had retrieved the animals and cleaned up the first round of manure it was dark and I was near tears. My injured horse could now barely stand on his back leg and within one day my promised hay would run out. The compassion and family warmth I sought seemed to be locked away under the winter ice, and the standoffishness of locals was more confronting than the steppe had been.

Akbakai was not founded on any basis of livability or community. People came here to make fast money, but became stranded in a place lacking in water, ambushed by an extreme climate and devoid of basic services. At least half of the population were engaged in contraband gold dealing and stealing, and fatalities were a formality in the mine. Some called it 'the place that even god forgot'.

Stumbling back to the mud hut in the dark I called my family in Australia from my satellite phone. They were merrily drinking red wine and dining on roast turkey. My phone battery froze before I finished the conversation, and with that I clambered inside. Misha and Grisha didn't hold back.

'Where have you been! We bought you vodka, but I'm afraid that it's already all gone…could you spare 200 tenge for another bottle? By the way, it has been a good year in the mines, only 12 fatalities. I wouldn't mind the payout that their families get, I tell you!'

We were soon in the throes of their Christmas celebrations, feasting on boiled pigeon and toasting to the glory of friendship.

Misha and Grisha passed out into their inebriated comfort zone while I lay awake trying to make sense of the past 24 hours.

It astonished me that people would come to the grandeur of the Betpak Dala, destroy all natural beauty in sight, litter the place with scrap, and then live right in the midst. They had created an island of problems in a sea of calm, and now I was stranded.

It made me feel ashamed for having turned my back on the steppe. Even in the harshest of weather it had offered a sheltered gully, patch of grass or some other kind of nurture. As nomads have known for millennia, it provided sustenance and was to be trusted.

Reflections aside, where would I go within a day, when the hospitality and hay ran dry? A storm was building, one horse could not go on, and the nearest village was another five days' ride across open steppe. I could only hope that morning brought answers.

Tim Cope, author of Off the Rails: Moscow to Beijing by Bicycle, *has crossed Siberia by bicycle and rowboat, and is currently following the trail of Genghis Khan, 10,000km from Mongolia to Hungary, by horse, camel and foot.*

PREVIOUS: The oldest Kazakh traditions date from the 13th century when Genghis Khan's mounted soldiers swept across the plains from Mongolia through northern China.

OPPOSITE: The arid landscape and bitterly cold winters ensure that vegetation is generally sparse and barely manages to support the few gold-mining villages scattered throughout the region.

The Roof of the World

John Mock & Kimberley O'Neil

Looking at the map, Afghanistan's Wakhan Corridor juts eastwards some 300km from northeastern Afghanistan towards China, like a finger of land separating Tajikistan from Pakistan. Three mountain ranges – the Hindukush, Karakoram and Pamir – converge here to form the Bam-i-Dunya, the 'roof of the world'.

We have come to famously remote and starkly beautiful Wakhan to follow the Oxus River to its source in the icy heights of the Afghan Pamir. Our journey traces the footsteps of past explorers – Marco Polo in the 13th century, Lord Curzon, who became Viceroy of India, at the end of the 19th century, and in the 20th century, British archaeologist Sir Aurel Stein and mountaineer HW Tilman. We travel not in service of an empire, but to experience this fabled landscape first-hand by travelling with the people, staying with nomads and listening to the ghosts of ancient caravans.

Wakhan has two distinct parts. In Lower Wakhan, the Oxus River, or Amu Darya as it's known in Persian, flows along the valley floor, past villages inhabited by hospitable Wakhi people. Five thousand metres of vertical relief commands the southern horizon where snow-capped 7000m Hindukush peaks tower over the valley. The Amu Darya or 'mother river' forms much of Afghanistan's northern border with Tajikistan and Uzbekistan as it courses more than 2400km across Central Asia to the Aral Sea. Beyond Lower Wakhan rises the Afghan Pamir, where we're more likely to see bighorned sheep

or brown bear than another person. These rolling grasslands, at more than 3500m, are the domain of the last remaining Kyrgyz nomads, who roam this lofty landscape. *Rabot* (travellers' shelters) and petroglyphs depicting warriors, hunting scenes and Buddhist history, offer us visible evidence of the ancient Silk Road that ran through Wakhan, linking ancient China with the Mediterranean.

At Kashch Goz, a Kyrgyz summer settlement of five felt yurts, the headman greets us. Several Wakhi men from Sarhad-e Broghil are here purchasing livestock. An Afghani trader is here, too, bringing grain and opium to barter with the Kyrgyz for livestock. He is from Jalalabad, and looks almost foreign among the Mongol Kyrgyz, with his pale skin, green eyes and curly light-brown beard. Young Kyrgyz women in bright-red skirts and long-sleeved maroon velvet tunics are tending the herds and flocks of yaks, sheep and goats. Inside the headman's yurt, his wife serves us bowls of fresh cream, and warm bread made with milk rather than water. His mother sits near us, propped up by richly appliqued pillows on an ornate Turkoman rug, as her grandson carefully prepares her opium pipe. Afternoon sun lights the smoke as it drifts upwards towards the central smoke-hole. This is Kyrgyz nomadic life in the Pamir. We could be in another world, another time. We are isolated and far away from the world we know.

Leaving the Kyrgyz camp, we head to the Bozai Darya. Above the stream's bank sit the tombs of Bozai Gumbaz, 'the domes of the elders'. Made of

sun-dried brick plastered with mud, these ancient tombs have been visited by every Western explorer who has visited the region, and are marked on every map. There is no sign of who built them or when – no writing to mark who may lie buried in them – just the ochre domes rising silently above the grass-lined stream.

We head east across the expansive, sandy flood plain and into the Wakhjir Valley, ascending along its broad terraces. Nomads spend winter in this valley, which, although higher in elevation than Kashch Goz, is less exposed to the frigid winds known as the Bad-i-Wakhan that sweep all Wakhan. We pass several now-vacant sites – Qizilotuq, Tekeli, Khitai Qeldi, Keskentash. Here, too, domed tombs indicate heavy mortality. Wakhjir is a typical Pamir valley: the mountains are ragged, snow-topped peaks, not sharp-edged like their Karakoram neighbours. Snow sits easily on the mountains year round, for their slopes are not steep enough to avalanche. The valley floor is broad and U-shaped, scoured by previous glaciation and well watered by the continual snow-melt, making grass abundant. At Guretuk or 'walk past the grave', we do just that to reach a small site where we pitch our tent on a grassy swale next to a clear stream with expansive views down valley.

We pass more empty camps, each with tombs – Duldul, Karatash and Aqtash, the highest site in the Wakhjir. The cloudy weather holds, and although it keeps the water level in the side streams low and easy to ford, it also keeps the air decidedly cool, especially with the near-constant wind in our faces. A lammergeier, obvious by its distinctive tail, soars overhead, likely preying on marmots. Lammergeiers are a sign of Mongol royalty and we take it for a good omen.

As we pass more clay-brick domes up valley, we see that rather than tombs these seem to be *rabot,* shelters with vents for smoke high up the dome and a tiny, arched ground-level entrance. Despite the snow and storms, caravans passed through the Pamir in winter, the only time the Kyrgyz were not present. Descendants of the Mongol emperor Genghis Khan, the Kyrgyz were once infamous as horseback raiders, who plundered and looted those who crossed their territory. Only in winter could the slow-moving caravans be assured of safety from raids, and preferring the cold and storms of nature to the cruelty of men, they chose the arduous frozen crossing of the Pamir. These shelters are for travellers unlucky enough to get caught in a sudden blizzard.

Leaving our camp site at the base of the Wakhjir Pass, we labour through a summer snowstorm towards the glacier filling the valley's head. The horns of Marco Polo sheep lie occasionally along the rocky riverbank, evidence of the animal's abundance and its unlucky fate from rock fall, or hunting. Through the swirling snow, we see the black cave in the glacier's terminus from which flows the icy source of the Oxus River, a corner of our planet unvisited by Westerners for more than a century.

John Mock and Kimberley O'Neil, a hardcore trekking couple, have logged more than 10,000km, 60 passes and 50 glacier traverses through the Karakoram, Hindukush and Himalaya, and are now pioneering new routes in Afghanistan.

PREVIOUS: In the 19th century British strategists ceded a strip of land known as the Wakhan Corridor to Afghanistan to create a buffer between territories annexed by Britain and Russia.

OPPOSITE: The Persians knew the Wakhan as 'the roof of the world' and its remoteness ensured it remained undeveloped during the Soviet occupation and Taliban regime.

The Many Perspectives of this Ice Cathedral

Heather Kirkpatrick

I peer into a labyrinth of ice. My world is blue, its hue increasing with depth. Mysterious turquoise caverns with curvaceous bulges and ripples surround me.

My body is wedged comfortably between two crevasse walls, as far as I can squeeze into the glassy, tapering bottom.

I am 30m down from the Brown Glacier's surface, 1000m above the sea and 4100km southwest from Australia on an active volcano. This place, with its 368 sq km of land, is just a speck in the vast Southern Ocean. I am on, or perhaps I am in, Heard Island.

Heard Island is the world's most pristine sub-Antarctic island, having avoided the introduction of reindeer, cats and rats, which have caused havoc on the other islands. Its 12 major glaciers result from thousands of kilometres of uninterrupted ocean, its southern latitude of 53 degrees and the 2745m massif of the Big Ben volcano.

As I abseiled below the surface of this frozen river of ice, the scouring, chilling, relentless wind suddenly left, as though I had closed a door. With only a slit of bright sky above I descended into this still, mystical world, spinning from my harness to absorb the many perspectives of this ice cathedral.

Shavawn calls to me before she descends and seconds later a shower of light-snow crystals falls from above. I hear the approaching jangle of the metallic climbing hardware swinging from her harness. Minutes later she is beside me and we prepare for the slow journey up.

For five hours, we methodically sample and package cores of ice at 20cm intervals as we ascend. Laboratory analysis will match the samples to a climatic history of the area. Heard Island's glaciation and isolation make it an excellent study location for our changing climate. Glaciers that were seen terminating at the sea nearly 60 years ago now finish hundreds of metres inland.

In between sampling, we slide the ascendeurs on our ropes, trusting the camming action of their small teeth to hold our body weight. Doug and Martin are anchored near the crevasse edge, ensuring the additional safety ropes attached to us remain tensioned.

As I haul myself over the lip of the crevasse, my blue world dissolves.

I adjust to the harsh glare of the sun on the glacier and the perspective of a wide landscape once again. The westerly wind chills my face, the only part of my body not covered by layers of thermals and Gore-Tex.

I look up at the swirling crescent-shaped clouds behind the mountain some 2000m above. Jagged rocky buttresses divide the steep tumbling glaciers. Piles of avalanche debris and large ice séracs indicate the mountain is very much alive. So much so, that two weeks ago I stood on the coast and watched the volcano shoot high plumes of smoke, discolouring its snowy slopes as the black volcanic dust settled.

In the other direction the Southern Ocean stretches endlessly. We travelled across it for 20 days. Often I was firmly braced in bed as the

ship pitched and rolled, for what seemed an eternity. I spent hours dreaming of an icy land with black beaches pounded by surf.

Beside the crevasse, Shavawn, Doug, Martin and I munch, drink and banter whilst digging out anchors and loading backpacks. The guys are pretty cold, after hours of managing the ropes on top. To avoid skiing into crevasses, we divide into pairs and attach a 15m rope section to our partner. Our teams carefully weave between obvious slots and icefalls. I appreciate the visibility and relative balminess of this evening as Doug and I ski in tandem. The weather is in sharp contrast to a blizzard we experienced here last week.

On that occasion we had not always been able to stay upright on our crampons in the ferocious wind. The wind was stripping the glacier surface free of snow. My only visibility had been about one metre of speckled pink rope in front of me. We had previously recorded the safest route home on our handheld GPSs and Doug was in front following the 'Go To' arrow on his GPS screen. The destination had seemed a mystery at the time as we headed into the oblivion of a howling, white void.

It had been impossible to read any terrain due to vast volumes of stinging snow being transported horizontally every second. A couple of times the rope had suddenly yanked on my harness as Doug's foot broke through a snow bridge spanning a crevasse. Our rope tension had ensured I did not have to rig up any crevasse rescue systems. Huge 10cm to 20cm pieces of corrugated rime had hung from our clothing and Doug's beard as the wet freezing maritime storm had plastered us in a way only Heard Island could. Just above 600m elevation we gained visibility again.

This evening the weather is kind to us. Our two teams exit the glacier's side and we leave a cache of equipment at 600m, placing rocks on top. Many rocks. With light packs we ski solo another few hundred metres down, leaving the crevasse fields behind. I complete one telemark turn after the other. My heart is singing as the four of us carve our way down this sensuous path to our home on the coast.

The moon rises as we remove our skis and walk the final kilometre home.

I choose to walk in my own space, that solitary cocoon that allows me to immerse myself in the ambience of the island. Rocky slopes lead to vast velveteen carpets of brilliant-green cushion plants. Clumps of tussock grass flutter as the sound of the ocean rises in a gradual crescendo.

A familiar symphony of the barking of fur seals, the belching of elephant seals and the chatter of king penguins greets me as I arrive at the coast. I drop my backpack and head to join the others in the communal cooking hut. I stop as I hear the haunting call of a sooty albatross. I watch it wheel in the deepening sky as I revel in another delight of this faraway isle.

Heather Kirkpatrick is a freelance journalist and outdoor instructor. She enjoys writing, broadcasting and filmmaking from remote locations around the planet and lives in Hobart, Tasmania, between her travels.

PREVIOUS: Isolated and remote, wild, windswept Heard island provides a breathtaking landscape to find a space of your own.

OPPOSITE: The island is remarkably unlike any other Australian territory, with glaciers covering around 70% of the land and permanent snow covering a further 2%.

OVERLEAF: Heard Island is home to four species of penguin – gentoo, macaroni, rockhopper and king – which are the island's top predators and as such have the run of the land.

32°N 77°E
HIMACHAL PRADESH, INDIA

Making the Most of My Indian Odyssey

Nicholas Thomson

With a spare 36 hours, I decided to make the most of my Indian odyssey and leave Delhi for the mountain air. As India heads north to its border with Kashmir, the bustle gives way to a more casual pace. The Himalayas reach out to the sky, the roads become windier, the buses become that touch more dicey. Manali is one of those utopian locations. It was originally a summer holiday retreat for the British colonial rulers. Now it's become a mecca for international backpackers seeking enlightenment in hillside ashrams and small guesthouses dotting the hillside overlooking what resembles a tiny Alpine village. The local population is the classic crucible of cultures, religions and races, with Hindus, Muslims, Tibetans, and Indian and Pakistani Kashmir people all residing in the clean mountain air eking out livings and accommodating tourists.

Being a fairly relaxed traveller, I didn't give too much thought as to why I only had a small daypack for a 15-hour trip, ill equipped for massive changes in climate and weather. It is also fair to say that having enough Indian rupee was an overrated concern as I sorted out my Zen experience in the most beautiful of locations. After an afternoon exploring the foothills, playing some local cricket and seeking accommodation, I was ready for Tibetan vegetable *momo* and sleep. Awaking to a fine day I climbed as high up into the mountains as I could manage. The combination of mountain air and herbal infusement had me floating and dreaming of spending seven years in Manali. It was all too good.

As the snow came down, I realised my bus was soon to depart from town. I ran down the mountain, dripping with sweat and wet through from the snowy drizzle. Without time for a warm shower and without a change of clothes, I rushed onto the bus. Finding myself the only foreigner on board, the need to bond quickly became apparent. My long-term love of cricket began to serve me well. Just as I was warming up, the bus stopped suddenly as we crossed the Himachal Pradesh border. On to the bus stormed the Indian military. Given the sensitive political environment, the location close to Pakistan and the Gudjarat riots, I should not have been surprised when I was ordered off the bus.

'You are a drug trafficker! Who only comes to Manali for one night with a daypack? Where are your trafficked drugs? Where is your passport? Who are you?' I was numb as I looked into the barrel of a Chinese-issued AK-47. I meekly responded: 'I am not a drug trafficker. My passport is in Delhi. I am very sorry.' 'How much money do you have on you?' 'None.' Not helpful. 'You are going to military jail.'

It was about now that I realised that I was in the middle of nowhere, without a passport, accused of being a drug trafficker or an al-Qaeda runaway, under heavy suspicion, unable to bribe, hypothermic and scared.

All the other passengers were ordered off the bus and asked to identify their luggage, as the thought of me with only a daypack was unfathomable to the military. They were convinced I was carrying large quantities of hash in another

bag. Their suspicion turned to frustration when it became apparent I had no other bags. They reluctantly sent everyone else back onto the bus and held a conference on the foreigner. Seeking out the most affable soldier, I saddled up next to him by his jeep as they discussed what to do with me. Me, the drug smuggler, Pakistani sympathiser and very light traveller. I had spent my remaining rupee on a rapidly disintegrating, low-quality black pashmina that I had bought for a friend. The rain bucketed down and I was ignored as the army personnel talked under an umbrella. The pashmina served as the only thing preventing complete hypothermia.

The distressed look on my face became panicked when the bus was waved on, my new-found Indian friends unable to help me. I was turned into the barracks. As I coughed my way through a cigarette I hoped for a miracle. All of a sudden, the bus stopped and reversed and one cricket-mad Indian passenger produced a mobile phone. Indian national security was called, the Australian embassy was contacted and the hazy memory of my passport number spurted out. Yes, I checked out.

Back on the bus to rapturous cheers, a massive relieved smile on my face and the feeling that I had escaped a complete nightmare.

There were high-fives all around and we continued our comparisons between Steve Waugh and Sachin Tendulkar. The bus driver summoned me up to the front of the bus for a chat with himself and his smiling companions in the front cabin. 'That must have been scary for you, foreigner.' 'Yes, it was awful.' I will never forget what happened next as the irony of the situation played out in full. 'Would you like to smoke?' the driver smiled as he lifted the engine cabin to reveal 20kg of tightly packed Kashmiri hash. One of his sidekicks started laughing: 'Where do you think your driver is from?' I had no idea. 'He is from Pakistan.'

The fact that the wheel came off as we approached Delhi was lost on me. I was safe, back from Manali and soon to be in the warm shower of my Delhi hosts. They looked on in amazement yet complimented my stupidity of rural Indian travel without a passport, as I told them stories of my 36-hour mission to Manali.

Nicholas Thomson has spent the last five years working as a drug-use researcher with Chiang Mai University, Thailand. His job is primarily to coordinate research projects and this puts him in some interesting places across South and Southeast Asia.

PREVIOUS: The Manali–Leh Road cuts a disturbingly thin passage, flanked by sheer cliffs, through some of the country's most mountainous terrain, which is notoriously prone to landslides.

OPPOSITE: Bathed in shadow, Himachal's magnificent sandstone cliffs take on majestic blue-and-silver hues in contrast to the surrounding plains.

Getting There is Half the Fun

David Waag

There are only a handful of people on the bus. My wife and I sit alone on one side about three quarters of the way towards the back. It is a classic government bus. More reminiscent of a school bus with its bench seats, stark metal interior and sliding windows, it offers little comfort on the harsh dirt road down which we hurtle at breakneck speed. The ride *up* into the Sangla Valley had been exhilarating to say the least. The narrow, precipitous dirt trail of a road, still under repair following a catastrophic flood the previous year, was enough in itself to make the trip memorable. However, combined with the joys of public bus travel in India, the ride had been downright unforgettable. The journey had never taken on any death-defying qualities, though. At least not until now.

We are headed back down the Sangla Valley and I am honestly as scared as I have ever been in my life, and I have been in some precarious jams in my time. The driver, dressed in military fatigues for macho effect I am sure, simply defies all rational thought with his driving skills. We barrel at top speed into blind corners, play chicken with oncoming traffic and lurch around as he decides on a whim to avoid various road obstacles. I never imagined fearing for my life on a public bus, but it is happening.

If travelling in India teaches you one thing, it is patience. Between the poor road conditions, the sometimes overly comprehensive system of stops and the often cramped conditions of the public bus system, it takes a special attitude to get from point A to point B. Some genius once said, 'getting there is half the fun'. Had he been in India he could have added – and takes three quarters of your time. Short of a good cup of *chai,* nothing comes easily when travelling in India and really that is a big part of the attraction of travelling there.

However, given our current white-knuckle scenario, I question my judgment. The Sangla Valley, described as a true Shangri-la by many, is a stunning place, located in the upper reaches of Himachal Pradesh in northern India. Framed by spectacular mountains, the Baspa River cuts a dramatic gorge down the valley. The villages are living museums of ancient wooden architecture and the people especially friendly. The dramatic, snow-covered Himalayan peaks set a striking backdrop to an already unique scene. Roads into the valley literally cling to the edge of steep cliffs and the drive up valley, albeit about as hairy as a road can get, is nothing short of spectacular. Mind-bending views emerge around every corner. The road edge drops several thousand feet into the river. The consequences of slipping off the road are unimaginable.

Our current situation though, careening down the very road we drove up a couple of weeks earlier, is downright frightening. We are truly fearful for our lives. The driver appears to be taunting us as he gets even more animated in his driving. He even receives encouragement from a passenger sitting directly behind him. We are in awe that this is really happening. We are both stubborn, well-travelled folk and it

seems ridiculous to abandon ship, but neither of us has ever experienced anything like this. We saw the skeletal remains of buses that have made the unspeakable journey off the road. We are nowhere near another village and we have no idea when or if there is another bus, but we see few other options. We can hold on for dear life and hope for the best, or we can regain control by getting off the bus. As silly as it sounds, the prospect of standing on the side of the road with no village in sight seems the most rational thing to do.

An opportune moment presents itself when the driver stops to allow an oncoming vehicle to cross a single-lane bridge. It is now or never and with hearts apounding and without announcing our exit, we dash for the side door and jump out. I clamber up the roof ladder, toss our packs off the rack and shimmy back down as the bus begins to move forward again. My wife and I look at each other and laugh out loud. Instantly, we feel better. Standing on the side of the road, packs in hand, feels so much more sensible than sitting on the bus wondering when we will pitch over the edge or run head-on into another vehicle and pitch off the road. Our abandoned bus roars off down the road in a cloud of dust while we sit in the dirt contemplating our next move. Never has standing in the middle of nowhere felt so good.

David Waag is an Oregon-based writer with a passion for mountains and skiing. His travels have taken him to remote mountain ranges in India, Alaska, China, South America, Iceland and Canada.

PREVIOUS: The five primary colours of traditional cotton prayer flags represent the five elements of the sky, air, fire, water and earth, and are inscribed with prayers believed to be activated by the wind.

OPPOSITE: 'Hairy' and 'white-knuckle' are two adjectives commonly used to describe the journey through the Sangla Valley by those who get to sit *inside* the bus.

Horns Like a Pretzel

Patrick Witton

Altitude sickness can do weird things to your system. It can put a hammer in your head. It can get your heart racing as if pumped with pure caffeine. It can make you see mango trees. In Nepal. It can turn what looks like a morning stroll along a path with no more hindrance than a rickety bridge and a fat yak, to be what it really is: a slow slog into the crumpled corners of the Himalaya. We are not the thrill-seeker types: a gang of five with ages ranging from 12 to 62, and a strong Nepalese entourage there to pitch tents, carry provisions and conjure feasts. But a suggestion from our trusty guide to venture to Thame, the village beyond the edge of our map, is one that stirs the explorer within.

Maybe the 500m ascent of yesterday should be considered. Our breath is a little thin. We're not sleeping too well. Why am I seeing spots? Has that chicken got a woolly hat on? Why do that yak's horns look like a pretzel? Well, we won't be bagging peaks or swinging from karabiners. And the village of Thame is only a *little* bit off the map. Plus, that little granny over there just did the hike from Thame to where we are at Namche Bazaar this morning, with thongs on. And she'll be heading back in a tick, carrying a sack of rice and 5L of kero she picked up at market. We might be a few days' walk from the nearest road (and it's blocked by Maoist rebels, anyway), but Thame's just up the trail a bit. No biggie.

The crowds of Namche Bazaar's Saturday morning market thin out quickly as we take the path west towards Thame. We head into the Nangpa La Valley, which widens enough to cradle the fields and pebble-fenced villages of Thamu and Thomde. But soon after, the jagged peaks start to squeeze the strip of sky above us. We wander onward in a thin-blooded fug, spinning roadside prayer wheels and *namaste*-ing to crowds of kiddies, entrepreneurial Buddhist nuns and anyone else confronted by us: a slow-moving wall of polar-fleece.

Soon the track thins to a width that can only take us one at a time. Our guide reminds us to take the higher ground when confronted by oncoming yak traffic. And one circumspective look down the crumbling valley, to the milky churn of the Bhotekoshi River, drives the point home: we're one yak's bum sway away from being *momo* mince. And when they're weighed down with enough corrugated iron to roof a preschool, you can't trust any yak to be sure-hoofed.

The Himalaya has a way of playing with your sense of scale. Or maybe it's that ol' lack-of-oxygen factor. Mountains that look close enough to touch can be days away, and bridges that look like they're made out of dental floss can take the weight of a rebel army. Likewise, our destination looms large soon after the start of our trek. From where we rest, munching nuts at the base of a Buddhist stupa, our guide points out Thame and the clear trail that will carry us there. Seeing how close it is, we wobble on with a tad more vigour. We'll be there in an hour? Two hours max? Our guide diplomatically changes the subject to hydroelectricity, respiratory diseases or chocolate (our favourite subjects).

As we dawdle on, our muscles lose their integrity. Knees take on the properties of jelly. One in our party spends a bit of time behind bushes, another seems to be sleepwalking, another puffs like a rutting koala. We stop passing through villages, and instead pass by glacial scree, off-duty yaks, and some daredevil Himalayan goats risking death for those juicy tufts of grass that grow on the edge of plummeting chasms.

The Bhotekoshi River rises up towards our path and squeezes past a pile of badly balanced boulders. We cross a bridge that resembles a cheese grater, bolted above the river's tightest, most furious point.

From the other bank of the Bhotekoshi, the path curls quietly, eerily, up the ever-narrowing valley. Intervillage traffic has dropped off completely, and we see no-one until we arrive at the first rock-walled fields of Thame. As we slowly stumble on, it becomes apparent that this place is special. Thame is strapped to the side of the now vertical valley wall. We can see the blue-tinged houses plonked atop each other, and the monastery taking prime position at the top of the tumble of dwellings.

Looking behind us, to the valley we crawled up, we can see the majestic peak of Thamserku smothered in watermelon-coloured light from the fading sun; meanwhile the thermometer in Thame crashes. Beyond Thame's houses, the valley folds its mile-high edges over itself and disappears in a swirl of snow. For us, with our cyclops torches, moon boots and camel slacks laden with a thousand buckles, this is the end of the road.

With camp assembled, one of our party vanishes into their polar-fleece, another goes to scrutinise the amenities and never returns. I start up a conversation with a yak. I think I meet a man with a bone necklace and knot of red hair. What altitude are we at? Best I go to bed. As a valley squall pushes Tibetan topsoil into my tent and up my nostrils, I dream of yaks and ripe mangoes.

Patrick Witton is a near-Melbourne-based author who may not have conquered Everest, but vigorously shook his fist at it.

PREVIOUS: Yaks have two layers of hair, densely-matted under-hair and straggly outer hair – a perfect blanket for a body that can weigh up to a tonne in an environment where sub-zero is the norm.

OPPOSITE: The Himalayas have witnessed many changes since they were formed 70 million years ago. Fossils show that giraffes and hippos thrived where humans now camp.

Searching the Mountains for Prey

Michael Kohn

I feel like the Stay Puff Marshmallow Man. With a few dozen layers of fleece clothing, a down jacket, woolly cap and ski gloves, I really should be warm. But I am not. My fingers are frozen solid and my face stings from the cold. I don't even feel my toes any more. They went numb days ago.

Yet I continue to walk. Day after day I follow these three Kazakh men as they search the mountains for prey. The hours pass slowly as the hunt drags on, and still there is no kill. We have been at this for 10 days and there have been several near catches. The hunters spot a fox or rabbit and release their golden eagles; the giant birds swoop down and reach out with their talons, but luck has eluded them. Still, we try.

Clambering up to the ridge, we look over a plain that could be Antarctica. There is nothing in the distance but a vast field of snow and rock, a hazy horizon and a dome of blue sky. The temperature is -15°C, the warmest it's been in days.

The hunters are braced for the elements. Dressed in thick, padded coats, felt boots and fox-fur hats, they look like battle extras for a film about Genghis Khan. Their resilience astonishes me. While I've been munching on cookies and snacks they only smoke a few hand-rolled cigarettes, and seem content.

There is no trace of the 21st century, or the 20th century for that matter. Out here, in Mongolia's far west province of Bayan Ölgii, time seems to have stood still. The small, mountainous region is home to a few hundred nomadic families who have staved off modernity and preserved their traditions far better than their cousins in modern-day Kazakhstan.

Geography plays a part in the isolation. To the south lie the deserts of Xinjiang, to the north are the forests of Siberia and to the west are the former nuclear testing grounds in Kazakhstan. To the east lies Ulaanbaatar, a six-day drive over unpaved desert-scape. While the Russians and Chinese developed the neighbouring regions, Bayan Ölgii was largely left to its own devices.

In a place like this, I learn, history is relative. The distant past resembles the present and events that occurred long ago, like the triumphs of Genghis Khan, are spoken about as if they occurred last week. The hunters have only vague notions about the outside world and yet their relationship with their natural surroundings is beyond my own comprehension. Change, however, is inevitable. The Internet, infrastructure and mobile phones are on their way; SUVs and precision-hunting rifles can't be far behind. There are also worrying reports about uncontrolled development and poorly enforced environmental laws killing off wildlife and felling forests at unsustainable rates.

Shaking off any ill-thoughts, I continue to follow the Kazakhs around the ridge. They ride slowly atop shaggy horses while I follow on foot. I had gone on horseback days earlier but realised that this only limited my ability to take photographs. My Kazakh friends love posing and I didn't want to miss a moment of their steely looks, which I could not capture while also looking after a half-wild horse.

The hunters stop short at a sunlit canyon. It looks like a good place to spot prey. They dismount. Yasiin and Kadal creep to the edge of the cliff with the eagles balancing on their arms. They crouch low to the ground. Kavai, the youngest, stands with his eagle to their right, a metre or two away. He tips a rock down the slope.

One shout is joined by two more and the three eagles rise simultaneously. Two fly straight down the slope and one, strangely, off to the right. The hunters roar and wave their arms. Further below, about 30m down the slope, I see it; a small fox glowing in the morning sun. The fox stands unmoving on the edge of a rock, paralysed with fear as death approaches. Flying side by side, with a combined wingspan over 3.5m wide, the eagles extend their craggy yellow talons. They bounce off the rock and soar skyward, the unfortunate fox in the eagle's vice-like grip.

The hunters roar with joy at the victory. Leaping on their mounts, they stand in the stirrups and charge down the slope like medieval warriors. We reach the fracas of feathers, wings and beaks and watch as the eagles squeeze the life from the fox. Suddenly, a gun seems so undignified.

The proud hunters pose stoically for a picture with their trophy, and then Yasiin strings the fox to his saddle. Because he is the oldest, they say, Yasiin keeps the first kill of the day. After a lifetime of hunting with your friends, I guess that what comes around eventually goes around.

That night, I sit in Yasiin's mudbrick home watching the old hunter skin the fox by the light of a candle. A dung-fuelled stove warms our hands as we drink bowls of milk tea ladled out by Yasiin's wife. His children hover over textbooks as a radio announcer delivers news from the capital, Ulaanbaatar, 1600km and a world away from here.

With careful detail, Yasiin schools his son in fox-skinning technique. Once the pelt is removed, the eagle, named Asalbek, is allowed to eat. The 1m-tall bird, hooded and tethered to the floor, can smell that the fox is being cut up for this benefit. The pieces of meat are placed in a metal bowl in front of him and his knife-like beak greedily reaches in. Yasiin's son, Nursaltan, strokes the soft pelt, turns it inside out and hangs it on the wall to dry.

From under his extra-large fox-fur cap he whispers to me that once he's old enough, he'll be a hunter like his father. I make him promise to be my guide and with a shake of the hands, the deal is sealed. Change might be headed for Bayan Ölgii, but Nursaltan's eyes tell me that its soul will remain the same.

Michael Kohn has travelled to more than 60 countries. His longest stint was a three-year stopover in Mongolia, where adventures included a 200km bike trip along the Russian border and the completion of his first marathon by the shores of Lake Khövsgöl.

PREVIOUS: The tradition of eagle hunting is believed to have originated in Central Asia around 6000 years ago and was introduced to the region by Mongols in the 13th century.

OPPOSITE: Tavan Bogd is the highest spot in the Altai Mountains and is undoubtedly one of the most remote and unforgiving regions anywhere.

The Flip Spilled Everything

Ben Kozel

Life really can be turned upside down. In fact, it takes less than seven seconds. It happened to me in northern Mongolian *aimag* (province) of Khuvsgul, about 40km downstream of where the Ider and Mörön Rivers merge to create the Selenga River.

A 4m-long yellow inflatable raft represented life for two companions and me. Everything that made it possible to exist in that wilderness, as far as we were concerned, was contained within the raft. Without it we would likely have been reduced to pitiable scavengers, perhaps even driven to the very edge of humanity. The raft was our mother ship, the proverbial bosom at which we suckled, and to which we clung for sanctuary.

The flip spilled everything. Four big dry bags (holding all our personal gear, passports, money, tool kits and film footage) floated away. A perilous swim in the snag-riddled channel had salvaged three of them. The fourth had narrowly escaped. Other items, meanwhile, never stood a chance. A large box of food sank, so too both camera tripods. And in what seemed like the work of a conscious entity, the swirling water had even managed to unbolt the left oar from its mounting. It, together with our only spare, lay somewhere on the bottom.

Yet things might so easily have been worse. But for one of the cam straps (which we used to secure two white-water kayaks at the stern) hooking onto a branch stub, the whole raft would have been whisked away.

Indeed, the bough from which that stub protruded had played both villain and saviour. We'd all seen it coming. A brutishly thick thing it was, more than 4m long, extending horizontally out over half the width of the channel. It was never going to yield, unlike the thicket through which we had crashed and scraped for more than 10 minutes. As soon as we'd taken a wrong turn, and the vegetation had closed in on both sides, oars made no difference in deciding where we went. The banks of the Selenga had burst, and a muddy torrent charged over the landscape, through woodland and scrub.

The worst winter in 50 years had dumped a huge quantity of snow on the mountains of northwestern Mongolia. Now a warmer than average spring saw all that snow melting fast.

My companions were two Canadians, Colin and Remy. At least, there had been two of them until about 20 minutes after the flip. For as soon as we'd secured the upturned raft and unstrapped one of the kayaks, Colin had shot off in pursuit of the fourth dry bag. This bag held all the video footage documenting our journey thus far. And its worth had blinkered Colin to both the danger of kayaking through raging flood waters, and the need to discuss a rendezvous plan. In the frantic heat of the moment, he'd left wearing nothing but a pair of cotton trousers.

Remy and I stayed at the site of the flip, picking up the pieces. The water level continued to rise, threatening to evict us from the meadow on which we made our stand. Both of us were acutely aware of how difficult it was going to be to negotiate the flood waters with only one oar. Manoeuvrability was the key to making sure we

didn't flip again. The consequences could be even more tragic next time.

We dismantled the rowing frame and reassembled it, *a la* Lego Meccano–style, with the lone oar positioned over the raft's stern. Here it could be swung from side to side, like a fish tail, or else be used as a rudder. We had salvaged a semblance of power and control over our destiny.

Yet control was a slippery thing to keep hold of in that flood land. A whole day passed with no sign of Colin. His whereabouts and welfare consumed me. It was as strong a feeling of helplessness as I could remember. I struggled to block visions of an upturned kayak, pressed relentlessly against the thicket, his pulpy, waterlogged body inside. High above us, jet aircraft silently plied the route between Japan and Europe, their business-suited, scotch-sipping passengers oblivious to the drama unfolding in the wilderness below.

Some comfort came from knowing that because the flood channels were braided around a maze of islands, it may not have been possible for Colin to find his way back. Even still, I recoiled from the thought of what it must be like outside the protective confines of the mother ship. What was he eating? And where had the poor bugger slept! It was unlikely he'd find any local hospitality to fill the void. The Selenga Valley is sparsely populated. And in the context of Mongolia having the lowest population density of any country on earth, this was saying something.

The snub of the Selenga essentially boils down to a distrust of rivers. The often-confined nature of river valleys is a world away from the open, gently undulating steppe that Mongolian horsemen adore. They regard rivers, like forests and mountains, as the domain of monsters. For the first time, perhaps I could see their point.

Forty hours after the flip, Remy and I relaunched the raft. The modified propulsion setup worked well. And it was this, coupled with a now obsessive vigilance, and meticulous approach to fork selection, that kept us clear of the potentially lethal vegetation.

Hours passed. We approached a log hut, perched on marginally higher ground. Suddenly, a horseman appeared from behind it, galloping towards the bank. Half a dozen more men swarmed out and followed on foot. All were shouting and waving for us to stop. The fellow on the horse, with a livid scar cutting the length of his face, could have passed for a seasoned Mongol warrior during the reign of the mighty 13th-century warlord Genghis Khan.

As I stepped ashore, one man rushed forward, unfolding a large piece of paper. Scribbled diagrams depicted a timeline of events. Looking at them more closely, the corners of my mouth began to turn upward. It was the first time in over two days I'd had reason to smile. The diagrams showed a raft, a kayak and several egg-shaped bags. And among them were three stick figures, labelled 'Colin', 'Remy' and 'Ben'.

Ben Kozel is lured by the remote and the wild. He prefers the slower journey – rowing an old boat, or leading camels – giving people and place time to get under his skin.

PREVIOUS: From Sühbaatar to its mouth the 1480km-long Selenga River flows down a gentle slope that allows Mongolia access to the broad fertile plains of Siberia.

OPPOSITE: At times the river rolls furiously through grey-walled gorges rising up hundreds of metres above the raging rapids.

25°N 102°E
YUNNAN,
CHINA

An Unexpected Mountain Desert

Korina Miller

Hor-Schpt. I'd been unceremoniously spat out of the bus window. The decrepit, groaning vehicle was impossibly long and its never-ending aisle was filled with chickens, children and those characteristically Chinese not-quite-canvas travelling bags that seem to expand to the size of small yaks. Getting to the door was a fool's mission and so I'd opted for the locals' exit, with a couple of helpful pushes on my rear and my small pack thrown out after me. And there I stood in Baishuitai (Baishuiwhere?), with knees so weary they couldn't even knock, after 108km of some of the most perilous road I had ever experienced. After massive rains, the dirt road had been at times as sticky as melted marshmallow, at other times as slippery as soap suds, requiring the majority of us passengers to exit the bus (via the window) and push the bus's back end back up onto the narrow, mountain track.

I'd arrived from Zhongdian, that glorious, nearly remote–feeling Tibetan town in the upper reaches of China's southwestern province of Yunnan. Baishuitai's tourist card is its less-than-rarely-visited limestone plateaus. I went and had a look (led by villagers who couldn't imagine why else I would be in Baishuitai) and was left with the strange and somewhat startling impression of having walked on nearly solid, iridescent water.

Contrary to the villagers' assumptions, the plateaus weren't what drew me here. I'd come to do the two-day trek from Baishuitai to Daju, on the other side of the Jinsha River and Tiger Leaping Gorge. But I'd come with my own assumptions, namely that I'd manage to meet up with some fellow trekkers at one of the village's guesthouses. This now seemed rather unlikely, given that I was the only guest at the only guesthouse in town.

I knew that doing a solo trek through the mountains and villages of China's borderlands wasn't a wise move. Nevertheless, the return bus journey seemed far more suicidal. So the next morning I gathered my nerve and provisions: a bottle of water, a piping hot *baba* (thick flat-bread), a couple of oranges and a hand-scribbled map that was my only guide. 'It's a gorgeous trek,' the illustrator of the map had assured me. I figured she'd damn well better be right.

Off I set down the dirt road, the dust swirled up by the occasional passing donkey cart. Soon enough I found the trail that led up into the woods. Once I'd accepted (or at least convinced myself) that this was my fate, I began to relax and enjoy the unfathomable vistas of wooded valleys with waterways and tiny hamlets too small to be considered villages. This was not the China I knew, not the China of sardine-can humanity, clogged air and piles of rubbish. This was a vestige of wilderness in a country better known for having the earth's largest population and some of its worst environmental practices. And I felt duly awed by its utter remoteness.

I reached the first sizable village at dusk and as I walked through in search of the guesthouse, I had that unnerving experience of leaving a trail of stares and silence in my wake. Foreigners

were about as common here as penguins, but I found a room and a startled, though gracious, host and felt galvanised for the next day's hike.

Day two was filled with more dramatic, lush views and even more silence – something which is as elusive as the panda in China. Despite the trail crisscrossing back and forth over the road, there'd not been a donkey cart all day.

The trail climbed up and up and the thin air of this mountainous region gave me two left feet and a drooping mind. As the afternoon wore on, I decided to take a shortcut that looked like it would cut out some of the crisscrossing and stepped off the edge of my crumpled map. The path took me down, down, down and then landed in a pile of undergrowth. I fought my way through only to find myself in an utterly unexpected mountain desert. Sand so powder-like it might have been imported from a tropical beach, but surrounded by coniferous trees instead of palms, and many miles and metres from the sea. Where was I? Lost.

My oranges and *baba* were long gone and my water was foolishly low. My sense of direction had evaporated a few crisscrosses ago. I walked, panic close behind, into the middle of this nowhere place. Just as panic took my hand, I saw what I decided must be a mirage over a distant dune: the huge angular black hats of three Yi women.

Yunnan Province is home to more than 20 diverse ethnic groups and the Yi remain one of the more obscure. Known as China's bandits, they've always fascinated me, not in least because of the women's fantastic wardrobe of embroidered tops, flowing skirts, bright Pippi Longstocking tights, running shoes and hats that must stand half a metre off their heads. The Yi have got quick smiles, a language that sounds like wind chimes and they smoke like chimneys from thin, ruler-length pipes. They believe that cameras steal their soul and have an entirely wary, somewhat shy manner with outsiders. This isn't surprising considering the poverty and ethnic injustices they've suffered.

Eventually our paths met on that odd, sand-strewn terrain and I think they would have carried right on by if I hadn't stopped them and attempted to ask the way. We sat together in that unheard-of desert, them bemused and me intrigued and it remains, to this day, one of the most surreal experiences of my life. They smoked and tittered to one another, their enormous hats swaying to and fro. 'Daju. Daju. Daju,' I said, trying different tones and inflections to make myself understood. Silence. Then a storm of laughter that I could only join in with. They pulled at my hair and tested the quality of my jacket between their fingers and then sat back, unhurried and relaxed. As the sun warmed us and the pipe went round and round, the tranquillity was palpable. Their presence filled the desert.

Finally they rose and pointed across the sand. 'Daju.' Evidently they had understood after all. So on I went. And while the story of the trek continues, complete with a maze of goat trails, a dodgy dugout crossing and a frozen bus ride, for me it ends in that desert, which, as I sat with those unusual women, had become my destination. The rest is just a footnote.

Korina's hunger for adventure has propelled her to the world's furthest flung corners for the past 13 years, taking her across five continents as a writer, backpacker, student, hiker, swimmer, teacher, hotelier, ocean-follower and mountain-lover.

PREVIOUS: The Jinsha ('Golden Sands') River froths and thunders down the mighty Jinsha River Gorge and passes through Tiger Leaping Gorge, believed to be the deepest river canyon in the world.

OPPOSITE: The river's power is notoriously deceptive as it charges along at speeds of 8m per second, causing even the most extreme sports junkies to admit it may never be rafted.

OVERLEAF: Yunnan's local ethnic minorities have farmed rice in hillside terraces for thousands of years, retaining the traditions of seed exchange and rice worship.

Angkor in Wartime

Daniel Robinson

A late-model Honda Civic whisked me across the Golden Gate Bridge, through 'the City', past the tract housing lampooned by Pete Seeger as 'little boxes on the hillside, little boxes made of ticky-tacky' and on to San Francisco International, where a spacious 747 was waiting to take me to Bangkok. Banks of public telephones lined the walls of the departure lounge but I hardly noticed.

It took 17 days to get an official invitation, and then a visa, to the Socialist Republic of Vietnam. On my last day in Bangkok, I used an AT&T card to place a final call to the US: 'I'll be in touch again when I can.' Vietnam Airlines laid on a timeworn, pointy-nosed Tupolev Tu-134, all of whose passengers were keenly aware that an identical aircraft had crashed on approach to Bangkok less than a year earlier. During the flight to Ho Chi Minh City, I could see Cambodia's dense jungle far below.

The time was June 1989, just a few weeks after the Tiananmen Square Massacre in neighbouring China. In Cambodia, a civil war that pitted the Vietnamese-backed Phnom Penh government against the genocidal Khmer Rouge still raged. Although Vietnam had put an end to Pol Pot's killing fields back in 1979, the US, the Western Europeans and the UN continued – obscenely – to recognise the Khmer Rouge as Cambodia's sole legitimate government. Phnom Penh's only diplomatic missions were in countries allied with the Soviet Union; for reasons of geography, the best place to try for a Cambodian visa was Vietnam.

During the Vietnam War – referred to by many Vietnamese as the 'American War' – US troops talked about being 'in-country' (as opposed to anywhere else in the world), and even in the late 1980s, as I researched Lonely Planet's first guides to Vietnam and Cambodia, I had a sense of flying, not 'to', but 'into' Vietnam. Rules totally unlike those in the democratic world, few of them explicitly spelled out anywhere, delineated – but only vaguely – what was permitted, what was forbidden and what was risky, if not to you then to your local contacts. Most everything a foreigner might do seemed to fall into the latter category. The unease in the eyes of

many locals, delighted to meet someone from abroad after years of isolation yet frightened of the possible consequences, and the habit some people had of breaking off in midsentence to scribble out the rest of their thoughts, hoping to elude perhaps-imaginary listening devices, made fear a constant, relentless presence.

The Cambodian consulate in Ho Chi Minh City was in a neighbourhood of French-era villas just two blocks north of the former American embassy. I suspect that the novelty of my visa request, the regime's hunger for international legitimacy and a general state of consular underemployment conspired to create a surprising degree of both goodwill and efficiency. The visa was ready within a few days and, after deciding not to pay US$22 for a three-minute phone call to the US, I hopped on the daily bus to Phnom Penh, which was considerably cheaper than the US$46 flight. My fellow passengers included a number of uniformed Vietnamese troops heading back to the front after home leave. One of them, playing with his AK-47, accidentally fired a shot out the window, producing guffaws and scolding from the other passengers. He smiled sheepishly. Things were getting curiouser and curiouser.

Perhaps because Cambodia was in a state of war and war always produces a degree of chaos, Phnom Penh, derelict and shell-shocked, was considerably more laid-back than Ho Chi Minh City. My hosts from the General Directorate of Tourism, a friendly bunch who hardly ever talked about the members of their families killed by the Khmer Rouge, were appalled to hear that I had travelled overland – despite the fact that the Moc Bai–Phnom Penh highway was considered the country's most secure. It was clear, though, that their sternness did not reflect a totalitarian mindset but rather heartfelt concern that something might happen to me, in which case they'd be in deep shit. Losing a foreign guest was definitely something to be avoided.

Amid the freewheeling wartime disorder, international phone calls were hardly monitored. In fact, thanks to a Soviet satellite link, you could call pretty much anywhere you wanted, politely assisted by an

English-speaking operator with a thick Russian accent. I wondered who she was, seated at her telephone exchange in faraway Moscow… I managed to place a call to Jerusalem – 'I'll be in touch again when I can' – before setting off for one of the most fabled and mysterious places on earth: Angkor. Deep in the rainforest in a part of Cambodia notorious for Khmer Rouge activity, the magnificent temples had been virtually inaccessible for almost two decades.

As we gained altitude, the Kampuchean Airlines Antonov An-24 turboprop filled with a fog so thick I couldn't see across the aisle – something to do with the Soviet air-con system coping badly with high humidity. As much as possible, we flew over the Tonlé Sap lake to avoid ground fire and after 40 minutes we landed without incident at Siem Reap. No matter what happened, including a medical emergency, I'd be stuck in an isolated patch of government-controlled territory until the next flight out – back to Phnom Penh – four days later.

A French aid worker named Claire and I were the only people staying at the 62-room Grand Hôtel d'Angkor, built in 1928. The sentries posted around the building at sundown were there just for us. Day and night, irregular shooting echoed through the surrounding jungle. Soldiers goofing off? A firefight with Khmer Rouge guerrillas? There was no-one to ask. Remembering the hotel's phone number was easy: it was 15. Sending a telegram to Phnom Penh or even phoning was said to be possible – sometimes.

As an expression of human architectural genius, 12th-century Angkor Wat is the equal of Chartres, Tenochtitlan or the Taj Mahal, but because of the war Claire and I had the sprawling temple all to ourselves. We rode there in the back seat of a black Russian-built sedan, accompanied by a driver, a French-speaking guide and a young government minder whom we dubbed 'l'Espion' (the spy) and who had more in common with Inspector Clouseau than he probably knew. It was cruel, I know, but as we wandered around the virtually deserted town of Siem Reap, Claire and I amused ourselves by giving l'Espion the slip. A look of profound relief and thanksgiving flashed across his beardless face each time he found us. His expression seemed to say: 'We're all in this together, here at the end of the line. We're all surrounded by the same impenetrable jungle, we all face the same unseen dangers – so why don't we just be nice to each other?'

'Good news,' our guide reported one morning, 'we've received military authorisation to visit Preah Khan. No-one has been allowed there since 1982.' We drove to the Bayon, with its hundreds of gargantuan, icily smiling visages of Avalokitesvara, and then continued north along overgrown roads, catching occasional glimpses of heavily armed soldiers. We entered the temple through the West Gate, slowly making our way past bas-relief scenes of gods and devils and through vaulted stone galleries, many of them partly collapsed. Bats flitted in and out of the ancient, intricately carved stone eaves, while underfoot, creeping plants competed for space and light and muffled each footfall. In the central sanctuary, on the side of a stupa, we came upon a dead bat being devoured by voracious red ants.

Suddenly, a group of government soldiers wearing unkempt uniforms and *kramas* (checked cotton scarves) and carrying AK-47s burst in. They spoke animatedly with the guide, who turned ashen and then translated: the temple had been mined to prevent Khmer Rouge infiltration. Our authorisation, it would seem, had not been properly coordinated with local forces. A deadly, bright-green Hanuman snake slithered through the undergrowth; one of the soldiers beat it to death with a stick. Shots echoed in the distance.

Slowly, carefully, deliberately, I made my way outward from the centre of the temple, scanning the undergrowth for the telltale glint of a nylon filament tripwire. The car, so black and ordinary, came into view through the vegetation. 'If we can only make it to the tarmacked road,' I thought. Keeping a good 10m between myself and the others – lest someone get unlucky – I tiptoed along the barely discernable path. A tarantula scurried under a rock. The seconds ticked by with excruciating slowness.

Daniel Robinson researched and wrote Lonely Planet's award-winning first guides to Cambodia and Vietnam. He had more success in avoiding minefields than he did in evading the Vietnamese secret police, who eventually expelled him.

PREVIOUS: A few remaining accounts from the 13th century depict Angkor as one of the most magnificent cities in the world and today its famous ruins remain a potent source of national pride.

OPPOSITE: Between AD 802 and 1431 Khmer kings constructed a series of no fewer than 80 temples at Angkor. Today the ruins of 40 temples are all that remain of a once-magnificent empire.

Rowing Across Lake Baikal

Ben Kozel

The surface heaves like the chest of an animal. This is water glutinous and brooding, so unlike any I have ever known before. I take a five-rouble coin from my pocket and flick it overboard. The surface breaks with a reassuring 'ploop'. Yet the coin seems to sink too slowly. I watch it descend for much longer than I had expected to. Free falling, it turns over and over, followed each time by a glint of steadfast clarity and brilliance. It's as if both sides of the coin know they will never see light again. At last, it disappears from view. But in my mind's eye, I continue to follow it down, down more than a kilometre to where it will lay in eternal darkness.

It is 10.30pm. By our best estimates we are halfway across the lake; about 20km from both the east shore and west shore. It has taken nine hours to row this far.

The horizon is stark in contrasts. Looking to the northeast and to the southwest, sky meets water. But to the northwest, the precipitous flanks of the Primorsky Range loom over our bow like castle ramparts. In this place, exhilaration is rivalled only by a sense of vulnerability. Baikal commands nothing less than awe.

I lever the oars through water that appears almost black. Supreme transparency and great depth ensure this water absorbs virtually all the light incident upon it. Wraithlike, Baikal hungers for energy. The water temperature here is only a couple of degrees above zero. Air coming into contact with the surface is instantly chilled, so that it hangs heavy and thick. And like some sort of vaporous zombie henchman, it squirms its way up jacket sleeves and trouser legs, pitilessly seeking out the warmth that has dared enter this realm.

Summer had dawned three weeks earlier, but the last chunks of ice had melted less than half as long ago. This says much more about Baikal than it does about the region's climate. An ice crust 10m thick takes a long time to thaw. So much so that the breaking of Baikal's crust is at least a month out of sync with all other lakes and rivers in southern Siberia.

It's all thanks to the sheer volume of water involved – 23,600 cu km, or 20% of the Earth's fresh stocks. If all the world's rivers were to empty into Lake Baikal for a year, they still would not quite fill it. Indeed, such is the scale of Baikal that local Russians refer to her as a sea. The irony is, however, that the lake contains not a trace of salt; her water is amongst the purest in the world.

The mood on board the boat is subdued, as if the cold constrains mental function to some absolute minimum. Nothing, however, could be further from the truth. Baikal's immensity causes you to retreat within yourself and contemplate the purity of your own soul. Simultaneously, you give yourself over entirely to her aura. You long to connect with her.

Then suddenly it seems that she has responded to such longing. A head rises out from the water, and looks on through shiny black eyes. Is it one of her minions? An ambassador despatched to receive us into the very heart of this

kingdom? Or is this seal just a curious resident? In fact, nerpa, the Baikal seal, is just one of almost 3000 species of animals and plants found nowhere else on Earth. Certainly it's fair to say that although geologists are only making reference to a localised spreading of the Earth's crust when they describe Baikal as 'a living lake', such an idiom rings true on several other counts as well.

With the onset of dusk my unease builds. But there is no throwback to irrational childhood fears at play here. The weather is deteriorating. To the west, a squall spills over the Primorsky Range and scurries southward across the lake. Electricity flashes in that part of the sky. My whole body shivers, but this time it is not because I'm cold. What does lightning mean for us as the only object for kilometres in every direction?

Soon the wind is driving swells up to a metre in height. To achieve any forward progress I must time each oar stroke to coincide with the trough between two crests. That the wind blows directly on our nose is auspicious enough. I don't want to imagine what fury would be unleashed against us if it should swing around to become a southwester. Landfall in that direction is more than 200km. Over that sort of distance, the waves generated by even a moderate wind would make those we are now battling against seem like ripples in a bathtub.

So enormous is Baikal that it creates its own weather systems. Storms can strike with little warning, and deliver 3m swells, easily capable of capsizing our boat. If that happened, what then? Even if we could muster enough strength and balance to haul ourselves up onto its bucking belly, there is almost nothing for numb fingers to hang onto. It would amount to the longest rodeo ride in history. Long before then, however, hypothermia would promise to claim us. Unable to dry out, we'd freeze to death in our sodden clothing.

At best, we are marking time. As the boat dips and props, and I struggle to maintain rhythm, my mind recalls the words of a Russian I'd met a few days before in the city of Ulan Ude. Upon hearing of our plans to row across Lake Baikal he had insisted we stock up on vodka. 'For celebrating?' I had asked, naively thinking that it would be an feat to celebrate. He had then regarded me with an expression that seemed to question how much I knew about where I was going. 'No' he had replied, 'For warmth.' There was a brief pause before he added 'And for courage.'

Ben Kozel is lured by the remote and the wild. He prefers the slower journey – rowing an old boat, or leading camels – giving people and place time to get under his skin.

PREVIOUS: From late January to early May, Lake Baikal freezes over and around Listvyanka the ice can be up to almost a metre thick.

OPPOSITE: Lake Baikal is so large it creates its own distinct microclimate. Fogs occur regularly throughout spring and autumn, and in summer violent storms are common.

214

Teetering on the Edge of a Watery Void

Joe Cummings

'G'day mate!' I opened my eyes and looked up from my sling chair. It had been a hard morning's work canvassing the Carita area for an update of Lonely Planet's *Indonesia* guidebook and I was enjoying a brief rest on the beach. The Australian standing over me in denim cutoffs, shoulder-length dirty-blonde hair and a muscled, sun-reddened chest didn't wait for a counter-greeting.

'A few of us are hiring a boat to have a look at Crack-a-toe. Tomorrow morning, around five thirty. Four hours out, fours back. Wanna come along?'

I didn't want to rise that early and I really needed to be moving along to the next area on my itinerary, West Java's Badui region. Fascinated by stories of mysterious priests who never left Badui Dalam – a zone at the centre of Badui that was off limits to all outsiders, I hoped to grab a peek into the heart of this little-known area. The Sundanese claimed that the clairvoyant Badui priests instantly knew when anyone intended to breach the invisible lines between Outer and Inner Badui. If they sensed the threat was real, these priests could conjure a powerful hex that would cause debilitating illness, even death, to the potential interloper.

But this was an opportunity to see Krakatau, site of the largest volcano eruption in human history. I had talked to the German owner of the backpackers' resort where I was staying and he had said the only boats to Krakatau were those chartered from the Indonesian park service post further south in Labuhan.

When questioned about his arrangements, the Aussie said he'd found a cheaper local alternative – a fishing boat whose owner was willing to take a group of around 10 paying passengers for a total of 200,000 rupiah. That would work out to about US$10 each if they could fill the boat. Briefly weighing the loss of one day against the opportunity to observe and photograph Krakatau at such an affordable price, I decided Badui could wait.

It was difficult to abandon the comfortable palm-thatched bungalow at 5.30am. The Sundanese *nelayan* (fishermen) and a brilliant sunrise greeted our group of 10 at the beach. As I rolled up my trousers to wade to the wooden *African Queen*–style boat, the Aussie chided me, 'What's the matter, mate, afraid to get your pants wet?'

Once we left the protection of Carita Bay, the boat's small gas engine strained against the chop and the promised four-hour crossing to Krakatau took 6½ hours.

The remnants of Krakatau's great crater rim were impressive. Carpeted with tropical scrub, the green, crescent-shaped islands surrounded a new cinder cone that had risen since the volcano's 19th-century eruption. The Javanese called the new cone Anak Krakatau, 'Child of Krakatau'. Thin curls of smoke issued from vents in the cone's black, granulated surface. Sulfurous lava leaked from one side of the cone into the sea, sending billowing spirals of white steam skyward. We produced the appropriate gestures of awe, snapped photographs, and hiked to the cone's summit for lunch.

Because the outbound voyage had taken so long, the fishermen were anxious for us to leave after only 45 minutes. The sky was clouding over as we reboarded the boat, and a general nervousness set in. We were a couple of hours east of Krakatau when the storm began to blow and the engine failed. The crew wasn't able to bring the engine back to life. As the sun dropped over the horizon, we drifted southwest with the current, away from Java and the rest of Indonesia.

With the storm came 3m swells that slapped against the boat's sides and washed over the deck. The craft shuddered on each impact, lifted with the swells and teetered on the edge of a watery void as I clung to the stripped mast to avoid slipping over the bow. When smaller swells buffeted the powerless boat, I tried to ride the deck as if it were an oversized surfboard, flexing my knees with the bumps to avoid being thrown into the sea.

For some it was quite a struggle. They retched and pinched their faces; if I could have heard anything above the *musique concréte* of wind and sea, I imagined a tremendous tearing, scouring, gargling sound. A Scotch traveller balanced on the foredeck next to me. We had occupied that spot since just before sunset, when the big swells were making trouble but before the storm had arrived in earnest. We shared the belief that the reason every one of our boatmates – including the Sundanese crew of three – was sick was that they hadn't fixed their minds on the horizon after the first sign of rough seas.

So the Scot and I stood there on the deck, with our hands clutching the low cabin roof for stability, while focussing on the fading rays of the sun setting over Krakatau. In between intentionally distracting chat about the malt whiskeys of Scotland, the ashrams of India and whatever other compost travellers like to churn, we vowed to hold the image of that reddish horizon in our minds even when it was no longer visible to the eye.

After a while, as the larger waves crashed over the deck at five-minute intervals, the salt water began to sting sharply through my soaked clothing. By midnight, with high winds and no relief between apartment-sized waves, we felt the cold deeply. Sitting in the cramped, open-sided, vomit-and-sea washed cabin was no relief, especially since, in that 1.2m-high space, I couldn't flex with the surf or focus on the imaginary line where sky meets sea. Around 3am the swells deepened yet again and the Sundanese still couldn't get the engine going. The oldest of the three prostrated himself in the engine hold and began murmuring prayers to Allah. Looking into his eyes, I could see he reckoned Judgment Day had arrived. Earlier in the night our Australian patron had used every epithet in his vocabulary to curse the Sundanese crew for the engine failure. Now he was shaking vigorously – in just a tank top and shorts – with cold, and alternating between gasping sobs and bursts of laughter. The Scot, his Swiss girlfriend and I pulled the Aussie into the low cabin, wrapped him in Javanese sarongs, and formed a tight circle around him in an attempt to warm his body and calm his hysteria.

The ordeal came to an end after the sun rose the next day and the storm abated. The Sundanese were able to dismantle and rebuild the engine using nothing more than a hammer and chisel, replacing a blown gasket with some hastily tooled leather scraps. Twenty-six hours after we had departed Carita Beach, the boat found its home mooring. Celebrating what seemed a shared miracle, we hugged each other and kissed the sand.

I never made it to Inner Badui, having decided that the secrets of the priests might best be left out of guidebooks.

Joe Cummings has knocked around Asia for Lonely Planet for the past 25 years. He resides in Thailand, where he divides his time between writing, acting and music.

PREVIOUS: When Krakatau erupted at 10:02am on Monday 27 August 1883 the resultant tsunami swept away scores of villages along the coastal regions of Java and Sumatra, claiming 36,000 souls.

OPPOSITE: Where there's smoke there *is* fire. At its current rate of growth Anak Krakatau could match the tremendous force of its famous parent's explosion when it erupts sometime around the year 2050.

The Heart of Borneo

David Lukas

I don't know where the term comes from, but for the world traveller there's a certain irresistible draw to the 'heart of Borneo'. Could it be that unlike Africa's 'heart of darkness', there is something haunting yet approachable about the interior depths of this island?

Perhaps only vaguely aware of this mystique, I had decided to take a weeklong break during the year I was working at a remote research site on the west coast of Borneo (an area now known as West Kalimantan). After 10 months of living deep in the midst of unexplored rainforest with only a couple of companions, you'd think that any sane person taking their only vacation of the year would head for the bright lights of cities and new faces. Instead, my coworker Nick and I journeyed to the provincial capital of Pontianak, ignored its museums, restaurants and eclectic mix of cultures, walked straight into the airport and asked for tickets to the furthest point in the interior that planes could take us.

For someone who had been long submerged in deep forest, the two-hour flight in our wobbly little Cessna was a baffling transit over an impossibly vast and complex landscape of mists and meandering rivers. As we left the coast and everything I knew about Borneo behind, I felt I was falling through the clouds into a sea of green. I had no idea where we were going or what to expect of the lay of the land, and nothing was clarified when the plane dumped us off at a tiny grassy airstrip and turned to leave. We had been left in a small bustling village on the banks of a mighty river in the middle of nowhere.

This was in 1987 and the village of Putussibau has since become famous as the gateway for travellers heading for the remote interior and the sprawling Betung Kerihun National Park that all trans-Borneo adventurers must traverse. But at the time Western visitors were a novelty and we stuck out like sore thumbs as we made our way to the market and bought crayons, drawing paper and coffee. With nothing more than these items, an extra shirt or two, binoculars and a bird book, we left the village and started walking up the nearest side river, trying to push our way into the remote unknown as far as our limited means allowed us.

Whether by sheer luck or stroke of genius, we had taken exactly what we needed. For several days we followed narrow tracks through a lush, overgrown countryside peopled with longhouses and scattered outposts. Although each village became progressively smaller and more threadbare, the people grew increasingly curious and gracious as we ventured upriver into areas that few Westerners had ever visited. Along the way, children were delighted by our gifts of crayons (not to mention our ludicrous attempts to draw). Adults and village elders crowded excitedly around our binoculars and bird guide. And it turned into a giant party when everyone decided to try their hand at making paper aeroplanes with the drawing paper.

Our original goal of finding some kind of wild, deep Borneo wilderness was nearly derailed by the courtesy we found in these humble villages,

where every household along the way absolutely insisted on treating us to meals, topped off with cups of high-octane coffee drowned in sugar. But we eventually reached the last village and an end to the trail.

Here we joined a hunting party in their impossibly narrow dugout canoe and continued on, entering the giant primeval forest that had once carpeted the island of Borneo. We travelled upriver, pausing along the way to fish in deep green pools, and finally stopping at the upper limits of their known lands to build a simple lean-to of thatched palm fronds draped over an elevated pole.

That night, seated there next to a small smoky fire, I experienced an odd moment of joy that here, at my own limits of adventure, I was both submerged in wildness yet close to home. I now knew that at any point in my life I would be able to walk away and within two to three days, return to the sanctuary of this place. I had bridged the gap between somewhere and nowhere and it gave me a deep sense of peace.

David Lukas is a lifelong student of the natural world, whether travelling far and wide or studying the wildlife of his backyard wilderness in California.

PREVIOUS: The famous Bornean jungle is still standing despite the disappearance of more than three million hectares of forest across Kalimantan between 1997 and 2002, mostly in 'protected areas'.

OPPOSITE: The lowlands of Borneo are dissected by a network of waterways that support the majority of the population, but are threatened by major pollution following years of intensive logging.

222

I Went to Wittenoom & Survived

Simone Egger

With a population of 12, you notice when a car stirs up the red dust in Wittenoom. But it's the microscopic blue dust from an old mine that has caused the biggest stir, and heralded the doom of Wittenoom.

The invisible asbestos fibres that carried through the air back in the '40s and '50s killed many miners – asbestos being a cause of mesothelioma (a rare lung cancer that was tragically not so rare among Wittenoom's population, which swelled to 7000 at its peak). Western Australian visitors centres are forbidden to recommend that travellers visit the town, and it's already been omitted from some maps. The access roads are poorly maintained, and much of the town's infrastructure was bought up and bulldozed by the government in the '70s.

But a dozen residents refuse to budge: their solitary residence a show of solidarity for the town's survival. I wanted to know what kind of place inspires a handful of people to defy government warnings, effectively choosing to live like pariahs among grown-over gravestones, with only 11 other humans. (I also had few options, without a tent. Wittenoom has the nearest budget-priced beds to the glorious Karijini National Park.)

The traditional lands of the Banyima, Kurrama and Innawonga peoples, the vast semidesert Karijini National Park is famous for its gorges – a network of red-terraced chasms that plunge 100m below the brittle surface. Inside these giant corridors, fern-filled gullies, waterfalls and streams are allowed to flourish – shielded from the debilitating sun by towering rust-coloured walls on either side. I had spent the day walking through nature's ancient hallways reaching a cool waterhole. Someone had thoughtfully left a tyre inner tube on which to float through this water-filled passage. Bliss.

The rubble-strewn road into Wittenoom is arduous. In town, the streets are empty: a red-dirt crescent loops past overgrown front gardens, with no houses left to front. A rusted petrol bowser stands resolutely on its concrete foundation next to an abandoned roadhouse. A tangle of Hills Hoist clotheslines jut out of the ground like twisted antennae. Among the debris and faint foundations, still visible through the ever-encroaching grass plants, is the Gem Shop. Inside, Ron and Mary Ebsary's lifelong collection of gems is displayed, along with cheeky souvenir T-shirts and bumper stickers saying: 'I've Been to Wittenoom & Survived'.

I found Wittenoom Guesthouse easily, its carefully tended lush garden like an oasis. I arrived unannounced and ill-prepared for the lack of options for buying food. (The half-packet of wilted muesli bars in the backseat of the car was suddenly looking rather precious.) A wiry, silver-haired man with a permanent squint from decades of living in a near-shadeless land answered my knock. Paul proffered a cold drink and showed me around the fibro dwelling. Virtually unchanged from its days as the convent, it has four private rooms and one long dorm, serried with single beds, which looks out to the old corrugated-iron schoolhouse and chapel.

Paul Fitzgerald came to Wittenoom in 1962 as pastor for the southern Pilbara region – an area roughly the size of Guatemala. He's since moved on from delivering faith to delivering mail and reporting the weather five times a day to the Bureau of Meteorology. He tends to the town's original Bedford fire engine and runs the guesthouse. In the middle of nowhere, Paul's hospitality made me feel like I was at the centre of the universe. He made me the first home-cooked meal I'd had in a month. He taught me how to play a card game called Kings, and let me win, so that I'd keep playing – opponents aren't easy to come by in these parts. I briefly interrupted the game to see what was making the series of low thuds outside the house. It was the sound of the powerful bounds of a group of kangaroos, now bowed over the water troughs lapping up the precious water Paul provides for them to drink.

Like the red dust from which it's composed, this rugged landscape gets under your skin. If you go beyond the old mine site – past fading warning signs and scarred rock faces – you find Wittenoom Gorge. All of Karijini National Park's two-billion-year-old gorges flow into Wittenoom Gorge, making it the most dramatic. It's also the least visited – hardly seeing a human for the past 40-odd years.

All the government warnings say not to go to Wittenoom. Every instinct I have says to go. I went to Wittenoom and survived. Here's hoping Wittenoom survives.

Simone Egger has clocked up countless kilometres covering Australia for half-a-dozen Lonely Planet guidebook titles. She's found the country's arid middle-of-nowhere towns to be fertile ground for stories.

PREVIOUS: Beyond the dereliction of Wittenoom lies some of the most spectacular scenery, lookouts and walking trails leading into the gorges of the Karijini National Park.

OPPOSITE: The park is the traditional home of the Banyjima, Kurrama and Innawonga Aboriginal peoples, with evidence of their early occupation dating back more than 20,000 years.

226

An Australian El Dorado

Andrew Bain

To reach Uluru, the great red paperweight at the centre of Australia, you must drive about five hours from Alice Springs through a big swath of nothing. To reach Lasseter's Cave, part of a legend seared as deeply as Uluru into the Australian consciousness, you must keep driving west, leaving the sealed road and towing a dust storm behind your vehicle for another 200km. And this is the easy approach.

Our journey to the cave was more indirect, travelling for more than a week from the roadhouse at Kulgera, beside the Northern Territory–South Australia border and actually nearer to Lasseter's Cave than is Alice Springs. We would pass below the cave and several hundred kilometres beyond, into lands wandered seven decades before us by the eponymous Harold Bell Lasseter.

For all outward appearances, Lasseter could have been one of the last outsiders here. For days we would see no towns, just the architecture of the outback – tiny Aboriginal settlements and the imposing ramparts of mountain ranges with names that even few Australians would recognise: Petermann, Musgrave, Rawlinson, Sir Frederick, Mann and Tomkinson. We passed roads that still existed on maps but through lack of use had all but disappeared back beneath the bush.

Almost everything on our circuitous route appeared to have a touch of nowhere: Giles Meteorological Station, the only manned weather station in an area of about 2.5 million sq km; Surveyor Generals Corner, the meeting point of three state borders, where we were told we were the first people to be granted permission to camp by the Pitjantjatjara people; and, ultimately, the cave where Lasseter spent his final days.

In 1897 Lasseter attempted to walk from Alice Springs to the goldfields of southern Western Australia, across some of the harshest desert country on the planet. Along the way he claimed to have stumbled across a rich seam of gold. Thirty-three years later an expedition, with Lasseter as part of the team, set out to search for the reef. The expedition disbanded in a clash of personalities, leaving Lasseter to continue the search alone. At one point he claimed to a dingo shooter that he'd again found the reef.

While returning towards Uluru, Lasseter's camels bolted on a dune in the southwestern corner of the Northern Territory. He took refuge in a cave – to become Lasseter's Cave – by a waterless, sandy creek bed, about the only sort you find in central Australia. It was January – midsummer – and the temperature would almost certainly have been around 40°C. Blind and weak, he lived in the cave for 25 days before staggering out to both his death and immortality at once.

In the decades since his death, Lasseter's Reef has become an Australian El Dorado, a mystery as fabled as that of the Loch Ness monster: does the reef exist or doesn't it? What continues to propel the story is that it took place in lands still all but unexplored and visited by so few people. Such a mystery can't be sustained in an area you know – there are no lost reefs in Sydney – but it's

easily projected onto an empty desert canvas like that which straddles the border between the Northern Territory and Western Australia.

Several years before I'd come on this journey into Lasseter country, I'd spent 14 months riding a bicycle around Australia, pedalling across the Nullarbor, the Top End and through the wild Kimberley, but nothing had seemed so removed as this lonely desert land. Mountain escarpments that would have thrilled climbers and hikers may never have been climbed. Horizons blurred behind heat hazes, and dingoes and camels wandered carelessly along the roads. Australia is a land of nowheres but this was a redefinition of the word.

Travelling with me, among others, as I headed for the cave was Bob Lasseter, Harold's son. For the past 40 years, Bob had spent much of his life out here – far more than his father – visiting the area more than 20 times in search of the reef, though what he sought was not gold but his father's reputation.

Like Bob's previous visits, our own journey was preoccupied not by the gold itself but by the landmarks that were the supposed clues to its location. In his diary, Harold wrote of natural features that were visible from the reef – a peak shaped like a Quaker's flat hat; three hills that resembled women wearing bonnets. Four decades on, Bob was still looking for these landmarks. The problem wasn't that they didn't exist, but that they did so in such great numbers.

So many peaks out here seemed flat-topped, and those that weren't, appeared rounded like bonnets, invariably in threes. Even climatic conditions and light conspired to become desert alchemy, as one morning we climbed above our camp to the crest of the Sir Frederick Range. A dawn mist hovered atop a salt lake below. Beyond, three rounded hills peeped above the mist. Three women in bonnets? Twenty minutes later the haze lifted, and the three hills became no more than formless bumps on a far range. Was something as fluky as the weather critical to unlocking the mystery of the reef?

As we swung back east, we entered the last days of Harold Lasseter, visiting the dune where his camels bolted, crossing trackless country to the lonely spot where he died, and finally on to the shallow cave that bears his name. We stayed at the cave a couple of hours, sitting in the shade of gum trees to escape even the winter sun. Twenty-five days here in summer could only have seemed like hellish eternity to a dying man.

From the cave we drove out to Uluru, where Harold himself had been blindly heading when he walked from the cave. Until that day I'd never been to Australia's great rock star, and suddenly I had no wish to be here. Against the emptiness of the past days Uluru, with its buses, hotels and people, seemed like a CBD built from rock. We drove straight on.

Andrew Bain is a Melbourne-based writer who has cycled around Australia – a journey that became the book Headwinds *– and trekked and paddled his way through various bits of five continents.*

PREVIOUS: Sealed roads built over the last 50 years might have made travel easier, but have done nothing to lessen the dangers associated with being stranded in the outback.

OPPOSITE: After 11 weeks spent traversing the formidable unrelenting desert terrain, it was expert bush-ranger Bob Buck who eventually discovered the tracks that would lead to Lasseter's remains.

28°S 137°E
LAKE EYRE, AUSTRALIA

Where Water is the Exception

Ben Kozel

Water graces the Warburton Creek just once every 10 years. Perhaps that's a cynical, and somewhat ambiguous, way to introduce a 'watercourse'. But let's be absolutely clear about one thing. In the northeast of the state of South Australia, water is the exception; it is definitely not the rule.

Indeed, launching kayaks in what is, statistically, the driest and hottest region of the continent, feels like a perversion of the natural order of things. It flies squarely in the face of convention. It seems to deny everything you grow up believing is and is not possible in the outback.

Ten days have passed since the water peaked. The trunks of the eucalyptus and melaleucas that crowd the banks are stained to a height 2m above the present creek level. Here in the first week of April 2004, the Warburton Creek resembles a river one might find draining the southern, much wetter parts of the country.

In truth, though, such a comparison has little meaning. For what distinguishes the Warburton from the majority of its southern cousins, and what I become more acutely conscious of with each paddle stroke, is the fact that it remains a wild river. The human trace barely exists here. The absence of dams, the complete lack of damage caused by mining, pollution or bad farming practices, carries me away to a time before the European settlement of Australia.

Self-propulsion, therefore, promotes a sense of being in harmony with the Warburton. To pass through such a wilderness *sans motor* is to connect with it in ways all but precluded by an incessant drone and whiff of carbon monoxide. This elicits much cosier interludes with the creek's residents. Several times each day the long neck of a darter is seen lunging snake-like through the water, before the bird disappears back below the surface to continue fishing. Galahs and mulga parrots add splashes of colour to logs and other deadwood. Small insectivores twitter amongst the tangle of lignum. Black kites circle the sky above, or else perch in the coolibahs and river red gums, vantage points from which they occasionally swoop to snare an unwitting fish in their talons. In the shade of an overhang, a southern boobook owl attempts to roost discreetly. Then a family of dingoes swims across the Warburton no more than a dozen metres in front of the kayaks. Less enchanting are the fly hordes. They start molesting before the sun's first rays have licked over the horizon and continue until after dusk. Removing a head net means choking on one within minutes.

From the seat of a kayak it's easy to be lulled by this riverine wonderland. Life, bountiful life, is assured. The suggestion that all of this abundance is fleeting seems anathema. But step away from the bank, and life's tenuous grip on this landscape is very quickly revealed. Either side of this thin green ribbon, the bleak and sun-scorched Tirari Desert extends as far as the eye can see. Sand dunes appear as mountain ranges on the otherwise featureless terrain. The temperature soars, the air thins. I can feel the moisture being sucked out of me.

232

Irrespective of the magnitude and endurance of the creek's flow, the besieging desert cannot be denied. For even in this, its rare soggy incarnation, the Warburton does not offer passage beyond the arid zone. Although the nearest ocean still lies over 600km to the south, she will soon have run her course, bequeathing her silty cargo to an enormous salt lake. Lake Eyre is the terminus of the world's largest internal drainage basin, the ultimate destination for all the water that has, up to this point, managed to defy a relentless evaporative force.

Despite the vast amount of water that flowed down the Warburton, the 2004 inundation of Lake Eyre is not the one-in-30-year event that sees waves lapping at its margins. The kayaks are restricted to the Warburton Groove, a narrow depression extending a hundred or so kilometres into the lake. And even here the depth is marginal. Paddle blades dig into the soft muddy bottom with every stroke.

The landscape here is epic in scale, yet it is acutely fathomable. It's possible to see great distances in every direction across the flat expanse of the lake. To the west and east, the crests of faraway uplands (nothing more than higher than average sand dunes) seem to hover above a band of shimmering emptiness.

Twenty kilometres into the Groove, GPS readings show an altitude of 15m below sea level. And if the thought of approaching Australia's lowest point isn't enough to make the heart beat a little faster, the seamless merger of water and sky guarantees an overwhelming sense of eeriness. Only the occasional gull-billed tern, head down and scanning for a meal, can shatter the illusion of this place existing as a kind of void.

Out here, perspective is everything. Bizarre as it may seem, the uncertainty, allied with travel through this remote environment, so little known by the white man, offers me great comfort. I brush off the hardship as a rite of passage. And I regard the mighty Lake Eyre not as a lethal trap for the unwary, but as a gateway to the soul, a place where it is impossible not to learn more about oneself. Façades rust into irrelevance. It is a place that strips you right back to some pure essence of being. What is dismissed by many as the archetypal 'middle of nowhere', is perhaps for me nothing less than the ultimate 'somewhere'.

Ben Kozel is lured by the remote and the wild. He prefers the slower journey – rowing an old boat, or leading camels – giving people and place time to get under his skin.

PREVIOUS: Approximately once every 30 years torrential rains fill the lake to create the fabled 'inland sea' that captured the parched imaginations of Australia's early white explorers.

OPPOSITE: The stark inhospitable 9000-sq-km expanse of Lake Eyre is the world's largest salt lake floating upon an unseen ocean of mud.

Cold Toes in Babushkina

Tim Cope

Cold in my toes gave way to numbness as I pedalled blindly into moody swirls of snowflakes. The blizzard had rushed over the taiga forest, blotting out the sky and tearing into my thin clothes. Most frightening was that it had also erased any sign of my travelling mate, Chris.

When night swallowed the murky greys I gave up looking, pushed my loaded bicycle into the forest and rushed to make a fire. Although still autumn the temperature was around -20°C. On a regular evening I looked forward to watching dinner boil but a quick search determined that while I had food supplies, Chris had the pots. It was not a scenario we had planned for when setting off on recumbent bikes from northwest Russia to ride 10,000km across Siberia and Mongolia to Beijing.

By morning the storm had abated and a silence unique to the muffling effect of fresh snow had overcome the forest. I broke camp and waited on the roadside until Chris came along. He had sheltered a few kilometres back in the confusion of yesterday's blizzard. Worries eased over a double serving of porridge, we swapped stories, and soon the adventure was back in motion.

Several kilometres distant, the forest gave way to a huddled collection of snow-ambushed timber homes. Crooked chimneys puffed away busily and locals moved about in thick furs. The opportunity to pick up some extra sweet biscuits was too good to pass up, and while I waited outside the local shop a woman and her daughter approached.

'Would you like to come back to my home for some hot mushroom soup?'

Soon we were sitting in the kind of warmth we hadn't known for some time. The soup thawed us to the bone and returned elasticity to extremities. 'Eat!' demanded Tanya.

Partway through the meal I noticed a tingling in my feet. Peeling back my socks I was shocked by bulbous lumps of purple and white on the ends of my big toes. Tanya caught on.

'Frostbite! Show me your shoes!' She picked up my hiking boots and tossed them into the outhouse in disgust.

'You should have been wearing Valenkee!' she screamed, referring to Russian felt boots.

More panicked than I, she hauled us down to the medical clinic. A queue cleared the way.

'Make way, Australians coming through!'

Then we were in the doctor's office. I sat down and pointed my toes into the air as Tanya bleated out the details. Bushy moustache quivering, the doctor stood up aghast.

'You are going to have to stay here for about 10 days to rest. I will need to operate immediately.'

He pushed me into another room, lay me on a bench, and began sharpening some scissors. I searched my Russian-English dictionary for 'numb', 'painkillers' and 'Will it hurt?'

'You can read while I do this if you really want,' he chuckled, before snipping away and tossing lumps of purple-white flesh into the bin.

'I am not going to ask you to pay for this, but could you bring me a baby kangaroo next time you visit?'

My toes were bandaged and Tanya rushed us home where she put an old record player on and danced with Chris. So began our time in the village of 'Babushkina'.

By evening I was more at ease. The owner of the house was a 75-year-old babushka affectionately known as 'Baba Galya'. Tanya and her daughter were guests visiting from northern Russia. Galya arrived bundled up in fur, with a kind smile, adorable eyes and sense of concern. Although total strangers, we had been embraced with the care and support of a family.

At dinner pancakes, fish pie, pickled cucumbers, cottage cheese with homemade jam, salted mushroom salad and oil-saturated fried potato were piled high.

'C'mon, you can do better than that, you're eating terribly! Eat, Eat!' chanted Galya. This was topped off with a shot of vodka. '*Chut chut* (a little) is allowed,' Galya maintained, '…but would we really be guilty if we had just a little more?' Her eyes were watering with laughter.

At dawn I woke to see Galya hauling firewood into the home in the midst of another blizzard. It was clear that just surviving in these conditions, let alone entertaining guests and living alone as an elderly woman, was harder than our journey would ever be.

By breakfast Tanya had planned our schedule for the next few days. Among appointments were lunch with the dentist, dinner with the timber workers, a visit to the local school, an afternoon with the doctor's family and a *banya* (bath) at 'Baba Sveta's'. As we went through the paces of this hospitality the sense of togetherness was striking. People helped each other with everything from firewood and water to washing and food. As my toes healed, I became focused on the intricacies of the community.

It appeared that many of the men were sickly and shrivelled, and certainly less hard-working than Baba Galya. This was probably due to a combination of hard labour and alcohol. Drunks often came knocking on the door in the middle of the night for vodka. As Baba Galya explained, those who were too lazy or drunk to collect wood, berries and mushrooms, to grow potatoes and to maintain their homes, eventually used up the community's goodwill. The winter brought with it a high rate of death for alcoholics and the homeless.

There was perhaps some sense of justice in this, but I wondered how the disadvantaged, and poorly paid workers without family survived. The zest that most people showed was humbling.

By the 10th day my toes had healed and we no longer had an excuse to call Babushkina home. The event had crushed plans to continue riding through winter and so the bikes were to be retired to Galya's garage until spring. On the last evening all of our friends gathered for a party. Rolling laughter, vodka and toasts ruled the night and we danced to a song with the lyrics 'Babushka! Babushka! Babuskha!' We thanked the community and told them that for us Babushkina was paradise, and Galya was surely the queen.

Early next morning we climbed into a fogged-up Lada and waved goodbye. As we passed beyond the welcome sign to Babushkina, I reflected that so much had happened in such a short time. It had forced us to throw off the spectre of plans and expectations and accept the reality of the journey. The soul of this faraway community had given us the insight and foundations that would surely pave the way to Beijing.

Tim Cope, author of Off the Rails: Moscow to Beijing by Bicycle, *has crossed Siberia by bicycle and rowboat, and is currently following the trail of Genghis Khan, 10,000km from Mongolia to Hungary, by horse, camel and foot.*

PREVIOUS: Siberian forests have long held sway over local people's imagination, and are rumoured to contain many ghosts as well as the mysterious Siberian forest cat.

OPPOSITE: The severity and length of the Russian winter generally increases as you move eastward. In the northeastern mountains temperatures often hover around -40°C.

On the Dusky Track

Michael Kohn

In relative terms, we're still dry. This will change soon. Nori, Tom, Tristen and I depart Halfway Hut under clear skies and tramp for three hours to Lake Roe Hut. We dump our bags in the 12-bunk hut and head for a nearby mountain called Tamatea. Nori and I make it in less than two hours. It's treacherous near the top, where there's a snowfield to cross and a couple of steep sections of granite rock. We ascend the final few metres, stand on the highest point and scan the 360-degree view of majestic peaks, glacier-carved fjords, Dusky Sound, the Tasman Sea and shimmering lakes. It's so clear I think I can see Mt Cook, 200km away. We announce our arrival with congratulatory back slaps and several *yeeee-haaas*!

I sit for a while and meditate. The dead silence that fills the air is so loud that my ears begin to hurt. Descending now, I use my rain shell as a sled and skitter down the snowfield before we navigate the ridge.

We pass Tom and Tristen. They stopped for lunch and are now pelting each other with snowballs, but soon they will also bag the peak. Down at the Lake Roe Hut, Alex and Suzanne, the last in our trekking group, are sunning themselves on a rock. Suzanne says the snow grass and tarns remind her of her dear old Scotland.

Our second night on the Dusky Track is similar to the first. Nori and Alex are obsessed with keeping the fire going. The air outside our hut is filled with the sounds of their boots smashing branches apart. Suzanne fills her time talking to anyone who will listen. Tom and Tristen attempt to repair their disintegrating camping gear and regale us with stories of Kiwi history. For Tom especially, this is a walk into the past. One hundred year earlier, his great-grandfather, Sir Thomas MacKenzie, explored this same route, named a pass after himself, and lost his compass in the process.

We are a motley crew. Alex (a Welshman) and Suzanne (half Scottish, half Canadian) are budding ornithologists, and have spent the past five months studying penguins in Dunedin. Nori (from Osaka) spent the summer working on a communal farm outside Christchurch. Tom and Tristen, students from Christchurch, have just completed engineering degrees. I am a backpacker. The Dusky is my last adventure in a nine-month romp from Japan to New Zealand. And it's as far away from home as I've ever been.

The one thing that binds us is the Dusky. We had started together, on the ferry across Lake Hauroko, where we had been forced into a small, select community that would coexist for the following 10 days.

We blow out the candles, flick off our torches and sleep.

In a country with many trails and hiking routes, the Dusky is renowned for its difficulty and distance. The 84km track cuts through some of Fiordland's most inhospitable territory – rugged alpine terrain and sandfly-infested swamp. The department of conservation warns away inexperienced trampers and recommends that seasoned walkers carry a mountain radio or emergency locator beacon – we have neither.

Tom's great-grandfather is our inspiration to beat the Dusky. But the track is unrelenting and gives us no favour. It is occasionally marked by orange tags stapled to trees, or snow poles where there are no trees, but it is a neglected route – rarely trod and often blocked by fallen trees, swollen rivers and menacing mud pits.

Day three sees us inching our way down a trackless slope to the valley floor. I borrow Tom's fishing rod at Loch Maree Hut and catch a 40cm trout. It is pregnant and Nori jumps out of his boots at the sight of fresh sushi. I am already running out of food, but we find oats in the hut and a 2L plastic bottle of 'Mass Fuel' high-energy drink mix. Food rationing begins in earnest.

We load up our water bottles with Mass Fuel and hike to Supper Cove in a driving rainstorm. After 45 minutes we reach a spot where an American man had fallen off a cliff just three months earlier, plummeting 15m to his death. We gingerly step past a cairn marking the fateful spot.

Slogging through knee-deep mud we happen upon two young Kiwi hunters, Tony and Craig. They are moving fast and in my haste to keep up I strain my bum knee beyond its limits. I am forced to stop. The hunters tell me to wait; they will go to the next hut and bring their dinghy upstream.

I hobble down to the river bank and wait, shivering, in the driving rain. In turn, each of my trekking mates passes by. We joke about a helicopter rescue but I promise that I will crawl out of this swamp if it's the last thing I do. Forty minutes later, I hear the low hum of an outboard motor. I am saved.

At the Supper Cove Hut, we have our ritual hanging of the socks, and I join the hunters in a fishing trip. We catch a massive load of what Craig calls 'shit fish'; creatures with large mouths but almost no meat.

Two days later, we are Mass Fueling our way to Kintail Hut. I am ahead of everyone, but they catch up when I veer off course and get stuck in a mud pit. At Kintail we rest briefly but Tom and Tristen head off into the wilderness, determined to honour great-grandfather Thomas and walk over the treacherous MacKenzie Pass.

Come morning, Nori and I hike to Centre Pass, scramble up Mt Memphis and reach Upper Spey Hut by 5pm. It's getting dark when we hear shouts in the night. Tom and Tristen! They look like hell. They recount their adventures, recalling a near-tragic fall and the loss of Tom's fishing rod and the canister of Mass Fuel. They also regret not recovering the great-grandfather's compass, but they still consider the hike a success.

It's the last night on the Dusky. Nori cooks us 'Crazy Cooked Milk Rice' and Tom breaks out a bottle of booze.

Slightly hung over in the morning, we tramp together to the end. Just five minutes before the road we find the trail engulfed in flash-flood waters. The Dusky would not quit. Carefully negotiating the torrent by clinging to roots protruding from the river bank, we escape with our lives to the shores of Lake Manapouri and the ferry pick-up point – 10 days of mud and stench forcing the smartly dressed tourists to the stern.

That night, a shower had never felt so good.

Michael Kohn has travelled to more than 60 countries. His longest stint was a three-year stopover in Mongolia, where adventures included a 200km bike trip along the Russian border and the completion of his first marathon by the shores of Lake Khövsgöl.

PREVIOUS: In 1770 Captain James Cook arrived at the entrance to the sound just as night was falling, naming it Dusky Sound because it was too dark to enter safely.

OPPOSITE: During the rainy season the Sound is resplendent with hundreds of waterfalls flowing down the fjord's steep granite sides and covered in luscious vegetation known to Maori hunters-gatherers for centuries.

Where Dreams & Endeavours Collide

Craig Scutt

Only when it was my turn to moon-walk could I fully appreciate how easy Armstrong made it look back in 1969. My first step was fine, but as I moved my right foot forward for the next step I could already feel I was losing my balance. To stop myself falling I overcorrected, flinging myself to the left. I repeated this comedic process four or five times before Dr Kim Enjie, there to welcome me in his official capacity of LS1 Director, offered his arm for support and escorted me to the moon buggy, in which we took the bumpy ride to the settlement.

The first and only lunar settlement, known as LS1, is situated high up on the northern rim of Peary crater, just a short moon-buggy ride from the lunar North Pole. The 73km-wide crater is the best site for human settlement for two reasons.

First, the crater floor lies in permanent shade, shielded from the sun by shadows created by mountainous walls of rock that ring the spot where, long ago, a meteorite crashed into the surface. Here a lake of ice water remained frozen close enough to the surface for it to be exploited by humans. The frozen mass was first suspected in 1994 following analysis of pictures sent back to earth by the unmanned Clementine mission. It was the breakthrough advocates of lunar settlement had been waiting for, and became the impetus and starting point for plans aimed at colonising the moon.

The second advantage of establishing a settlement close to the Peary crater is its position in relation to the sun. The high elevation of the crater's northern rim, and close proximity to the pole, ensures it is bathed in almost continuous sunlight. Temperatures here are relatively stable, usually between -20°C and -50°C. This is resort-style weather compared with the wild variations experienced elsewhere. The mean surface temperature for the moon is 107°C during the day, and -153°C at night. The hottest temperature ever recorded was a rock-melting 123°C, and the coldest an element-hardening -233°C.

The most extreme temperatures recorded on earth are mild by comparison, ranging between 56°C and -89°C. The ability of humans to thrive in the harsh moon environment is the culmination of decades of research, training and perseverance.

LS1 is a feat of engineering that rivals anything undertaken on the earth. An international team of scientists was able to melt the reservoir of ice, unlocking an invaluable resource of drinking water that could also be used for irrigation and converted into breathable air. The elements oxygen and hydrogen could also be separated to make the rocket fuel that will soon be used for the inaugural manned flight to Mars.

Underlying lunar and space exploration is the species' remarkable ability for adaptation. At no time was this clearer to me than when I took those first steps on the dusty lunar surface. As I stepped off the lunar module, I recalled the timeless words spoken by Neil Armstrong, as he became the first man to walk on the moon: 'One small step for a man, one giant leap for mankind.'

My first night on the moon, and every one thereafter, was spent in a small cylindrical chamber, like the kind you might come across in

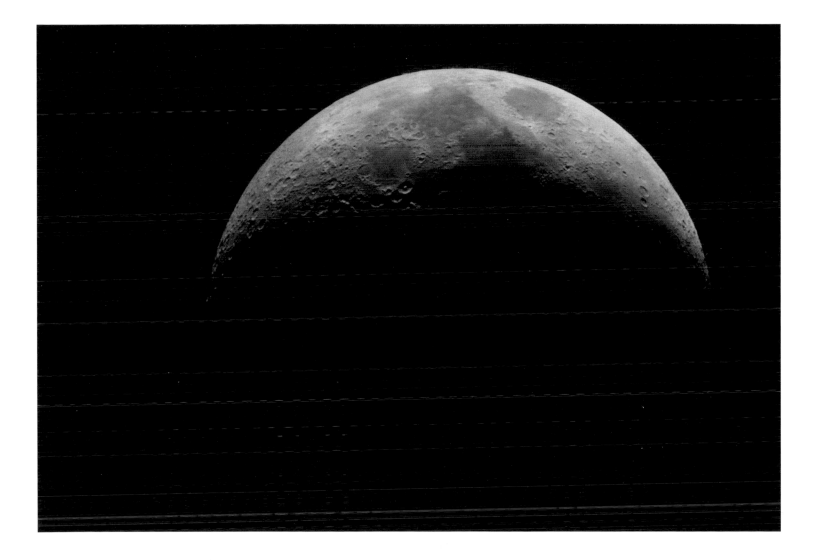

Tokyo. This tiny impersonal zone, barely the length and width of a large man, would be my bedroom for a whole year. Because gravity inside LS1 is the same as it is outside, roughly one-sixth that of the earth, we had Velcro sleeping suits to keep us on the bed. These made it easier to relax and stay asleep. In many respects, once I had mastered moon-walking, lunar gravity was preferable to both weightlessness and earth gravity. The important thing was always to maintain a regular regimen of exercise to avoid muscle wastage.

My first lunar dawn was something of a surprise. The 'night' blinds, which cut out the sunlight to give us an illusion of 'night' and 'day', peeled back over the reinforced glass to reveal that nothing had changed outside. I understood the phenomenon of perpetual light, but seeing is truly believing. Confronted by exactly the same light as I had witnessed the previous 'day', spread languidly over the surface, I felt unnerved. This flat mass of colour was like a beached animal. Immovable. Defiant.

In this perpetual light the surface of the moon is not silver, as it is seen from the earth, but a pale, jaundiced yellow. Its lifeless, haunting beauty is like the memory of a loved one who comes to you in a dream.

Sidney Greenberg said that 'life is a journey, not a destination.' As a single destination, the moon has done more to inspire the journey than any other.

This barren rock has been orbiting our planet for more than four billion years. It has witnessed the formation of the earth's oceans, the cooling of the land; it has been a twinkle in the eye of dinosaurs and worshipped by our ancestors. To stand upon it is to become part of a larger world, where the twin currents of dreams and endeavour collide, creating legends of which I am now part. But instead of making me feel immortal or like a god, I am struck by how far from being gods we are. Humans are not the alpha and the omega, and yet we are a part of it. Here on the moon, I can see the string that binds the universe. The sun, the earth, the moon, everything that exists, is part of a great, continual oneness, which it is our destiny to explore.

'Look,' said Dr Enjie, 'for there is the most precious vision you could ever see.' Beyond the glass, across the surface of the moon, far beyond my puny reach, the blue earth rotated on its side. Such was the water planet's beauty that it seemed to shine a thousand times brighter than the sun.

'What time is it?' asked Dr Enjie.

'12:43 Greenwich Mean Time,' I said.

Said Dr Enjie, 'Your family will be having lunch.'

Lost in our yearning for home and loved ones, we conceded to the inevitable ache of loneliness that accompanies extreme isolation. But there was something else. An understanding, a complete appreciation for what we had left behind. I had journeyed 384,403km to the moon, and learned, above all else, how much I loved the Earth.

Craig Scutt has lived on three continents and thinks everywhere's a good home. He hopes to come back as a Lonely Planet photographers' camera lens.

PREVIOUS: Contrary to popular belief, there is no 'dark side' of the moon because – except for a few deep craters near the poles – all parts receive sunlight at least half of the time.

140°

120°

100°

80°

60°

40°

20°

0°

20°

Getting Nowhere

MARIANA TRENCH

Story: *The Lowest Place on Earth*, p8.

Location: The Mariana Trench is at the bottom of the Pacific Ocean, 338km southeast of the Mariana Island of Guam.

Getting There: If you don't have access to a bathyscaph hitch a ride on one of the military submarines using the Trench as a convenient north–south passage to navigate the Pacific.

Movement: By specially designed submersibles only. At present manned vessels do not go below 6500m.

Geography/Geology: The Mariana Trench marks the convergence of two enormous tectonic plates, the Pacific and the Philippine. About six million years ago the plates began a mighty collision, which forced the Pacific Plate downwards, through a process known as subduction, to create a gouge in the ocean floor that is 1800m deeper than Mt Everest is tall. The Trench is 2542km long and 69km wide.

History: The deepest part of the Trench was discovered in 1951 by the British survey ship *Challenger 2*, hence it is referred to as the Challenger Deep. In 1960 Swiss scientist Jacques Piccard and US naval officer Donald Walsh became the first, and so far only humans, to venture to the bottom, and in doing so set a unbeatable world record for deep-sea adventure.

Things to Do/Highlights: If you were to see a creature at the bottom of the Trench chances are you'd be the first person to lay eyes on it, instantly making you a part of history.

Proximity to Civilisation: The nearest other humans will be your support team waiting on the surface. To reach them you must pass through an 11km vertical corridor of 'heavy' water exerting enough pressure to crush a truck.

Don't Go Without:
1. Nerves of steel – succumbing to cabin fever is not an option.
2. Checking the oxygen supply in the submersible.
3. A paper and pen – this is definitely an experience to write home about.
4. A good book to read on the journeys down and up.
5. A loyal support crew – the conditions on the surface have been known to become life-threatening for waiting vessels.

Inspired: Screenwriter Shane Solerno based his script for the Hollywood horror *Meg* on the story of a man who discovers *Carcharodon megalodon*, the gigantic prehistoric mother of the great white shark, lurking in the deep waters of the Mariana Trench.

TONGA

Story: *Living on Tonga Time*, p12.

Location: The Tongan archipelago is in a far-flung corner of the South Pacific Ocean, to the east of Fiji and about two-thirds of the way between Hawaii and New Zealand.

Getting There: Wing your way to the main island, Tongatapu, over the endless blue of the South Pacific with Air New Zealand, Air Fiji, Air Pacific or Polynesian Airlines.

Movement: Island hop by plane, take to the waters on a ferry or reset your watch to laid-back Tonga time by negotiating a passage on a private vessel.

Geography/Geology: The Happy Isles comprise 169 islands – 36 of which are inhabited. The total Tongan land mass is equal to an area four times the size of Washington DC. The islands are fringed by 419km of idyllic coastline and coral reefs which are amongst the finest in the world.

History: The mists of time have obscured when exactly people washed up on Tongan shores and who those first inhabitants were. Some scholars believe the islands were probably settled in about 500 BC by people from the Samoan islands. Dutch navigators were the first Europeans to clap eyes on Tonga in 1616 followed by Captain Cook in the 1770s. Tongans take pride in the fact that Tonga never ceded its independence and Tonga remains the South Pacific's last Polynesian kingdom.

Things to Do/Highlights: Tonga offers the opportunity to experience a living, breathing Polynesian culture. Perhaps the biggest magnet for visitors, though, are the blue waters of the South Pacific which lap the islands. Visitors can immerse themselves in sea kayaking, scuba diving and snorkelling, surfing, yachting and game fishing.

Don't Go Without:
1. An underwater camera – you won't want to leave without having captured the astonishing array of marine life on Tonga's reefs.
2. Reef booties – all that beautiful coral can have a cutting edge or two. Pop in some antibiotics as well because cuts can become infected fast.
3. Polarizing sunglasses – to minimise the glare of the Polynesian sun on those endless blue waters.
4. Two towels, one for the bath and one for the beach – you'll be spending a lot of time in the water.
5. All your own surf supplies because materials for repairs are hard to come by.

Inspired: In April 1789 the crew of the *Bounty*, seduced by their experiences of paradise Polynesia-style, mutinied against Captain William Bligh off Tonga's island of Tofua.

ALASKA, USA

Story: *Not Lost, but Searching*, p16.

Location: Mt Marathon is the stunning backdrop to the small town of Seward (pop 2500), which lies at the head of Resurrection Bay on Alaska's Kenai Peninsula.

Getting There: Head for Seward by following the Seward Hwy about 200km south of Anchorage.

Movement: During the ascent runners work hard to keep their legs and heart from failing, then let gravity create an adrenaline and fear-fuelled rush on the way down.

Geography/Geology: Mt Marathon's snow-covered summit is 921m from the base, which is less than a kilometre from the town. Behind the mountain and extending down the coast lies the massive Harding Icefield.

History: According to local lore, one gold miner bet another he could run up and down Mt Marathon in less than an hour. He lost, taking 62 minutes, but the wager inspired a race, which officially began on 4 July 1915. The annual competition gave the mountain its name and is credited with creating the sport of mountain racing. The fastest time was set by Bill Spencer in 1981 and stands at 43 minutes, 23 seconds.

Things to Do/Highlights: Pushing your body to the limit as you join 800 other masochists to race up and down a mountain is proof that everyone has inside them an inner Iron man or woman bursting to get out.

Proximity to Civilisation: Even though Seward is less than 4km away it's unlikely that anyone would hear you scream if you happened to have an accident on the mountain.

Don't Go Without:
1. Applying for the race early – it's so popular that there is often a scrum for race slots when applications open to the public.
2. Protective gear such as a helmet, goggles, knee and elbow pads to avoid those nasty scrapes.
3. A search-and-rescue party so you don't have to spend too long in the undergrowth.
4. Massage oil for a post race rub down.
5. Being noisy – bear encounters have been known on the trail, runners and hikers are advised to make a noise so they don't surprise, and agitate, bears with their presence.

Inspired: In 2001 the Alaska Press Club presented first place in the award for Best Sports Photo, Daily Newspapers to M Scott Moon, for his dramatic image entitled 'Mount Marathon Slide'.

65°N 148°W

ALASKA, USA

Story: *Knee-Deep in Powder-like Snow*, p20.

Location: Most of Alaska juts out like a peninsula from the extreme northwest of Canada into the icy waters of the Arctic Ocean (to the north) and the Pacific Ocean (to the south). Alaska is separated from Russia by the narrow waters of the Bering Strait. To the south, a smaller portion of Alaska is a coastal strip hugging the Canadian landmass.

Getting There: If you're coming from the US mainland, you can take the road trip of a lifetime up the Alcan (also known as the Alaska Hwy). If that's not your style, you can book a berth on a ferry or cruise ship up the Inside Passage or fly in from a number of US cities. There are few direct flights from beyond the US into Alaska so most travellers come via the US.

Movement: Travelling around Alaska's vast and rugged terrain is unlike travelling in any other state or country. If you want to venture off the beaten track, hop aboard a bush plane, which can take you to some of the 75% of Alaska unreachable by road. What roads there are will take you to spectacular scenery whether on two wheels or four. Ferries and catamarans also connect some of Alaska's far-flung communities.

Geography/Geology: Alaska's terrain is dominated by two massive mountain systems: the Pacific Mountain System in the south and southeast, home to Mt McKinley (otherwise known as Denali), the highest peak in North America, and the Rocky Mountain System to the north. In the far north lies the Arctic Coastal Plain, a sweeping area of permafrosted tundra sloping towards the Arctic Ocean. The largest land area of Alaska is Interior Alaska, an immense plateau rippled by foothills, low mountains and great rivers.

History: Alaska's first intrepid inhabitants arrived from Asia some 40,000 years ago across what is now the Bering Strait but what was then a land bridge. Europeans arrived in the form of Russian fur traders and whalers who brought guns, alcohol and disease in the mid 1700s. The Russian-American company colonised much of coastal Alaska until on 9 April 1867, William H Seward, the US secretary of state, engineered the famous Alaska Purchase with the US purchasing Alaska for a mere $7.2 million. Alaska was the site of a major gold rush in the 19th century. Surprisingly, it was not until 1959 that Alaska was admitted into the Union as the 49th State.

Things to Do/Highlights: Enjoy the light show of a lifetime – the aurora borealis (northern lights). Alaska's vast natural beauty is the perfect backdrop for outdoor adventures and activities. Track down some of Alaska's abundant wildlife and diverse flora or release the daredevil within and embark on a glacier-climbing or mountain-climbing odyssey. If you still have spare energy, hike off into the wilderness or paddle Alaska's pristine waters.

Don't Go Without:
1. Capsicum spray – the best line of defence against any unfriendly bears you might bump into.
2. A handheld signal flare – handy for locating you if you get lost in the wilds or as the next best line of defence against bears.
3. Plenty of mosquito repellent – the summer air is redolent with the buzz of a billion mosquitoes.
4. Photographic equipment – the most cherished memories you'll take home from your trip will be photos of Alaska's powerful scenery.
5. A tent – camping is king in Alaska and with a tent you'll always have cheap accommodation even in remote and otherwise expensive places.

Inspired: The novel *Coming into the Country* (1977) by John McPhee. Still one of the most riveting literary portraits of Alaska yet written, McPhee shifts from the wilderness to urban Alaska to a winter spent in remote Eagle to observing Alaskans during the 1970s.

61°N 144°W

ALASKA, USA

Story: *The Alaska Factor*, p24.

Location: The Chugach State Park spreads out just beyond the foothills of Anchorage. The Glacier Ranger District encompasses most of western Prince William Sound.

Getting There: Head southeast from Anchorage to the Chugach Mountains.

Movement: Skis are the logical choice for travel. Daunting access is made reasonable by a short flight.

Geography/Geology: The Chugach literally backs up to Anchorage, Alaska and stretches 320km south along the Pacific Ocean. Rugged, with forested lower slopes and glacier-covered summits, these mountains are a barrier for movement inland from the coast. At 4016m, the highest elevation is the peak of Mt Marcus Baker.

History: Governor Keith Miller signed the bill that created the Chugach State Park in August 1970. The land parcel borders Anchorage on all sides except west. With the immediate proximity of a major city and Anchorage's quarter of a million citizens, this a vast tract of pristine wilderness is almost unique on such a scale. Grizzly bears, wolfpacks and lynx are to be found in abundance inside the park and occasionally wander into the city.

Things to Do/Highlights: Watching as a bald eagle sweeps across the immense skies of this enormous, pristine mountainscape will ground you in nature forever.

Proximity to Civilisation: It might be reassuring to think that Anchorage is 'right next door' to the Chugach backcountry, but remember that the Chugach State Park covers a whopping 2023 sq km.

Don't Go Without:
1. A stove – there are limited water facilities in the park and you will need to boil snow to make safe drinking water.
2. Avalanche training – if you're heading into the backcountry you must be able to identify potential avalanche sites.
3. Flares – in case you need to attract a search party.

4. The warmest and most durable tent you can afford.
5. Booking ahead – if you intend to stay in one of the backcountry cabins dotted around the Glacier Ranger District.

Inspired: The Chugach State Park is home to some of the best skiing and snowboarding in the world. It also hosts some of the most dramatic avalanches. Cinematographer Steve Kroschel regularly ventures off the beaten track inside the park to capture dramatic footage of avalanches.

16°S 143°W

TUAMOTU ARCHIPELAGO, FRENCH POLYNESIA

Story: *Floating on the Ocean, Firmly Fixed on Land*, p28.

Location: Ahe lies in the northern part of the Tuamotu Archipelago of French Polynesia in the South Pacific.

Getting There: Whether you fly from the mainland or take a cargo ship from Papeete, you'll end up in a little outboard boat to pass through the narrow passage that leads inside the lagoon.

Movement: Given the atoll's proximity to the ocean, it's best to make like a fish and swim.

Geography/Geology: Ahe is an almost entirely enclosed coral atoll rising just above sea level – the summit is only 6m high. It was formed over thousands of years as reef built up around an eroding volcanic island, which eventually sank leaving only the ring of coral. Only a single narrow

passage affords entry into the lagoon. The sole village, Tenukupara, is located on the south side of the island.

History: Archaeological evidence suggests the Polynesians began inhabiting the Tuamotu atolls a thousand years ago. However, Ahe was virtually unknown, even amongst local Tahitians, until the discovery of rare Pacific black pearls, which locals now farm as a lucrative source of income.

Things to Do/Highlights: Ahe is paradise found for island lovers. Dive in the sanctuary of the lagoon, then idle up the beach and educate yourself at a pearl farm. Afterwards join locals for a celebratory song at the local church – the congregation is minute but the singing is infectious.

Proximity to Civilisation: The nearest 'big' island is Mainhi, 30km north, but when you look out from Ahe's lagoon there is no sign of land anywhere on the horizon.

Don't Go Without:
1. Skimpy speedos – on sundrenched Ahe, less is more.
2. A map of the region, just to remind yourself that you're not really alone in the middle of the ocean.
3. A copy of *Lord of the Flies* – read here, the literary classic will come alive.
4. A book of fish – always nice to know what you're gawking at.
5. A surfboard – the Tuamotu atolls are heralded as the 'final surf frontier'.

Inspired: Veteran Hollywood actress and icon Elizabeth Taylor named a fragrance Black Pearls. The remoteness of the Tuamotu atolls inspired the French government to test its nuclear capabilities in the region. Testing was halted in 1996 following international protest.

36°N 115°W

LAS VEGAS, USA

Story: *Invisible Stars*, p32.

Location: Las Vegas is a fluorescent oasis slap bang in the middle of the Nevada Desert, traditional home of the Pauite Indians.

Getting There: For a spectacular introduction make sure you arrive after dark. You can drive or fly to Las Vegas.

Movement: Max out on cool by cruising the Strip in an open top Cadillac.

Geography/Geology: If nature had her way, Las Vegas wouldn't exist. Thousands of kilometres of concrete pipes bring in water from across the desert to service the city's 131.1 sq miles, and keep the glitziest place on earth alive.

History: Paiute people lived in the fertile valley for a millennium before springs drew Europeans to Las Vegas in 1829. Boom came with the railway in 1902, and legalised gambling carried Vegas through the Great Depression. Raunchy European-style shows, prostitution and mobsters cemented its place in the cultural consciousness. Vegas is now the self-proclaimed entertainment capital of the world and has cleaned up its act considerably.

Things to Do/Highlights: Winning in the casino will make you feel like a movie star. People-watching can be taken to a whole new level in Las Vegas. Head down town and check out the new Lou Ruvo Alzheimer's

Institute building – it was designed by legendary architect Frank Gehry and proves that style is everything in this city.

Proximity to Civilisation: Las Vegas is an oasis of hyper-real civilisation in a sparse, sparse land; LA is 452 empty kilometres away.

Don't Go Without:
1. An Elvis costume.
2. Knowing the rules for poker.
3. Cash for chips – you can't come to Vegas and not place a bet.
4. Someone to marry, a la Britney Spears/Kevin Federline–style.
5. Sunglasses – at night the glare is like looking into the sun.

Inspired: A combination of psychedelic drugs and Las Vegas inspired Hunter S Thompson's gonzo classic *Fear and Loathing in Las Vegas*. The city is also the spiritual home for generations of professional gamblers who are treated VIP-style by the casinos.

39°N 114°W
GREAT BASIN NATIONAL PARK, USA

Story: *The Loneliest National Park in America*, p36.

Location: The Great Basin National Park is nestled high up on the border between the states of Utah and Nevada.

Getting There: Let the empty desert scour Vegas from your skin as you drive through just four small towns in 500km to reach the park.

Movement: Leave the car and become part of the silence by exploring Wheeler Peak, the glacier and the bristlecone pines on foot.

Geography/Geology: Great Basin National Park covers an area of approximately 31,000 hectares. The name is a reference to the fact that no creeks, streams, or rivers flow out of it to either the Gulf of Mexico or the Pacific Ocean. However, the term is slightly misleading because the Great Basin is actually made up of about 200 small basins.

History: The park was established in 1986, encompassing the historic Lehman Caves National Monument and Humboldt National Forest's Wheeler Peak Scenic Area. Jedediah Smith passed through the Snake Range in 1826 and John Fremont explored the area in 1843–44.

Things to Do/Highlights: A tour through the limestone caverns of the Lehman Caves will be a reminder of forgotten geography lessons as you marvel at the amazing stalactites, stalagmites, helictites (calcite formations that curve and seem to defy gravity) and shields (flat plates).

Proximity to Civilisation: Great Basin is 500km from Las Vegas and 500% completely different.

Don't Go Without:
1. A star map – the canopy above the Great Basin is one of the clearest in the USA, a perfect spot to play name the constellation.
2. A brand new water bottle – from which to drink the officially best-tasting water in Nevada.
3. Ankle protecting boots – there be rattlesnakes in them thar hills.

4. Plenty of snacks – there are two restaurants within 16km, but no general food store.
5. Fast-speed film and a good flash – if you want to take a decent picture from inside the caves.

Inspired: The landmark silent film *Covered Wagon* (1924) was shot on location in the Great Basin. It has been dubbed 'the Titanic of its day' and heralded the emergence of the modern Western.

36°N 111°W
PARIA CANYON, USA

Story: *The Unsocial Desert*, p42.

Location: The Paria River Canyon cuts a swathe through the borders of Northern Arizona and Southern Utah.

Getting There: From the small town of Page, head north along Hwy 89, over the Glen Canyon Dam and take a right turn to the trailhead.

Movement: Casual hikers without a permit can walk as many kilometres as they can return in a day; to do the entirety of Paria Canyon, you need five days, one permit, and some canyoneering experience.

Geography/Geology: The Paria River Canyon is simply a result of millions of years worth of wear and tear as the Paria River made its mark in the soft sandstone. As the stream carved out the intricate patterns of the slot canyon it simultaneously carried the soil down to the Colorado River, which helped to carve out the Grand Canyon.

History: From 200 BC, Ancestral Puebloans occupied what is now the Arizona Strip region; from AD 1100, Southern Paiutes dominated. In the 1860s, Mormon pioneers built a ranch at Pipe Springs. In 1890, the Mormon Church repudiated polygamy (in order for Utah to gain admittance as the USA's 45th state); in the 1910s, unrepentant polygamists relocated to the Arizona Strip, founding Short Creek (now Colorado City).

Things to Do/Highlights: The first time you squeeze through one of the canyon's orange, narrow slots is like entering a mythical labyrinth. And the journey only becomes more surreal and enthralling as you continue.

Proximity to Civilisation: Page is 48km away. A long way to crawl if a rattlesnake has bitten you.

Don't Go Without:
1. Filtered water – some of the natural springs have become contaminated with chemical residues from agriculture.
2. Lightweight hiking sandals – boots can become wet, heavy and uncomfortable, as the trail follows the river.

44°N 110°W
YELLOWSTONE NATIONAL PARK, USA

Story: *The Wildest Slice of the Wild West*, p46.

Location: Yellowstone National Park is located in the north-western corner of the state of Wyoming along the borders of Montana and Idaho.

Getting There: From Jackson, Wyoming, head north around 120km, then take the dusty Thorofare Trail.

Movement: In summer, lace up your boots or saddle up to head into the backcountry. In winter, guided snowmobile tours are another option.

Geography/Geology: Around 640,000 years ago a massive volcanic eruption covered the entire western US, a large chunk of the Midwest, northern Mexico and parts of the eastern Pacific, with millions of tonnes of ash. The event was instrumental in shaping the landscape of what is now the Yellowstone National Park. The Old Faithful and other, less well-known geothermal sites are testament to the high level of volcanic activity in this region.

History: Long a sacred rendezvous site for Native American tribes, Yellowstone was proclaimed the world's first national park in 1872 by President Ulysses S Grant. The railroad arrived in the late 1800s and hunting inside the park was banned in 1894. Bear management regulations restrict travel to designated trails for most of the summer.

Things to Do/Highlights: There are many fantastic moments to be had during a hike through the backcountry, but one of the most rewarding is when you finally stumble across the 24m waterfall of Plateau Creek, which, at a minimum three days' hike from nearest trail, is the most distant officially named waterfall in the Park.

Proximity to Civilisation: The Thorofare Patrol Cabin is 48km from the Nine Mile trailhead, at minimum a two-day hike or a long day's horseback ride.

Don't Go Without:
1. Reading the park's rules and regulations – particularly in regard to approaching wildlife.
2. Your own bicycle – if you fancy tackling roaming the main paths on two wheels.
3. Fishing rods – Yellowstone has some of the best fly-fishing anywhere.
4. Applying for a backcountry use permit.
5. Knowledge of appropriate bear precautions that need to be taken at all times.

Inspired: Settlers of European descent recognised early on the cultural significance of the land that would become the Yellow-stone National Park, and many famous artists of the day joined calls to preserve the area. In 1872 Thomas Moran exhibited paintings of Yellowstone, in a bid to promote the establish-ment of America's first national park.

47°N 109°W
MONTANA, USA

Story: *Solitary Walking Through Prime Bear Habitat*, p50.

Location: The Glacier National Park is in northwest corner of the US state of Montana.

Getting There: Fly in to Great Falls, Montana, then wind down the window and breathe in the cool fresh air as you drive up Hwy 89 to the park.

Movement: The only way to explore the best parts of Glacier National Park's magnificent backcountry is on foot. You'll find every type of walk in the park and there's plenty of roofed accommodation if you don't fancy sleeping with the bears.

Geography/Geology: The park's mountains began life as sediment deposited on the ancient sea-bed. These deposits slowly hardened into layers of limestone, mudstone and sand-stone until around 60 million years ago extreme tensions in the earth's crust began to warp, fold and finally break the layers. By the time the cataclysmic event was over a 480km-long portion of the crust had been pushed up and over soft layers of rock that had lain more than 80km to the east.

History: Recent archaeological surveys have found evidence of human inhabitation dating back 10,000 years. By the time the first European explorers arrived there were several indigenous tribes settled on and around the mountains. After decades of trickery on the part of European arrivals, the Blackfoot Indians finally sold the park to the US government in 1896.

Things to Do/Highlights: The Boulder Pass Trail provides access to some of the most rug-ged and beautiful high country areas in Glacier Park, not to mention awe-inspiring views of Boulder Glacier.

Proximity to Civilisation: Though the park offers all the requisite visitor facilities, 4100 sq km of prime wilderness means you can get as far away as you want.

Don't Go Without:
1. A squeaker horn – an easy and less embarrassing way of making noise as you hike through bear country.
2. Preparing for the worst weather – sudden snow-storms are common even in summer.
3. Booking a permit in advance – access to backcountry camp sites is restricted to ensure humans do not overrun this pristine environment.
4. Bear spray – if you think it will help.
5. Checking the trail status guides issued by the park rangers.

Inspired: One of the running shots of Tom Hanks passing a mountain lake in the Oscar-winning movie *Forrest Gump* (1994) was filmed at Glacier National Park.

27°S 109°W
EASTER ISLAND, CHILE

Story: *At the Feet of the Stone Giants*, p54.

Location: Slap bang in the middle of the Atlantic, practi-cally midway between Chile and Tahiti.

Getting There: Catch a plane from Santiago, Chile, or Papeete, Tahiti. Paddling to the island in an open canoe like the island's first inhabitants is not advisable.

Movement: Trek on foot and relish the freedom of being able to move around unrestricted by fences or warning signs.

Geography/Geology: The small 106-sq-km triangular shaped island is volcanic in origin and, unlike the Poly-nesian islands that were the likely home of Hotu Matu'a, it has neither rivers nor protec-tive reefs. Fortunately drinking water was available in volcanic craters and for several centuries magnificent forests provided resources for civilisation.

Do not expose to excessive heat or direct sunlight.

STAPLE HERE

PRINTED IN U.S.A. BY MAGNETIC TICKET AND LABEL CORP., DALLAS, TX REV. 2/11 CPN1113922

PASSENGER TICKET AND BAGGAGE CHECK
SUBJECT TO CONDITIONS OF CONTRACT

ISSUED BY AmericanAirlines® oneworld

DATE OF ISSUE 30 JUL 14 ISSUING OFFICE CODE ISI ISO US

ISS. AGENT ID. DT3 /SFO PLACE OF ISSUE SAN FRANCISCO

NAME OF PASSENGER (NOT TRANSFERABLE) DORN/CHERYL

FARE BASIS TOUR CODE

X/O	FROM / TO	CARR.	FLIGHT	CLASS	DATE	TIME	STATUS	NOT VALID BEFORE	NOT VALID AFTER
	SAN FRANCISCO	AA	197	Y	30JUL	540P			
X/O	CHICAGO OHARE	REVALIDATION							

ENDORSEMENTS/RESTRICTIONS
****

ORIGINAL ISSUE * *

ISSUED IN EXCHANGE FOR

FARE CALCULATION * BOARDING PASS *

* *
****

PNR CODE PNR CODE QOMCOP /AA
CONJ. TKT. NO.

GROUP 2
SEAT 13E

FARE

EQUIV. FARE PAID ********** FORM OF PAYMENT

TAX/FEE/CHARGE PCS CK. WT. UNCK. WT. SEQ. NO. ALLOW PCS. CK. WT. UNCK. WT.
****

TAX/FEE/CHARGE ***********
TAX/FEE/CHARGE ***********
TOTAL ***********

STOCK CONTROL NUMBER TX 00119353472681

COUPON AIRLINE FORM SERIAL NO. CK

AmericanAirlines®
BOARDING PASS

NAME OF PASSENGER
FCI DORN/CHERYL

X/O FROM SAN FRANCISCO
X/O TO CHICAGO OHARE
AMERICAN AIRLINES

CARRIER	FLIGHT	CLASS	DATE	TIME
AA	197	Y	30JUL	540P

REVALIDATION

GATE	BOARDING TIME	SEAT	SMOKE
57	510P	13E	NO

ADDITIONAL SEAT INFORMATION

PCS CK. WT. UNCK. WT. SEQ. NO. PCS. CK. WT. UNCK. WT.

GROUP 2

BAGGAGE ID NR.

COUPON AIRLINE FORM SERIAL NO. CK

DT3 /SFO

ADVICE TO INTERNATIONAL PASSENGERS ON CARRIER LIABILITY

Passengers on a journey involving an ultimate destination or a stop in a country other than the country of departure are advised that international treaties known as the Montreal Convention, or its predecessor, the Warsaw Convention, including its amendments, may apply to the entire journey, including any portion thereof within a country. For such passengers, the treaty, including special contracts of carriage embodied in applicable tariffs, governs and may limit the liability of the carrier in respect of death of or injury to passengers, and for the destruction or loss of, or damage to, baggage, and for the delay of passengers and baggage. For additional information on international baggage liability limitations, including domestic portions of international journeys, see AA.com.

NOTICE OF INCORPORATED TERMS OF CONTRACT

Air Transportation, whether it is domestic or international (including domestic portions of international journeys), is subject to the individual terms of the transporting air carriers, which are herein incorporated by reference and made part of the contract of carriage. Other carriers on which you may be ticketed may have different conditions of carriage. International air transportation, including the carrier's liability, may also be governed by applicable tariffs on file with the U.S. and other governments and by the Warsaw Convention, as amended, or by the Montreal Convention. Incorporated terms may include, but are not restricted to: 1. Rules and limits on liability for personal injury or death, 2. Rules and limits on liability for baggage, including fragile or perishable goods, and availability of excess valuation charges, 3. Claim restrictions, including time periods in which passengers must file a claim or bring an action against the air carrier, 4. Rights of the air carrier to change terms of the contract, 5. Rules on reconfirmation of reservations, check-in times and refusal to carry, 6. Rights of the air carrier and limits on liability for delay or failure to perform service, including schedule changes, substitution of alternate air carriers or aircraft and rerouting.

You can obtain additional information on items 1 through 6 above at any U.S. location where the transporting air carrier's tickets are sold. You have the right to inspect the full text of each transporting air carrier's terms at its airport and city ticket offices. You also have the right, upon request, to receive (free of charge) the full text of the applicable terms incorporated by reference from each of the transporting air carriers. Information on ordering the full text of each air carrier's terms is available at any U.S. location where the air carrier's tickets are sold. Additionally, American Airlines' contract terms are found on AA.com under the "Legal" link. You can reach American Airlines on the web, using the following link: www.aa.com/customerrelations.

REV. 3/11

m

History: Hotu Matu'a and his followers arrived around AD 400. The population reached several thousand, with the statue-building culture thriving into the 1700s until intertribal warfare brought the *moai* crashing down. Centuries of woe followed under a system of effective slavery imposed by outsiders, or *tangata hiva* (man from elsewhere), before the islanders finally won freedom in 1965.

Things to Do/Highlights: The quarry, Rano Raraku, is one of the wonders of the archaeological world and contains *moai* in all stages of construction.

Proximity to Civilisation: Aside from other tiny islands, Easter Island is thousands of miles from the nearest urban centres of Chile (3599km) and Tahiti (4000km).

Don't Go Without:
1. Reading Alfred Métraux's ethnology of Easter Island, written in the 1940s from first-hand accounts of stories told by islanders.
2. A visit to the doctor – this is one place where visitors need to have all their shots.
3. A small medical kit – probably best to try avoid a trip to the island hospital if possible.
4. Your own lock – if you intend to rent a bicycle.
5. Windbreaker – the climate is temperate, not tropical, and strong winds are common.

Inspired: The epic Hollywood action-drama *Rapa Nui* (1994), based on legends about the island's warring tribes – the Long Ears and the Short Ears – was shot entirely on location at Easter Island, and is a fascinating, quasi-educational introduction to the island's natural beauty and forgotten culture.

69°N 105°W

CAMBRIDGE BAY, CANADA

Story: *Alone in the Middle of the Tundra*, p58.

Location: Cambridge Bay is a hamlet located on the south coast of Victoria Island in the Kitikmeot Region of Nunavut, Canada.

Getting There: There are no roads to Cambridge Bay. It's strictly a fly-in community with three flights weekly connecting it to Yellowknife 850km to the south.

Movement: Snowmobiles are to the Inuit what mopeds are to the Italians – there's simply no cooler or more convenient way to get around.

Geography/Geology: Its proximity to the pole means that in winter you can see the midnight sun. The whole region is a rugged landscape of mountains and lakes.

History: Cambridge Bay was a traditional summer gathering place for the Inuit and the first Arctic explorers seeking the fabled Northwest Passage arrived in the 1800s. By the 1920s the Royal Canadian Mounted Police and Hudson's Bay Company had established posts. In 1955 the Distant Early Warning station opened, the settlement became a key transport link for the area and the community began to grow.

Things to Do/Highlights: Observing musk ox, an arctic ruminant that coexisted with mastodons and mammoths for millions of years. Going out on a hunting trip with experienced locals and returning to the welcoming lights of the town through a thick blanket of winter ice fog.

Proximity to Civilisation: Kitiga Lake is 18km from Cambridge Bay (pop 1300).

Don't Go Without:
1. Thermal underwear.
2. A fishing rod to catch your own Arctic char.
3. Reading about Inuit legends – they will make the icy world come alive.
4. Snow knowledge – the Inuit have 150 terms for different kinds of snow, and it helps to know which is which.
5. Snow goggles – you will develop snow-blindness without them.

Inspired: In 2003 a large, lonely planetoid was discovered orbiting the freezing outer edges of the solar system. Inspired by the Inuit legend of Sedna the Great Sea Spirit, the planetoid was named Sedna in her honour.

0°S 78°W

COTOPAXI VOLCANO, ECUADOR

Story: *The Perfect Mountain*, p62.

Location: The highest active volcano in Equador rises majestically out of the Eastern Cordillera mountain range, and is the prize jewel in the aptly named Avenida de los Volcanes (Avenue of Volanoes).

Getting There: Pre-book onto an organised expedition or simply fly into Quito, Ecuador's enchanting capital, and search for your own guide.

Movement: The walk from grassy paramo over sandy volcanic soil to snow crusts provides an odyssey of textures as memorable as the views. Climb lesser peaks in the Central Valley beforehand to acclimatise and savour the shifting bird's-eye perspectives.

Geography/Geology: Cotopaxi sweeps up from a highland plain climbing over 2km towards a glacier-covered summit elevation of 5911m. The famous crater is 600m x 800m in diameter and several hundred metres deep. An eruption in 1877 melted snow and ice on the summit, which produced mudflows that travelled 100km from the volcano.

History: Considered Ecuador's most destructive volcano, Cotopaxi has wiped out the nearby village of Latacunga on three occasions since the 1700s and has erupted 50 times since 1738. It was first climbed in 1872 by German geologist Wilhelm Reiss, and is now one of South America's most popular 5000m peaks. The most recent eruption of Cotopaxi ended in 1904.

Things to Do/Highlights: Standing on top of the world and peering into the steaming vent of an active volcano is guaranteed to take your breath away, even if you are too tired to appreciate it at the time.

Proximity to Civilisation: Cotopaxi is only 55km south of Quito but when you're standing at the summit, high above cloud cover, it's as if you're light years away from the bustling city.

Don't Go Without:
1. Acclimatising – altitude sickness affects even the most experienced climbers and poor preparation could prove disastrous.

2. Checking the danger alert for a volcanic eruption – some volcanologists believe one is imminent.
3. Binoculars – so you can become acquainted with the route before you make your ascent.
4. A balaclava – heading above 5000m it pays to protect your facial extremities.
5. Making a lip balm necklace – so you don't have to do a stop and search every time you want to apply a fresh layer.

Inspired: Inspired by a dream to start painting, local indigenous artist Julio Toaquiza depicts Cotopaxi in many of his artworks and leads a new school of indigenous art, which seeks to express the way of life, the thinking, and the feeling of the land's traditional owners.

7°N 77°W
DARIEN GAP, COLOMBIA

Story: *In the Swamp, Surrounded*, p66.

Location: The Darien Gap is an area of almost impenetrable jungle between Colombia and Panama and is the last gap in the Pan-American Hwy that connects South and Central America.

Getting There: After four days swimming down the River Atrato, leave the river in the area of La Honda and head northwest to the Panamanian border and the village of Paya.

Movement: The difficulty and dangers associated with trying to hack your way through the jungle should not be underestimated. You will shed blood, sweat and tears.

Geography/Geology: Including the two national parks adjoining the Darien Gap proper, the total area of undeveloped rainforest in the region is around five million hectares running along the border of Panama and Colombia. In 1981, Unesco designated the park as a Biosphere Reserve for its genetic value and extraordinary biological diversity – over 2440 species of flora have been recorded in the 500-year-old jungle.

History: There is an old saying that says, 'The Spanish conquered the Indians, the Andes, the deserts, and the Amazon, but they could not conquer the Gap.' Nowadays the technology exists to be able to bridge the Gap but doing so is a contentious and emotional issue. Indigenous peoples still resident in the area have made a legal claim to the land, and have rejected plans to drive a road through it on the basis of the environmental degradation that would be caused.

Things to Do/Highlights: If you think you're tough enough it is possible to arrange a cross isthmus trek tracing the hellish path taken by 16th-century Spanish conquistadors.

Proximity to Civilisation: Once away from the river it is unlikely you will meet anyone in the swamps and jungle.

Don't Go Without:
1. Mosquito repellent – although the insects here are so hardy it will probably prove useless.
2. Inoculations for just about everything, including malaria and yellow fever.
3. Heeding the cautionary travel advisories issued by just about every country, including Colombia and Panama.

4. No fear.
5. A guide who can show you the way and help calm your nerves when the jungle starts closing in.

Inspired: Indie filmmaker Brad Anderson based cult flick *The Darien Gap* (1996) on the story of a Boston bohemian slacker named Lyn Vaus whose ultimate daydream is to go trekking in remote Patagonia with the giant sloth of Indian legend, but is thwarted by the Darien Gap.

7°N 76°W
BAJIRA, COLOMBIA

Story: *Nothing to Do but Hope and Walk*, p70.

Location: The town of Riosucio lies across the Río Atrato in northwestern Colombia.

Getting There: Fly to Medellin, capital of the Department of Antioquia, then catch a bus bound for Turbo. At Bajira take the very long track that leads west towards Riosucio.

Movement: Certainly at the time of the expedition, moving into this area using the road from Medellin to Turbo meant passing through a number of 'front lines'.

Geography/Geology: Colombia is divided into four geographic regions: the three vast ranges and intervening valley lowlands of the Andean highlands, the Caribbean lowlands coastal region, the Pacific lowlands coastal region which contains the swamps at the base of the Isthmus of Panama, and the immense plains of eastern Colombia stretching out beyond the Andes.

History: Since the 1970s, leftist guerrilla groups have been at war with paramilitary groups backed by the Colombian government and the US, perpetuating instability. Both the guerrillas and paramilitaries have been known to abduct people, including foreign teachers and humanitarian aid workers, with alarming regularity. During the 1990s Medellin had the highest recorded homicide rates of any city outside a war zone.

Things to Do/Highlights: The friendliness of many of the locals is astounding given their intense poverty and isolation. If a family sacrifices its last chicken in your honour such kindness will be in you forever.

Proximity to Civilisation: The last border post marks the end of natural law; once you have crossed it your future is in the hands of the guerrilla fighters.

Don't Go Without:
1. Examining your motives.
2. Honing your negotiation skills.
3. Conversational Spanish.
4. Stating you don't want to be rescued – the sound of approaching rotor blades is a death warrant for guerrilla hostages.
5. A thorough psychological examination.

Inspired: *Plan Colombia: Cashing-in on the Drug War Failure* (2001) is a radical documentary challenging the view that the US government's Plan Colombia is effective in decreasing the production of cocaine and is instead bringing increasing levels of poverty and degradation to rural Colombia.

MIDDLE OF THE COASTAL DESERT, PERU

Story: *The Coastal Desert*, p74.

Location: The Coastal Desert of South America is squeezed into a strip of land separating the Andes from the Pacific Coast.

Getting There: Travel 50km to 100km east from almost any seaside settlement in Peru or northern Chile, and you can't miss it.

Movement: Trekking across the desert is a singular act of madness. An equally dramatic though far safer option is to drive or catch a plane that will take you over the Nazca Lines.

Geography/Geology:
The deserts of Coastal Peru and northern Chile form a continuous belt along the western escarpment of the Andean Cordillera for more than 3500km from the Peru-Ecuador border (5°00'S) to northern Chile (29°55'S). This region is dry for three reasons: (1) the Andes block rain-bearing winds from the Amazon Basin, (2) air masses moving towards the coast out of the South Pacific high pressure system produce little rainfall, and (3) northward-flowing cold water off the coast (the Peru, or Humboldt, Current) contributes little moisture to surface air masses.

History: During a slightly wetter past, today's Coastal Desert region was the site of several great pre-Inca civilisations, including the Moche and Chimú, Sipán, Lambayeque and the Sechín.

Things to Do/Highlights:
Head northwest of the town of Nazca and feel the hair on the back of your neck prickle as you explore the enigmatic lines and images spread over 450 sq km of desert.

Proximity to Civilisation:
Small towns are scattered across the region but don't let that lull you into a false sense of security.

Don't Go Without:
1. An honest map.
2. Well-worn hiking boots.
3. Boiled sweets – superb saliva stimulant.
4. Discarding anything that's not essential – any spare room in the backpack will be used for water.
5. Knowing your limits – you don't want to find you've reached them halfway across the driest place you've ever been.

Inspired: The arid coastal desert has been a considerable blessing for archaeologists studying the mummified remains of Inca and pre-Inca that have been preserved for centuries by the uniquely waterless climate.

PUELO VALLEY, CHILE

Story: *Beyond Road's End*, p78.

Location: The Park National Lago Puelo is tucked away in the extreme northwest of Argentina, alongside the border with Chile.

Getting There: The Puerto Montt morning bus runs the length of Reloncavi Sound to Puelo.

Movement: Hop a ferry and shuttle up valley to Llanada Grande, where you can pack your gear onto a horse and giddy up.

Geography/Geology:
Covering 23,700 hectares the Park National Lago Puelo is actually the smallest one in the Andean-Patagonia region. It is dominated by Lake Puelo and its tributaries, which include the Rivers Azul, Turbio, Pedregoso and Epuyén. The lake is glacial in origin and lies at the bottom of a valley, which drains along the Puelo River to the Pacific.

History: Puelo's first pioneers arrived in the early 1900s. Most were Chileans who had worked as sheep shearers on the great estancias of Argentina, kicked out by Peron's reform and looking for their own sliver of land to cultivate. Gaucho customs are still the norm.

Things to Do/Highlights:
As well as its dramatic vistas and refreshing microclimate, the region is also rightly famed for its fantastic fruit, in particular cherries, strawberries and raspberries. Patagonian berries taste just the way nature intended.

Proximity to Civilisation:
150km southeast of Puerto Montt and almost none of the road is paved.

Don't Go Without:
1. A local – who will guarantee you go the right way.
2. Deep Heat to soothe your muscles after a long day's riding.
3. Gloves – the reins can rub after a while.
4. Learning some Spanish – it will go along way to making this trip special, and the locals will appreciate you making the effort.
5. Spare magazines (in Spanish) as presents for the isolated locals.

Inspired: The area's remoteness has recently begun to attract newcomers in search of an alternative lifestyle away from the pressures of the city. Lago Puelo celebrates an annual 'forest festival', which includes a colourful crafts fair which galvanises the new 'hippy' presence.

MACHU PICCHU, PERU

Story: *Alone in the Ruins of Machu Picchu*, p82.

Location: Machu Picchu nestles in a high saddle between two peaks 80km northwest of Cuzco, Peru.

Getting There: Fly or bus in to Cuzco from the capital Lima, then take the train to the start of the Inca Trail.

Movement: The classic Inca Trail route is by far the most rewarding way to access the site and will give you some appreciation for the ingenuity and organisation of the people who built it.

Geography/Geology:
Machu Picchu is perched nearly 2500m above sea level on top of an estimably beautiful ridge between two differently sized peaks. Huayna Picchu is the smaller peak that lies in the background of the 'classic' shot of Machu Picchu, which means 'older' or 'bigger' peak. The site's name is therefore simply a reference to its geography, and was adopted because the original name, like the magnificent civilisation of the Inca, has been lost in the shroud of time.

History: Machu Picchu's history remains shrouded in mystery. Built in the 15th century, it eluded discovery by the Spaniards, was eventually abandoned by the Incas, and remained unknown to the outside world until Hiram Bingham reported rediscovering this 'Lost City of the Incas' in 1911. In 1983 the UN made it a World Heritage Site.

Things to Do/Highlights: In spite of the crowds at Machu Picchu there is always a spot amongst the ruins that you will find to call your own. The majesty and magic of these perfectly sited ruins amidst the rarefied air and luscious greenery of the Andes is beyond description.

Proximity to Civilisation: Machu Picchu is four hours from Cuzco, but at night, alone with ghosts and the llamas, you could almost believe you had travelled back in time to before the Spanish conquest of the Incas.

Don't Go Without:
1. Preparing to share the solitude with extraordinary crowds.
2. Believing the hype – Machu Picchu is every bit as magical as everyone claims.
3. A waterproof coat or even an umbrella as showers are likely.
4. Reading about Manco Inca, the last Inca king who it is believed retreated to Machu Picchu following an unsuccessful revolt against the Spanish.
5. Sketch pad – the incomparable beauty of this place will unlock your inner creativity.

Inspired: Artefacts collected by Hiram Bingham are the subject of a bitter dispute between Yale University and the government

of Peru. Peruvian President Alejandro Toledo has demanded the return of the objects, currently on display at the Yale Peabody Museum, as part of the national heritage of the people of Peru.

43°S 71°W
PATAGONIA, SOUTH AMERICA

Story: *Suddenly Rendered Immobile*, p88.

Location: Patagonia is the sparse rugged region at the southern tip of South America forming part of the territory of Argentina and Chile.

Getting There: Fly to El Calafate at the tip of the continent, pull on your backpack and head north.

Movement: For those going it alone, bus services ply their trade between most towns. Adventure and trekking companies offer tours throughout the region.

Geography/Geology: Patagonia covers 880,000 sq km, which is around one third of the total surface of Argentina. The largest area is the vast central plateau that extends from the Andes to the Atlantic Ocean. However, the formidable mountainous and glacial terrain for which it is most famous dominates the region. The Patagonian Andes is like a giant wall creating a natural border between Argentina and Chile. The region is one of four places on earth known to contain large deposits of dinosaur fossils.

History: Initially populated by migrating native peoples, most notably the Tehuelche. Europeans first noticed Patagonia when Ferdinand Magellan stopped there briefly in 1520, but it wasn't until a Welsh expedition in 1850 that non-indigenous people began to settle in the area. Interestingly, many Welsh place names still survive.

Things to Do/Highlights: The imposing splendour of the 60m high Perito Moreno glacier, located in the arm of Rico of the Argentino Lake, is one of the most jaw-dropping sights in a region of spectacular natural beauty.

Proximity to Civilisation: It is two lonely days south to the town of Esquel, struggling against winds that will cut through you like a knife.

Don't Go Without:
1. Immense stamina – if you intend to trek this rugged and difficult terrain.
2. Conversational Spanish – the ability to communicate with the few who inhabit this wilderness will add enormous value to your trip.
3. Windproof clothing and apparel – 100 km/h winds are not infrequent in Patagonia.
4. Checking for reports of the 'red tide' – an infrequent aquatic event that makes some of the local seafood inedible.
5. As many spare tyres as you can fit in your car if you'd prefer to follow the asphalt.

Inspired: The series of vignettes about local travellers that are presented in the film *Intimate Stories* (2005), directed by Carlos Sorin, are all set in Patagonia and convey what it feels like to be poor and live in this wilderness.

12°S 70°W
MANU NATIONAL PARK, PERU

Story: *The Jungle Came Alive Around Me*, p92.

Location: The Manu National Park lies west of Puerto Maldonado in Peru and overlaps the departments of Cuzco and Madre de Dios.

Getting There: You can choose from the luxury of a 25-minute flight from Cuzco or the cheaper and option of a one-and-a-half-day journey by bus and boat.

Movement: Manu has become one of the most important tourist destinations in Peru, even though access is limited to an outer buffer area. It is now a relatively simple trip whether by road, boat or plane.

Geography/Geology: Manu encompasses and protects over 2 million hectares of land that's extraordinarily rich in diversity. A single hectare of forest could have up to 220 species of trees. Many rare species of animals, such as giant otter and armadillo, and of course the fabled jaguars, can be sighted.

History: Set aside in 1973, Manu National Park gained international fame and was designated a Unesco World Biosphere Reserve in 1977. Until the early 1990s, however, only a few hundred people a year made it to this remote place. Indigenous tribes still live within the reserve, some of which are yet to make contact with outsiders and the diseases they bring with them into this pristine environment.

Things to Do/Highlights:
Everything about this mysterious, unfathomable jungle will get under your skin and remain in your dreams long after you have walked beneath its vast, bewitching canopy.

Proximity to Civilisation:
A flight from Cuzco can be made in 25 minutes, but the Amazon still feels remote by virtue of the Andes and the vast distances of the jungle.

Don't Go Without:
1. Patience – wild fauna is fantastically elusive.
2. Expecting delays – anyone travelling through dense jungle should allow for changes to their itinerary.
3. Plenty of insect repellent.
4. 100% waterproof clothing – keeping dry will drastically reduce your level of discomfort.
5. Your yellow-fever inoculation certificate – or you won't be allowed into the jungle.

Inspired: The extraordinary film *Keep the River on Your Right: A Modern Cannibal Tale*, tells the story of 78-year-old Tobias Schneebaum who wandered off by himself into the usually off-limits, uncharted territories of the Manu National Park.

20°S 66°W

ATACAMA DESERT, BOLIVIA

Story: *A Flat, White Expanse of Salt*, p96.

Location: The Salar de Uyuni saltpan is high up on the Bolivian high plateau at an altitude of around 3600m above sea level.

Getting There: From La Paz jump on a bus for the incredibly scenic and roughshod 10-hour trip to Uyuni.

Movement: Hire a jeep and a driver to take you from Uyuni across the largest saltpan in the world and up into the surreal volcanic landscapes of the Atacama Desert and its geyser fields.

Geography/Geology:
Forty thousand years ago this area was part of Lago Minchin, a massive prehistoric lake that gradually dried up, leaving the dissolved minerals in the lake's waters to form a salt plain that has a surface area of approximately 10,500 sq km, 10 times the size of Hong Kong. The surface crust is 10m thick and the total quantity of salt is estimated to be around 10 billion tonnes.

History: The Incas inhabited the edges of the Atacama Desert that border the saltpan, building irrigation channels to make the land arable. The saltpan itself is uninhabitable but is still a source of national pride and the major tourist attraction in Bolivia. The nearby volcanoes were revered as deities by the Inca and the region contains dozens of archaeological sites featuring their mummified remains.

Things to Do/Highlights:
Watching in horror as the oppressive heat causes the driver of your jeep to doze off, before realising that it hardly matters as in this flat stretch of wilderness there is absolutely nothing to crash into.

Proximity to Civilisation:
Driving the 400km between Uyuni, Bolivia and San Pedro de Atacama across the border in Chile, you'll pass through one tiny mud-encrusted village and stay overnight at a remote shelter.

Don't Go Without:
1. Mountain goggles – the salt flats are as blinding as snow.
2. Cocoa leaves – locals chew the leaves of the cocoa plant to give them energy at high altitude.
3. Moisturiser – if you don't want to end up with scales for skin.
4. A salt grinder – stock up on free unrefined natural salt.
5. As much water as you can carry – salt + heat = dehydration, big time.

Inspired: NASA has conducted extensive research here in its quest to discover the origin of life on Earth and on other planets, including Mars.

64°S 64°W

NEUMAYER CHANNEL, ANTARCTICA

Story: *A Continent with No Road Signs*, p100.

Location: Unless otherwise specified 'South Pole' refers to the Geographic South Pole – the southernmost spot on the planet at the intersection of the Earth's axes of rotation.

Getting There: It is possible to embark on a day trip to the South Pole from Punta Arenas, Chile.

Movement: The advent of snowmobiles means that scientists who live at Antarctica during summer are no longer dependant on pack animals.

Geography/Geology:
The South Pole is located on Antarctica. The world's fifth largest continent encompasses 14.2 sq km of land, 95% of which is covered by ice.

Antarctica is the windiest and coldest place on earth. The average inland temperature is -70°C. The Antarctic ice contains around 70% of the earth's fresh water. If it were to melt scientists predict the world's sea levels would rise more than 60m.

History: Norwegian Roald Amundsen led the first team to the South Pole on 14 December 1911. England's Captain Robert Falcon Scott and his team arrived one month later. Unusually harsh weather ensured Scott's men would perish just 20km from the supplies that would have kept them alive. In 1929 American Richard E Byrd led the first aerial expedition to the Pole in a Ford tri-motor aircraft.

Things to Do/Highlights:
Those seeking the ultimate wilderness endurance challenge should sign up for the Antarctic Ice Marathon. Running across snow and ice, athletes can expect average temperatures during the 42km event to be around -20°C.

Proximity to Civilisation:
McMurdo Station is over 1600km away across the coldest, most bewildering landscape on the planet.

Don't Go Without:
1. Being able to use the sun as a compass – the technique employed by Scott to find the Geographic South Pole.
2. Sleeping tablets – during summer the sun never sets, making sleep problematic.
3. Paints – so you can recreate the extraordinary colours and light unique to Antarctica.
4. A neoprene facemask – for protection against cold and wind.
5. A sleeping bag that will keep you warm in -40°C conditions.

Inspired: The extremely harsh Antarctic weather prompted the US and all 30 signatories of the Antarctic Treaty (1959) to build a 1632km road across the continent. The 'ice highway', expected to be complete by the end of the polar summer in 2006, will link the McMurdo Station on the coast to the Amundsen-Scott base at the Pole, reducing the number of dangerous flights to the region, and freeing it up for 'deep field research'.

18°N 63°W

ST MAARTENS, CARIBBEAN

Story: *A Perfect, Glassy Swell*, p104.

Location: St Maartens is an island in the Caribbean, 240km south east of Puerto Rico.

Getting There: Catch a flight to Princess Juliana Airport and then hire a car to go explore the island.

Movement: If you don't fancy paddling around on a seal-like surfboard there are plenty of boats available for charter.

Geography/Geology: Reefs that lie far offshore from an island are usually classified as barrier reefs, which become separated from the shoreline by wide channels when landmasses sink as a result of erosion and shifting in the Earth's crust.

History: St Maartens was spotted, and possibly named, by Christopher Columbus on 11 November 1493. For more than 350 years it has been divided between the Dutch and French after the Spanish subjugated the indigenous population. Nowadays 'the friendly island' is popular with tourists and celebrated for its beautiful beaches and surf spots, many of which are known only to locals. The island is also famous for it's friendly grey and Caribbean reef sharks.

Things to Do/Highlights: There is something profoundly humbling about looking at the land from the level of the ocean, floating on the surface of an instinctively familiar yet physically alien environment, and knowing that only your own flimsy, water-reliant muscles will get you home.

Proximity to Civilisation: The reef in question is around a kilometre offshore. A long way to paddle if you've attracted the attention of local sharks.

Don't Go Without:
1. A rash vest, hat and sunblock – sunburn and overexposure is the major health risk on the island.
2. Shark repellent – it's possible to buy a device that fits in a board leash and creates an electric shield against sharks.
3. Knowing your limits – surfing is a lot to do with confidence, if you think you're out of your depth then a connection with the reef could be imminent.
4. A disposable underwater camera – to capture the barrel from the inside.
5. Respect for the ocean – if things start to get hairy, get out of the water.

Inspired: In 1989 Larry Moore, former photo editor at *Surfer* magazine, discovered a reef break 160km off the San Diego coastline that could potentially hold up to 150ft swells. In 2001 Mike Parsons rode the biggest wave of the year – a whopping 66ft – at Cortez Bank, as the break became known. Since then it has been ridden on just four occasions.

60°N 44°W

AAPPILATTOQ, GREENLAND

Story: *Amid the Icy Vastness*, p108.

Location: Aappilattoq is a tiny village at the southernmost tip of Greenland.

Getting There: In summer fly out to Narsarsuaq from Denmark or Iceland. From there travel by helicopter or ferry to Nanortalik, where the once-a-week mini ferry will take you to Aappilattoq.

Movement: A fleet of coastal ferries run up and down the west coat from Aappilattoq in the south to Uummannaq in the north.

Geography/Geology: Greenland is the world's largest island. Its northerly location, at the point where the Atlantic meets the Arctic Ocean, means it is surrounded principally by cold ocean currents, so the coasts are constantly being cooled. This, combined with the radiation of cold from the inland ice, gives Greenland its arctic climate. Aappilattoq is situated near some of the world's most spectacular fjords, huge mountains of rock and ice that rise out of the freezing waters to peaks of almost 2000m.

History: Danish colonial policy and the global boycott of seal products in the 1980s all combined to kill off the traditional seal-hunting villages that were once dotted about the spectacular fjords of the Nanortalik region. Aappilattoq is the last true hunter's village to survive on Greenland's southern tip.

Things to Do/Highlights: North of Aappilattoq the abandoned settlement at Nuuk provides an excellent stop off point if kayaking around the fjords. The view from a nearby ridge (around 800m) is nothing short of mindblowing.

Proximity to Civilisation: The nearest 'big' town is Nanortalik, home to around 1540 residents, but the field ice flowing with the current from the east coast contributes to Aappilattoq's isolation, as it can make it impossible to sail for several months.

Don't Go Without:
1. Remembering the polite term is Inuit, not Eskimo.
2. Getting your camera polaroiled or the parts will freeze over in winter.
3. Expecting long delays – the airline is referred to as Immaqa Air, translated as Maybe Air.
4. An ANNA Emergency Kit – containing essential items such as a whistle, compass, flares, signalling mirror, aluminium foil wind sleeve and signal flag.
5. A Danish phrasebook may be helpful in the urban centres en route to Aappilattoq.

Inspired: Winner of the Camera d'or for Best First Feature Film, *Atanarjuat* (2001) is based on a centuries old Inuit legend. Although it was filmed on location in Canada, it gives international audiences a more authentic view of Inuit culture and oral tradition as it was the first ever Inuit-made film.

WATKINS BJERGE, GREENLAND

Story: *Gazing Out Towards the Vast Greenland Icecap*, p112.

Location: Greenland is an island between the Arctic Ocean and the North Atlantic Ocean, northeast of Canada and is part of the Kingdom of Denmark.

Getting There: The remote mountain areas in East Greenland are best approached by chartered aircraft from Iceland. Once deposited on some remote glacier, there are lifetimes of mountains and valleys to explore. Winter north of the Arctic Circle is long, cold and dark, so May to July are the most practical months to visit.

Movement: Getting around is likely to be on telemark skis, pulling your gear on a sled.

Geography/Geology: A flat to gradually sloping icecap covers all but a narrow, mountainous, barren, rocky coast, and there is continuous permafrost over the northern two-thirds of the island.

History: The Watkins Bjerge contain Greenland's highest peak, Gunnbjørns Fjeld (3693m). Referred to as Hvitserk (white robe) by early Norse sailors, who saw the snowy summit from Denmark Strait, the first ground sighting was made by a British expedition in 1934, and the summit reached by an Anglo-Danish party the following year.

Proximity to Civilisation: The small town of Ittoqqortoormiit, 350km to the north-east, is the nearest settlement in Greenland.

Don't Go Without:
1. 121.5MHz emergency position indicating radio beacon (EPIRB). The Greenland authorities won't let you out on the ice without one.
2. Your professional guide – solo trips are for mentalists and in any case are illegal.
3. Avalanche probes – better safe than sorry.
4. Avalanche transceiver – your only chance of rescue if you wind up buried beneath tonnes of ice.
5. Flares in case you drop your EPIRB down a crevasse.

Inspired: VP-5 recovery effort – more than 40 years after a US Navy plane, the VP-5, crashed into the ice killing all 12 crew on board, an expedition was launched to recover the pilot's remains. In 2002, veteran 'astronomical artist' Don Dixon painted *Greenland Meteor*, which depicts the power and splendour of 'a meteor that may have exploded over Greenland'.

EL HIERRO, CANARY IS.

Story: *The Edge of the Map*, p116.

Location: El Hierro lies off the northwestern coast of Africa and is the most westerly of the Canary Islands, so named because of the large dogs (Canes) found living on the islands.

Getting There: From Tenerife you can reach El Hierro by ferry in four hours, or fly with local airline Binter Canaria from any of the Canary Islands.

Movement: Given that many of the roads appear to be almost vertical it is best to explore by car, or using any vehicle that has an engine.

Geography/Geology: El Hierro was formed by volcanic activity and is said to contain over 1000 craters, although you'd be hard pressed to count them all. Despite being the smallest island in the Canary archipelago, it has an abundance of beautiful landscapes, including dense forests and unusual rock designs known as lajiales, formed by petrified lava flows.

History: The primitive and peaceful Bimbache existed harmoniously here until the arrival of the Spanish during the 14th century. Although the Bimbache king capitulated peacefully, the Castilian conquerors struggled to suppress revolting dissidents as they were unable to find drinking water anywhere on the island. Fortunes changed when a Bimbache princess was wooed by a Spanish officer and gave away the secret of the Ga roé – a sacred tree that wept water – which, according to legend, provided fresh water for the island's thousand or so inhabitants.

Things to Do/Highlights: Take in the waters at Pozo de las Calcosas, a natural spring with healing properties. Divers should head for the spectacular 'Cueva de Don Justo', Don Justo's Cave, a 6km volcanic tunnel bursting with marine life.

Proximity to Civilisation: Physically the island lies just 75km from the party capital of Tenerife, but El Hierro's tranquillity makes it feel light years away.

Don't Go Without:
1. Hard-soled shoes – the volcanic rock is as sharp as it looks.
2. A bandana – or anything to soak up sweat, as El Hierro can get surprisingly humid.
3. Underwater camera – to take advantage of the excellent visibility in the calm waters surrounding the island.
4. Planning ahead – to minimise the time you spend waiting for the ferry.
5. Looking at a pre-Columbus map on which El Hierro is shown as the end of the known world.

Inspired: The island of El Hierro is mentioned in Umberto Eco's novel *L'isola del giorno prima* (The Island of the Day Before, 1994), which is about a 17th-century aristocrat trapped on an island at the International Date Line.

ATLAS MOUNTAINS, MOROCCO

Story: *A Speck in the Sahara*, p120.

Location: Merzouga in Morocco lies south of the ancient oasis city of Rissani, not far from the Algerian border.

Getting There: Travel by bus to Rissani from Fès or Marrakesh, then take a taxi, minibus or rent a jeep to get to Merzouga.

Movement: Camel is the traditional and most reliable way to traverse the Sahara, allowing you time to absorb its eerie majesty.

Geography/Geology: The Sahara Desert is the largest desert in the world covering 5,635,000km. The name Sahara is derived from the Arabic word for desert. The range of topography features mountains, rocky plains, salt flats and vast tracts of sand dunes, which are its major draw card for tourists.

History: Ancient Egyptian, Greek, Roman and Arab civilisations all left their mark on this desert, which has long been the stronghold of nomadic Berber tribes. Arabic caravans have been traversing the Sahara since at least the 10th century. The desert regularly receives no rainfall for years on end, which is a major factor in ensuring the region remains sparsely populated – less than 2 million people live here.

Things to Do/Highlights: The first time you see real Saharan ergs, the classic wind-sculpted desert sand dunes, at Erg Chebbi, the moment will be imprinted on your mind forever. As will be the first time you attempt to climb up one!

Proximity to Civilisation: Rissani is 35km away but travelling across desert it is notoriously easy to lose your sense of direction, and this is not a place you want to lose the trail.

Don't Go Without:
1. Treats for your camel, unless you like being spat at.
2. Learning basic French and Arabic – Moroccans are famous for being cunning linguists and have been known to look down on those who have knowledge of just one language.
3. Getting some tips on how to climb ergs – doing so is definitely an art.
4. At least three lip balms for protection from the heat and sand storms.
5. A thick jumper – it gets cold at night.

Inspired: Morocco is an affordable and hence attractive option for film production companies

and some great footage has been shot on location in and around Merzouga. The surprise Hollywood hit *The Mummy* (2001), starring Rachel Weisz, was filmed here with the red dunes of the Moroccan Sahara standing in nicely for Egypt.

57°N 4°W
WESTER ROSS, SCOTLAND

Story: *A Glorious Illusion*, p124.

Location: Wester Ross is a remote and rugged region in the northwest Scottish Highlands about 300km from Edinburgh.

Getting There: Reach the Highland capital of Inverness by road, rail or air, and then hop on a bus that will take you into Wester Ross.

Movement: The area described lies within a privately owned deer estate, although public access for tramping is well established.

Geography/Geology: The Highlands is an ancient land, its craggy valleys and shimmering lochs carved by the action of mountain streams and marauding ice sheets. Many of the mountain summits are not much above sea level, whilst the valley floors have been denuded to create the sense of scale and height. The mountains of Wester Ross are extremely wet, wild and dangerous places.

History: There was human settlement on the coastal fringes of Wester Ross as early as the

Mesolithic (Middle Stone Age) period of about 10,000 years ago. In keeping with most of the Scottish Highlands, the region saw periodic depopulation, especially after the 18th-century Jacobite rebellions and during the 19th century when the mountains were developed for sheep rearing and for the shooting of game birds and red deer.

Things to Do/Highlights: Feeling your heart thumping against your ribs as you haul yourself to the top of a high crag, find a spot to shelter from the wind and let your soul rejoice that you are alive in the last great wilderness in Scotland.

Proximity to Civilisation: Small settlements are scattered along the lonely peripheral roads. The nearest large settlement is the Highland capital of Inverness 80km away.

Don't Go Without:
1. Making sure you are well equipped, experienced and physically fit.
2. Checking for current local information – especially around deer shooting season.
3. A walking stick – if you want to really get into rambling character!
4. The taste for an amazing tot of whiskey – or fifty.
5. Rock climbing gear – great climbing abounds in these parts.

Inspired: For centuries the original inhabitants of the Scottish Highlands defended their territory against the armies of Rome and England, and in the process became the stuff of legend. The Hollywood movie *Highlander* (1986) starring Christopher Lambert re-ignited the mythical past for a new generation to admire the Highland spirit, paving the way for Mel Gibson's *Braveheart*.

13°N 4°W
MOPTI REGION, MALI

Story: *Resting Through the Hollow Hours*, p128.

Location: The Djenné Rd junction on the Bamako–Mopti Hwy lies across the Niger River in southern Mali.

Getting There: Djenne is 15km from the road junction, no problem if you have your own vehicle, but if using public transport you'll have to wait for a kind passer-by to offer you a lift.

Movement: Even with a private vehicle, ferrying across the Niger River in the dark is ill advised.

Geography/Geology: Mali is part of the Sahel, the region where desert and savannah collide. Not surprisingly this area is at risk from increasing desert encroachment caused by a combination of environmental problems such as deforestation and soil erosion. The region is highly prone to flooding during the rainy season when the Great Mosque actually becomes an island.

History: Djenné, the oldest known city in sub-Saharan Africa, is situated on the floodlands of the Niger and Bani Rivers, 354km southwest of Timbuktu. Djenné's famous mosque is the largest Sahel-style mudbrick structure in the world, rebuilt in 1903 based on its 13th-century predecessor. The city has taken great care to preserve the mud architecture, which was named a World Heritage Site in 1988.

Things to Do/Highlights:
Little moves through the darkness. Lose yourself to the night instead, either at the crossroads or on the banks of the river near the boat embarkation area. The syrupy silence of a rural African night is like no other.

Proximity to Civilisation:
15km from Djenné and 10 hours from the reassuring comfort of daylight.

Don't Go Without:
1. Learning basic French – the country's official language.
2. A sleeping bag – if you intend to spend the night at the junction.
3. A torch in case nature calls.
4. Something to quench your late-night thirst.
5. An MP3 player to create your own soundtrack to accompany the stars.

Inspired: The film *Yeelen* (1987) is one of the most powerful and acclaimed African films ever made, and follows the journey of a young warrior of the powerful Mali empire of the 13th century.

90°N 00°W

NORTH POLE

Story: *Crawling Across the Vast Frozen Ocean*, p134.

Location: Literally on top of the world. Number N90.00.000 on the GPS.

Getting There: The 'classic' route is to leave from Canada's Resolute Bay and keep walking until the GPS lets you know when to stop.

Movement: Painfully slow, dragging a 180kg sledge over the frozen surface of the sea. Average speed: 2.4 km/h. Top speed of polar bears: 48 km/h.

Geography/Geology:
In winter the Arctic Ocean is around 16 million sq km of floating ice, shrinking to 9 million sq km in summer. During the coldest winter months the ice can be up to 5m thick but quickly thins during spring, which is the only safe time for polar expeditions. The Arctic is the most humid place on earth and is home to seals, polar bears and arctic foxes.

History: The first expedition to the pole is generally accepted to have been made in 1909 by Robert Peary, although a 1996 analysis of Peary's record indicates he must have been 40km short of the Pole. In 1952 US Air Force Lieutenant Colonel Joseph O Fletcher and Lieutenant William P Benedict landed a plane at the Geographic North Pole. Ralph Plaisted made the first confirmed surface conquest of the North Pole (by skidoo) in 1968.

Things to Do/Highlights:
Avoiding having your sled 'mugged' by a polar bear by barking like a dog and firing a flare stirs an overwhelming sense of relief as well as respect for these magnificent creatures.

Proximity to Civilisation:
You are the only living person in an area the size of a continent and the only thing connecting you to the outside world is a satellite phone.

Don't Go Without:
1. GPS tracker – or you won't know you've reached the pole.
2. Blood thinners to help prevent frostbite.
3. Sponsorship – only space travel and deep ocean expeditions are more expensive than a trip to the pole.
4. Extensive strength and aerobic training for what will undoubtedly be your greatest challenge, ever.
5. A 'peebottle' – taking a leak when it's –50°C outside is a delicate operation.

Inspired: The only permanent resident at the North Pole is alleged to be Santa Claus. Since 1982 Canada Post officially lists his address as: Santa Claus, North Pole, Canada, H0H 0H0.

45°N 6°E

MONT BLANC, FRANCE

Story: *Dawn at the Summit of Mont Blanc*, p138.

Location: Mont Blanc is part of the French Alps in southeast France, which forms the country's natural border with Italy and Switzerland.

Getting There: Travel by train to Chamonix then take the cable car and train into Chamonix Valley where you will start the ascent.

Movement: Slow, deliberate and measured is best on the way up, though you'll be forgiven a euphoric slide on the way down.

Geography/Geology:
Mont Blanc is the highest mountain in Western Europe. Its summit is officially 4807m above sea level but changes each year due to changes in local meteorological conditions. The Alps range was formed over a period of about 500 million years, resulting from unimaginable upheaval in the earth's crust. By around 300 million years ago granite and metamorphic rocks had already formed the base of the Mont Blanc massif.

History: The first ascent of Mont Blanc was made in 1786 by two men from Chamonix, Dr Michel Paccard and Jaques Balmat. The pair were spurred to the top by a reward from Horace-Benedict de Sassure, a physics professor from Geneva. Sassure himself was to become the third person to stand on the summit. The first woman to reach the summit was Marie Paradis in 1808.

Things to Do/Highlights:
Ascending the highest point in Europe is an end in itself. The meaning of such an act can only be fully appreciated by those who have been there and done it.

Proximity to Civilisation:
Mont Blanc is eight horizontal and four vertical kilometres from both the French town of Chamonix and the Italian town of Courmayeur.

Don't Go Without:
1. Advanced mountaineering experience.
2. Fully acclimatising.
3. Lady luck – mountain climbing is extremely dangerous and climbers need all the help available.
4. A headlamp – finding your way in complete darkness would be impossible.
5. Flattery – if on the Italian side you should acknowledge the summit is in Italy, likewise if conversing with the French then the peak is in France.

Inspired: To celebrate their centenary, Montblanc, the extortionately priced German pen and jewellery manufacturers, created a diamond-encrusted signet in the style of their logo, which 'pays tribute to the summit of Mont Blanc as a symbol of the highest standards of perfection and aesthetics'.

SAHARA DESERT, NIGER

Story: *Lost in the World's Largest Desert*, p142.

Location: The Niger desert dominates the Republic of Niger in northwest Africa.

Getting There: From Algeria, follow the Hoggar Mountains south until the dunes take over.

Movement: You are strongly advised to travel in a 4WD convoy. Drivers of 2WD vehicles have in the past not been allowed to join convoys because of their potential for breaking down.

Geography/Geology:
It's really quite hard to miss the Sahara: the world's greatest sandpit covers a massive 8,600,000 sq km across northern, western and central Africa, measuring 4800km from east to west and up to 1900km north to south. It encompasses a plethora of landscapes from the volcanic mountains of the Hoggar to the windblown rockscapes of the Djado Plateau. At 1,267,000 sq km, Niger's total land area is merely a fraction of the Sahara.

History: The dominate social force in Niger's remote desert region are the Tuaregs, descended from the Berber, who it is believed migrated into the Sahara around the 7th century to escape persecution from advancing Arabs. For centuries their power and wealth came from raiding the merchant caravans crossing the desert but conflict with neighbouring tribes throughout the 20th century has left many impoverished.

Things to Do/Highlights:
North of Agadez lies a remote sandstone outcrop featuring engravings carved into the rock, including two of life-size giraffes estimated to be around 8000 years old. An incredible site in the middle of nowhere.

Proximity to Civilisation:
If you are unprepared and break down away from the piste you could be waiting days or weeks for rescue. If you're lucky.

Don't Go Without:
1. A GPS, otherwise just follow those barrels, and make sure you have a compass as backup.
2. Water – for life and for bartering.
3. An emergency plan in case your luck runs out.
4. A satellite phone – or rent one if necessary.
5. Savouring your last free-flowing, water-wasteful 20-minute shower.

Inspired: Rebecca Popenoe's bestseller *Feeding Desire: Fatness and Beauty in the Sahara* (2003), based on fieldwork undertaken in an Arab village in Niger. It analyses the meanings of women's fatness as constituted by desire, kinship, concepts of health, Islam, and the social need to manage sexuality.

BOSNIA-HERCEGOVINA

Story: *A Rush into Perilous Night*, p146.

Location: The Neretva River forces its way through the Dinaric Alps and winds a 225km course through Bosnia-Herzegovina and Croatia.

Getting There: Fly in to Dubrovnik, Croatia, or Sarajevo, Bosnia, then head for the river valley on your preferred mode of transport.

Movement: If cycling is too strenuous then buses run the length of the road between Sarajevo and the Dalmatian coast.

Geography/Geology: Neretva is the largest river of the eastern part of the Adriatic Basin. Its beauty and the diversity of its landscape is unique. The lower valley contains one of the largest remnants of Mediterranean wetlands in Europe, as well as a rich monumental heritage reflecting human activity in this area for thousands of years.

History: The Balkan conflict of the '90s ravaged the land and left no town undamaged. There was international outrage in 1993 when the Old Bridge (Stari most), spanning the Neretva in the city of Mostar, was destroyed by shelling. The bridge was rebuilt and reopened in 2004.

Things to Do/Highlights:
Sitting at a café drinking strong, sugar-laden Turkish coffee whilst munching on *tufahije* – an apple and walnut cake served with whipped cream – and contemplating the remarkable transformation of a place so recently at war.

Proximity to Civilisation:
It's the valley's remoteness from normality that sets it apart. Along the Neretva River, you are never physically far from somewhere, but the ravages of war wrap solitude around this place like a bandage round a wounded soldier.

Don't Go Without:
1. Sensitivity – asking about the war is more likely than not to cause offence.
2. Booking accommodation in advance – the war destroyed many hotels and you can't always expect there to be room available.

3. Building up a caffeine tolerance – downing coffee is a national pastime.
4. Landmine training – if you expect to spend a long time in the region.
5. Travel insurance – medical facilities are limited, and patients are often expected to pay for their own equipment.

Inspired: After working extensively in Bosnia, former *Christian Science Monitor* writer and photographer Sara Terry launched the Aftermath Project – a non-profit foundation that offers grants to photojournalists documenting the aftermath of conflict. Michael Winterbottom's hard-hitting film *Welcome to Sarajevo* (1997) offers an insightful and confronting perspective on the Balkan conflict and how the West reacted to it.

WESTERN DESERT, EGYPT

Story: *Axle-Deep in Soft Sand*, p150.

Location: This immense desert to the west of the Nile spans the area from the Mediterranean Sea south to the Sudanese border.

Getting There: Drive 600km southwest from Cairo along the desert fringe of the Nile Valley until a sharp right turn leads down to the desert floor at Al-Kharga Oasis.

Movement: Wend your way northwest along ancient desert trade routes to Dakhla Oasis (190km), then 300km more to Farafra.

Geography/Geology:
The Western Desert is about the same size as Texas, covering 700,000 sq km, and accounts for about two-thirds of Egypt's land area. The desert's Jilf al Kabir Plateau has an altitude of about 1000m, an exception to the uninterrupted territory of basement rocks covered by layers of horizontally bedded sediments forming a massive plain or low plateau. Scarps (ridges) and deep depressions (basins) exist in several parts, and no rivers or streams drain into or out of the area.

History: Trade routes have crossed the Western Desert's arid expanse since prehistory, carrying everything from ostrich feathers to slaves. The major oases (Al-Kharga, Dakhla, Farafra, Bahariyya and Siwa) have been inhabited for millennia, and most have ancient tomb and temple remains.

Things to Do/Highlights:
Linger in the stunning White Desert before soaking in a mineral spring in Bahariyya Oasis, 120km north.

Proximity to Civilisation:
From Cairo, Al-Kharga Oasis is separated by 600km, hundreds of scorpions and millions of tonnes of sand.

Don't Go Without:
1. Trying to get a permit to drive to Siwa Oasis, where Alexander the Great declared himself a god.
2. The best guide you can afford.
3. Scarf – to protect you in a sandstorm and for great TE Lawrence impersonations.
4. Goggles.
5. Humility, in case you too get stuck in the sand.

Inspired: Much of the action in the film *The English Patient* (1996) originally took place in the Western Desert. The film made famous the rock art left behind by ancient nomads at Uweinat.

30°S 28°E

DRAKENSBERG, SOUTH AFRICA

Story: *The Engine Roars with Anticipation*, p154.

Location: The uKhahlamba-Drakensberg Park lies in the province of KwaZulu-Natal in the Republic of South Africa.

Getting There: The gateway to the park is a three-hour drive north from the coastal city of Durban.

Movement: Adventure abounds when you explore Africa at your own rhythm and pace. Travel with independence and confidence, and let the road take you where you belong.

Geography/Geology:
The mountains of the 243,000-hectare uKhahlamba Drakensberg Park were formed around 150 million years ago and form South Africa's major watershed. uKhahlamba translates as 'the Barrier of Spears' in reference to the extraordinary basaltic buttresses, peaking at over 3300m, rising sharply out of the rugged grasslands. The park is also home to the world's second-highest waterfall, the Tugela Falls, with a drop of 947m.

History: In 2000 Unesco designated the uKhahlamba-Drakensberg Park a World Heritage Site in recognition that it contains well over 20,000 rock-art paintings made by the San people, or bushmen as they are known. The San inhabited this area for at least 4000 years until they were driven out by a succession of African tribes and white settlers, who hunted them for sport. In 1837 Boers of Dutch descent traversed the land using ox-wagons during the historic Great Trek from Cape Town – a journey of unimaginable hardship.

Things to Do/Highlights:
It is fascinating to venture deep into the park to some of the more remote cave paintings left by the San whose ancient drawings reflect the spiritual peace and abundance of natural resources in what was once their homeland.

Proximity to Civilisation:
The peaceful southern edge of the park is about 180km west of Durban, the busy, beachside capital of Natal.

Don't Go Without:
1. Allowing for cold weather – even in summer thunderstorms can be expected.
2. Binoculars – it's fantastic to survey the land through the clear mountain air.
3. Bathers and a towel – the rock pools and crystal streams are very inviting after a few hour's hike.
4. Travel insurance – as mountain rescue can be very expensive.
5. A good tent – so you can head out into the real wilderness away from the permanent lodges.

Inspired: The classic movie *Zulu* (1963) starring Michael Caine was shot on location in a valley in what is now the uKhahlamba-Drakensberg Park. Apparently, Caine became desperately homesick during the three-month shoot.

15°S 35°E

MULANJE MASSIF, MALAWI

Story: *The Mystical Mountain*, p158.

Location: The Mulanje Massif dominates the landscape of southern Malawi near the city of Blantyre.

Getting There: Call in to the forestry office in Likhubula to organise your hike, maps and porters/guides, if required. There is a circular road around the mountain along which you can regularly take a minibus or *matola* (alternative taxi).

Movement: Local labourers run up and down the Massif transporting timber to the logging depot, but chances are you'll find a brisk hike tough enough.

Geography/Geology:
The Mulanje Massif is a granite inselberg, an isolated strand of igneous rock rising sharply out of the Phalombe Plain. Inselbergs are formed when their rock mass withstands erosion over many years, in this case 130 million, whilst the surrounding sedimentary rocks waste away to form a flat plain. The Massif contains the highest peak in South-Central Africa at 3002m.

History: David Livingstone was the first Mzungu to site the Massif in 1859, but archaeologists have since discovered evidence of human presence on and around the Massif dating back to the Stone Age. In 2000 it was designated a Unesco Biosphere Reserve.

Things to Do/Highlights: The enchanting scent of the Mulanje cedars reaches out across thin silent air, almost like the hand of time itself, to remind you that here, in this ancient land of Africa, our species was born.

Proximity to Civilisation: The Mulanje Massif is 100km southeast of Blantyre and possibly a lot closer to the realm of the *mizimu* (spirits).

Don't Go Without:
1. A guide – the route markers are weathered and hard to find, which can lead to some sticky free-climbing situations.
2. Checking for storms – the mountains can become treacherous in wet weather.
3. Shoes that grip.
4. Whiskey – the summit is low enough that a celebratory shot won't be too dangerous, and high enough that reaching the top is something worth celebrating.
5. A medallion that will protect you from the *mizimu*.

Inspired: South African author Laurens Van Der Post used the Mulanje Massif as the setting for his famous adventure travel book *Venture into the Interior*.

3°N 37°E

CHALBI DESERT, KENYA

Story: *High and Dry*, p162.

Location: Kenya's Chalbi Desert falls between the shattered lava fields surrounding Lake Turkana and the dusty scrubland around the Moyale–Isiolo Rd.

Getting There: Head north from the town of Maralal and try to take a wrong turn!

Movement: If you have an instinctive aversion to engines then saddle up for a camel trek across this formidable ochre desert.

Geography/Geology: Surrounded by volcanoes and ancient lava flows, Chalbi Desert is the hottest and most arid region in Kenya. The region is home to the Rendille and Gabra, traditional nomadic tribes who even today manage to maintain a culture based on livestock, notably the camel. Chalbi is referred to as Kenya's only 'true desert' and is home to thirsty hyenas and cheetahs.

History: The availability of water and forage for livestock is highly variable in this region, making mobility and cooperation essential for survival. An increase in the number of refugees from war-stricken Somalia and Sudan has added considerable strain on the region's resources. The introduction of new religious and cultural values in the form of Islam and Catholicism is also having an impact on indigenous lifestyles.

Things to Do/Highlights: If you somehow fail to get lost, Lake Turkana is an awesome spot and home to the isolated El-Molo tribe, who have become something of a tourist attraction. To the south, volcanic Mt Kulal offers some excellent trekking.

Proximity to Civilisation: It is a 90-minute flight by light aircraft to Nanuyki, which represents an impossible distance to cover on foot through this inhospitable, sun-baked desert.

Don't Go Without:
1. A shovel, rope, extra fuel, plenty of water and at least one spare tyre.
2. Checking locally for reports of recent bandit activity.
3. An egg to fry on the vehicle's bonnet.
4. Ripping up your map – if you want to get lost for real.
5. Keeping another map somewhere safe – when you realise it wouldn't be so great to succumb to the desert after all.

Inspired: Nearby Lake Turkana is featured in Fernando Meirelles's film *The Constant Gardener* (2005), based on the book by John Le Carré.

44°N 72°E

AKBAKAI, KAZAKHSTAN

Story: *The Place That Even God Forgot*, p166.

Location: Akbakai is situated in Kazakhstan midway between the Tien Shan mountains in the south and the Siberian Taiga to the north.

Getting There: Fly to Almaty, take the overnight train to Chu, and then bargain your way into a taxi that is headed 350km north into the Betpak Dala to the village of Akbakai.

Movement: Catching a cab might sound like the easy option, but a few kilometres down the wild vomit-inducing track, you'll realise that in this isolated region there are no easy options.

Geography/Geology: Situated in Central Asia, Kazakhstan is the ninth biggest country in the world, covering 2.7 million sq km, making it about the size of Western Europe. Its 5000km border with Russia in the north and west is one of the world's longest. Akbakai lies exposed in the middle of a long mountain ridge that is a magnet for bad weather, particularly strong winds.

History: The harsh steppe of central Kazakhstan has been the heartland of nomads since the time of the Scythians. Since then it has been washed over by waves of nomad groups, including the Mongols and Zhungars. Various branches of the Silk Route passed over this hazardous terrain. It was only during the early Soviet years that de-nomadisation, industrial development and collectivisation largely destroyed the nomad way of life. Some Kazakhs rumour that Genghis Khan is buried somewhere in the Betpak Dala.

Things to Do/Highlights: In many ways, the attraction of the steppe is trying to appreciate its inherent harshness. To breathe easier though, it's better to visit between March and June or September and November.

Proximity to Civilisation: 850km from Almaty, which is an almighty long way when the only word that can accurately describe most of the journey would be hellish.

Don't Go Without:
1. Car sickness tablets – the ride is rough enough to bring your guts up.
2. A valid visa permit for entry.
3. Proof of a negative test for HIV is required for anyone intending to stay longer than three months.
4. US dollars – foreign currency talks.
5. A jacket of the most wind-resistant fabric you can find.

Inspired: Generations of gold diggers have been lured to the Akbakai gold belt as it is one of the most mineralised in Kazakhstan – the deposit contains more than 2.5 million ounces of gold.

WAKHAN CORRIDOR, AFGHANISTAN

Story: *The Roof of the World*, p170.

Location: A mountainous region on the edge of the Hindukush, Wakhan (sometimes known as the Wakhan Corridor), which is sparsely populated and relatively poor.

Getting There: Fly from Kabul to Faizabad in Afghanistan, or from Dushanbe to Khorog in Tajikistan – then it's one day's drive to Ishkashim and another day's drive to the starting points for journeys into Wakhan.

Movement: To get to Wakhan you'll need a local guide and a donkey, horse, yak or camel to transport gear.

Geography/Geology: This is one of the most rugged, unforgiving regions on earth. Snow-capped mountains (many over 7000m) with very little surrounding vegetation dominate the wind-lashed valley that at some points narrows to less than 15km in width. The Wakhan Corridor has been strategically important for centuries, separating Pakistan and Tajikistan as well as sharing a 96km border with China.

History: Populated for more than 2500 years, the kingdom of Wakhan, where the Great Game (the 19th-century rivalry between Great Britain and Russia) played out, was given to Afghanistan in 1895 as a buffer zone between the two empires. Its borders with China and the Soviet Union were closed in the 20th century. The Soviet occupation in the 1970s and 1980s, and the subsequent civil war and Taliban rule, kept Wakhan closed to foreigners until the Karzai government was established in 2002.

Things to Do/Highlights: Life is hard in this region and there is something curiously compelling and symbolic about seeing vultures, with their 2m wingspans, circling high above a yak carcass for the first time.

Proximity to Civilisation: Wakhan is an arduous 4WD trip from wherever you start – at least three days by road from Kabul (about 600km) and two days from Dushanbe (about 500km).

Don't Go Without:
1. Knowledge – rocks painted red signal land mines in that area.
2. An open mind in relation to opium farming, the primary source of income in this desperately poor region.
3. Being prepared to eat a sheep's testicle – a Kirghiz delicacy.
4. The thickest, warmest clothes you can find.
5. Stamina – the Wakhi are tough people; to survive in their homeland you'll have to be too.

Inspired: Before the 1978 Marxist revolution, Wakhan was prized for its Ovis Poli (Marco Polo sheep) and attracted hunters in great numbers.

HEARD ISLAND

Story: *The Many Perspectives of this Ice Cathedral*, p174.

Location: Heard Island lies in the Southern Ocean 1500km north of Antarctica. It is part of the Australian Antarctic Territory.

Getting There: Travel is only by sea and options are to go with the very occasional tourist ship, or arrange your own transport for one of the world's more serious ocean crossings.

Movement: On the glaciers there is a real danger of plummeting into crevasses – listen to your guide's instructions and don't stray from the group.

Geography/Geology: Heard Island covers an area of 368 sq km dominated by the Big Ben massif, which includes Mawson Peak – the only active volcano in Australian territory. The island, like nearby McDonald Island, is formed of limestone and volcanic accumulations and sits on top of the underwater Kerguelen Plateau. More than 80% of the island is covered in ice.

History: Heard Island was officially discovered in 1855 by American sealer Captain John Heard. From 1855 to 1880, several groups of American sealers lived on the island in what must have been horrendous conditions. Within five years they managed to virtually wipe out the island's seal population, after which they left the island. Approximately 100,000 barrels of elephant seal oil was produced during this period. In 1947 the British government designated the island as part of the Australian Antarctic Territory. It was added to the World Heritage list in 1997.

Things to Do/Highlights: Looking across the northern beaches that are literally swarming with hundreds of thousands of seals will make your heart skip a beat. The remains of the sealer's abandoned, squalid huts at Atlas Cove are among the best preserved anywhere.

Proximity to Civilisation: The closest inhabited land is the Kerguelen Islands, 440km north across an ocean that, were you to fall in, would claim you in minutes.

Don't Go Without:
1. The appropriate permit from the Australian Antarctic Division, which has very strict quarantine considerations.
2. Sea-sickness medication – the Southern Ocean is rougher than rough.
3. Planning activities with safety as the top priority.
4. Identifying the impact your trip will have on the environment.
5. Insurance – all visitors to Heard Island are required to indemnify the Commonwealth from any liability arising from an accident.

Inspired: The World Heritage Convention requires that the natural splendour of listed territories should be presented to the outside world. To fulfill this obligation, a 2003/4 Australian Antarctic Program expedition worked with Wade Fairly, a filmmaker with experience working under extreme conditions, to record images and footage for public exhibitions showing how expeditioners live and work on Heard Island.

HIMACHAL PRADESH, INDIA

Story: *Making the Most of My Indian Odyssey*, p180.

Location: Situated in the central Himachal Pradesh, Manali is at the head of the Kullu valley, 200km north of the state capital Shimla.

Getting There: Buses leave Delhi regularly, but you may arrive irregularly on a different bus or one that has had several mechanical repairs along the way.

Movement: Along the roads military camps and convoys occasionally spring out to conduct random passport checks.

Geography/Geology: The village of Manali is the gateway to the Kullu Valley leading away to the north, whilst steep gorges ascend towards the Himalayas in the southwest. Manali lies at an altitude of 1926m, affording spectacular views of the nearby and closely defined snow-capped mountains. The Beas River bubbles majestically through the settlement to complete the romantic image of a secluded mountain hideaway.

History: Vaivastava, the seventh incarnation of Manu, found a fish floating in his bathtub. He was instructed to nurture it until it grew. He did and the fish warned him that a deluge would wipe out mankind and instructed Manu to build a vessel high enough to survive the water. We now know this vessel as Manali. Over the past decade Manali has grown from an outback Himachali town to a busy tourist destination.

Things to Do/Highlights: The Rahala waterfall is a healthy 16km hike away but the sight of the falls as you approach along the old road makes a trip worthwhile.

Proximity to Civilisation: Especially in winter Manali seems every inch as remote as the 570km it is from Delhi looks on the map.

Don't Go Without:
1. Your passport.
2. Diplomatic skills intact.
3. A Hindi phrasebook.
4. A trail map to navigate the high passes.

5. The warm clothes you didn't think you'd need.

Inspired: Director Anil Sharma's sensitive movie *Ab Tumhare Hawale Watan Saathiyon: A Curtain Raiser* (2004) was based on the 1971 India-Pakistan war. Several key scenes were shot in and around Manali.

32°N 78°E

LAHAUL SPITI VALLEY, INDIA

Story: *Getting There is Half the Fun*, p184.

Location: Sangla Valley is located in Kinnaur district of Himachal Pradesh in the northern Himalayas of India.

Getting There: The most convenient route is by rail, plane or bus to Simla, and from there, to Sangla by bus.

Movement: If the bus sounds too suicidal, vehicles can be hired at Simla, Delhi or Chandigarh to get to Sangla. The region has some fantastic trails for hikers.

Geography/Geology: Stretching for 95km, the Sangla Valley is irrigated by the Baspa River, which meets the Satluj at Karcham, and by several smaller streams and springs. The Sangla Valley is a gorgeous swathe of green, dwarfed by the surrounding mountains. The clear waters of the Baspa run between orchards of apples and apricots. Local inhabitants are fond of claiming that this is the place 'where the Gods live'.

History: The region's proximity to Tibet restricted access until

---

the early 1990s. Permits are now easily obtained. The proximity to Tibet also influences local religion as Kinnauris follow a mix of Hindu and Buddhist religions.

Things to Do/Highlights: Trekking through the Sangla Valley when the wooded slopes are a riot of colours with mountain flowers strewn across the expanses you realise why this place is cited as the 'most beautiful valley in the Himalayas'.

Proximity to Civilisation: The journey from Simla to Sangla is a distance of 230km, or about 10 hours in a white-knuckle bus ride.

Don't Go Without:
1. Taking your own food supplies if you intend to camp away from the main villages – the locals are very friendly and will probably offer you food but adding strain to the local subsistence economy should be avoided if possible.
2. A minimum of three days to take in the luscious scenery.
3. Anti-malaria medication.
4. Ensuring your car, should you choose to hire one, has very high ground clearance and working suspension.
5. Knowing that the wave of a red flag from the roadside means a landslide is in progress and that you should stop, immediately!

Inspired: The scenic beauty and tranquillity of the mountain valley has for centuries made it a destination for those seeking spiritual growth. Nowadays the region is flush with retreats offering guests the chance to practice yoga and meditation, as well as hiking and angling.

27°N 86°E

EVEREST BASE CAMP, NEPAL

Story: *Horns Like A Pretzel*, p188.

Location: Thame is a Nepalese village along the ancient salt trade route between Tibet, Nepal and India.

Getting There: There are flights to Lukla from where you can trek along the Dudkhoshi River and up into the towering mountains.

Movement: Follow the trippy trail less travelled as your mind wanders corridors tinged with the early symptoms of altitude sickness.

Geography/Geology: Thame lies at an altitude of 3,800m and is part of the Sagarmatha National Park, which also includes the world's highest peak, Mt Everest (8848m). The park covers a predominantly mountainous area of 1148 sq km and includes the upper catchment areas of the Dudh Kosi and Bhote Kosi Rivers. It is home to rare species such as the snow leopard and the lesser panda, and is World Heritage Listed.

History: The Solukhumbu region of the Himalaya was settled by Sherpas approximately 500 years ago. They migrated from Tibet, and brought with them many Tibetan-Buddhist customs that are still in practice today. Sherpa roughly translates as 'people of the east'.

Things to Do/Highlights: Watching sunrise over the 400-year-old Thame monastery, or *gompa*, will invoke serenity in a place that, along the mountain trails, is a physical manifestation of meditation. As Thame marks the beginning of the non-tourist trails you will be richly rewarded if you hunker down and keep on walking.

Proximity to Civilisation: Thame is about four-hour hike from the regional centre of Namche, which can turn into a long struggle to stay warm if the weather turns against you.

Don't Go Without:
1. Turning the prayer wheels at Namche Bazaar before you head off down the trail.
2. Glacier glasses – at high altitude it pays to have the right protection.
3. Chocolate purchased outside Nepal – good for energy and much better than the local stuff.
4. Riding a roller coaster – to prepare you for landing at Lukla's airstrip, perched on the side of a very steep valley.
5. Being very sure you are surefooted.

Inspired: Thame is home to many of the most respected Sherpa guides in Nepal, and is the birthplace of the legendary Tensing Norgay, who along with Sir Edmund Hillary became the first man to summit Everest in 1953.

49°N 88°E

TAVAN BOGD NATIONAL PARK, MONGOLIA

Story: *Searching the Mountains for Prey*, p192.

Location: The Tavan Bogd National Park is a protected wilderness in Bayan Ölgii, Mongolia's westernmost province. The region's capital, Ölgii, is just 225km from the border with Russia.

Getting There: Fly to Ölgii from Ulaanbaatar in four hours and hire a jeep to take you along an unpaved track into the park. The alternative is a brutal six-day journey by road from Ulaanbaatar to Ölgii.

Movement: The only way to get around Western Monglia is by jeep along roads in varying states of disrepair.

Geography/Geology: The Mongol Altai Nuruu range forms the backbone of Bayan Ölgii and has many peaks over 4000m, which are covered by permanent glacier or snow. The range, stretching from Russia, through Bayan Ölgii and Khovd, and concluding adjacent to the Gov-Altai range, is home to livestock that graze in the fertile valleys, as well as foxes, lynx and bears.

History: Hunting with eagles is a tradition that dates back two millennia and is described by Marco Polo in his book *The Travels*. Nomadic Kazakhs, from which the majority of the present population are descended, first arrived in the Mongol Altai in the 1840s. The Altai Tavan Bogd National Park was established in 1996 and contains Mongolia's highest mountain range, Tavan Bogd, which rises to a height of 4374m.

Things to Do/Highlights: The annual eagle hunting festival held high up in the aching beauty of these remote mountains provides rare insight into the Kazakhs' extraordinary bond with their environment and its animals.

Proximity to Civilisation: Tavan Bogd National Park is 80km from the regional capital Ölgii, far enough to get very saddle sore.

Don't Go Without:
1. Understanding of mechanics – many of the jeeps for hire at Ulaanbaatar are on their last

wheels; if you can spot the duds so much the better.
2. Knowing how to ride a horse – this is Mongol warlord country and no trip is complete without a stint on horseback.
3. Reading the history – Mongolia today still resonates with the time of the Great Khans.
4. A Mongolian phrasebook – the locals may speak a bit of Russian but not much English.
5. Clothes for all conditions – temperatures fluctuate wildly across the region.

Inspired: Even today 13th-century Mongol general Genghis Khan is still very much revered as the founding father of Mongolia. Inspired by the great military leader, who established the largest empire the world has ever known, Australian adventurer Tim Cope set off on a 10,000km journey on horseback to retrace Khan's footsteps from Mongolia to Hungary.

51°N 100°E

SELENGA RIVER, MONGOLIA

Story: *The Flip Spilled Everything*, p196.

Location: The headwaters of the Selenga River are in southern Mongolia's Khangai Mountains.

Getting There: From Moscow fly to Ulan-Ude, capital of the Buryat Autonomous Republic, from where it is possible to raft down the Selenga River all the way into Lake Baikal.

Movement: In summertime the ice melts making this the only time to travel, but also brings

the possibility of increased water flow and the river bursting its banks.

Geography/Geology: The Selenga River originates in Mongolia and runs a northern course of 1480km ending with the Selenga Delta as it empties into Lake Baikal in Russia. This delta region alone covers 54,000 hectares of nutrient rich wetland providing an extensive habitat for many rare species of fish, water fowl and mammals.

History: For centuries the Selenga and its tributaries have provided transportation routes connecting Russia with Mongolia and China. The surrounding region was once the heartland of the Mongol Empire, which extended from the Korean Peninsula to Hungary. In recognition of the rich biodiversity in the river, it's tributaries and surrounding area, Russia and Mongolia have developed a network of protected areas including a Ramsar wetland protection site at the Selenga Delta.

Things to Do/Highlights: Each spring around 5 million birds, including cranes, herons, eagles and hawks, converge on the Selenga River Delta for one of nature's most captivating events.

Proximity to Civilisation: The Selenga River is 500km northwest of the Mongolian capital Ulaanbaator, making it several weeks of shoulder crippling kayaking away.

Don't Go Without:
1. Attaching a GPS beacon to your supplies – you won't always be able to rely on Mongol horsemen being around.
2. Being open to a religious experience – many settlements alongside the river are founded on ancient sects such as Animism, Shamanism and old forms of Buddhism.

3. A wide-brimmed hat – the summer sun reflecting off the river is surprisingly fierce.
4. A lightweight paddle – you'll be thankful for it after the first 100km.
5. A marine radio telephone – in case you need to phone a friend.

Inspired: The book *Tibetan Buddhism in Buryatia* (2001), written by Luboš Bulka, recounts the historical narrative of how a mission of 150 Tibetan and Mongol monks in 1712 spread Buddhism along the course of the Selenga River.

25°N 102°E
YUNNAN, CHINA

Story: *An Unexpected Mountain Desert*, p200.

Location: Yunnan Province is the most southwest region of China, bordering Vietnam, Laos and Burma.

Getting There: Fly into Kunming Wujiaba International Airport and take a domestic flight to Lijiang from where you can catch a bus to Baishuitai.

Movement: Get off the bus in Baishuitai and hike across Tiger Leaping Gorge to Daju. Don't hitch a ride or you'll miss the views and that solitude that's oh-so-rare in this part of the globe.

Geography/Geology:
Yunnan Province covers 394,000 sq km through which the mighty Yangtze River rages between the Haba Shan and Yulong Xueshan mountains, in the process carving out Tiger Leaping Gorge – one of the deepest in the world. The gorge runs a length of 16km producing a series of spectacular rapids under steep cliffs plunging 2000m into the raging torrent. Legend says that in order to escape from a hunter, a tiger leapt across the river at the narrowest point, about 25m wide.

History: After 15 centuries of rule by minority kingdoms, Yunnan was annexed to the Chinese empire in the mid-13th century. Today the government sees the province as a backward hinterland, a potential tourist magnet and a vulnerable border region. Yunnan is home to more than 42 million people, a third of China's ethnic minorities, and over half the country's species of flora and fauna.

Things to Do/Highlights:
From the high trail the dreamy vista of terraces, greenery and cliffs plunging steeply down into the brown rumbling waters of the Yangtze will soothe all your city worries gently, gently away.

Proximity to Civilisation:
The trail runs for 16 solitary kilometres between Baishuitai and Daju. It's one of very few places in China where you can get intimate with nature, on your own.

Don't Go Without:
1. A phrasebook.
2. Tout tolerance – expect to be hassled at Baishuitai, the locals are increasingly dependent on tourist dollars.
3. A permit – travel in China is strictly controlled.
4. Toilet paper and a torch – if you plan to camp overnight.
5. Practicing your spitting technique – if you want to blend in with the locals.

Inspired: *South of the Clouds* (2004) by award-winning director Zhu Wen is set in and celebrates Yunnan Province's ethnic diversity, particularly the Mosuo people who still follow their traditional matriarchal culture.

13°N 103°E
SIEM REAP, CAMBODIA

Story: *Angkor in Wartime*, p206.

Location: Preah Khan is part of the city complex at Angkor, the capital of the ancient Khmer empire, lies in northwestern Cambodia.

Getting There: From Siem Reap, take the tarmacked road north through the rainforest past Angkor Wat and the Bayon.

Movement: From Preah Khan's western gate continue on foot – but keep to well-trodden paths to avoid leftover ordnance.

Geography/Geology:
The conventional theory is that the site at which Angkor was constructed was chosen for its strategic military importance and its agriculture potential. However, alternative hypotheses suggest the site was selected because it fits into an ancient 'planet-spanning sacred geography'. The city plan and arrangement of the temples supposedly mirrors the stars in the constellation of Draco at the time of the spring equinox in 10,500 BC.

History: Preah Khan was built in the late 12th century by the great Khmer King Jayavarman VII. Between 1927 and 1932 French archaeologists cleared the temple's jungle cover, which has since grown back. In 1992, Unesco declared the whole city of Angkor a World Heritage Site.

Things to Do/Highlights:
Reflecting on the destruction of the Temple of Ta Prohm by trees that have broken through the walls since the site was abandoned is a reminder of the transience of civilisation, and imbues deeper respect for the strength and beauty of the natural world.

Proximity to Civilisation:
Angkor's mysterious remnants of a forgotten civilisation are 235km northwest of Phnom Penh.

Don't Go Without:
1. Checking out the definitive 1944 Maurice Glaize Angkor Guide, which is now published online.
2. Buying a ticket – sneaking into the temple area is no longer tolerated.
3. Allowing yourself a few days if you want to see a cross-section of the hundreds of temples scattered around the heritage site.
4. A map of the area – it's huge and navigation without a map is difficult unless you hire a guide.
5. Change to buy food and drink off the local touts – they need the money and you'll need the refreshment.

Inspired: Dozens of movies have been filmed in and around Ankor Wat, including the Hollywood blockbuster that shot Academy Award-winner Angelina Jolie to fame as *Lara Croft: Tomb Raider* (2001).

LAKE BAIKAL, RUSSIA

Story: *Rowing Across Lake Baikal*, p210.

Location: Lake Baikal is in southeastern Siberia, in the Republic of Buryatia and the Irkutsk region, Russia.

Getting There: Fly in to Irkutsk then take the scenic nine-hour train ride where you will eventually disembark at Port Baikal.

Movement: Charter a Yaroslavets, one of the sea boats that ply Lake Baikal, and join the short-list of human beings who have visited numerous remote bays only accessible by water.

Geography/Geology: Baikal is immense. It is an enormous rock-hewn bowl 640km in length, 80km wide and 1620m deep. Almost a quarter of the world's fresh water is contained in Lake Baikal. If engineers made every river on earth flow into it, then it would take a year to fill up. At around 25 million years old, the lake is also the oldest freshwater deposit and has amazing clarity that can allow visibility of up to 50m.

History: The earliest written accounts of Lake Baikal are to be found in Chinese texts that refer to people now believed to be the local Kurykany tribe who settled in Priolkhonye around AD 500. In 1992 Lake Baikal and the surrounding area, which supports habitats for bears, elks and lynxes, was designated as a national park.

Things to Do/Highlights: The 18km Great Baikal Trail from Listvyanka to Bolshoye Kotui is a fantastic introduction to this unique ecosystem. Sampling the local delicacy of omul salmon is to die for.

Proximity to Civilisation: Less than 80km from the Siberian city of Irkutsk, but a whopping 5185km, and five time zones, to the east of Moscow.

Don't Go Without:
1. Vodka – 'for warmth…and courage'.
2. Gloves – to prevent rowing blisters.
3. A picture by which to identify the Sagan-Daila herb – it is said to have magical properties.
4. Munchies for the long, cold hikes around the lake.
5. Enough petrol to get you back to the petrol station – if travelling by road.

Inspired: During winter Baikal represents the kind of extreme environment that attracts those who want to redefine their limits. In 2003 five Dutch skaters did just that by crossing the lake from the south to the north, covering more than 600km in 18 days.

KRAKATAU, INDONESIA

Story: *Teetering on the Edge of a Watery Void*, p214.

Location: Krakatau volcano lies in the Sunda strait between the islands of Java and Sumatra.

Getting There: Travel agencies in Carita Beach arrange Krakatau day trips costing US$30 to US$50.

Movement: As you approach the volcano across the strait it is easy to imagine the terrifying tsunamis that once rushed out from the spot you are heading towards.

Geography/Geology: Indonesia has more active volcanoes than anywhere on earth. Krakatua is one of 130 volcanoes in the region, and lies directly above the subduction zone of the Eurasian Plate and Indo-Australian Plate, at what is thought to be an unusually weak part of the crust. Two-thirds of the original Krakatau Island was obliterated when it erupted in 1883. Eruptions since 1927 have created a new, smaller island group known as Anak Krakatau (child of Krakatau).

History: Krakatau volcano, one of the world's largest, has erupted repeatedly throughout history. The most well documented event happened in 1883, when a massive eruption spewed over 25 cu km of rock, lava and ash, triggering tsunamis that wiped out hundreds of towns and villages, killing over 36,000 people. The explosion created the loudest sound ever recorded, which was heard over 4600km away. Volcanic ash darkened skies over the entire Earth for nearly a week, and for at least a decade afterwards brilliant red sunsets were the norm.

Things to Do/Highlights: The smoking rim is impressive from afar but to actually stand on the rim of the most famous and deadly volcano in history is as extraordinary as it is spectacular.

Proximity to Civilisation: Java's Carita Beach is 40km across the wild and unpredictable waters of the Sunda Strait.

Don't Go Without:
1. Warm, waterproof clothes in case you spend the night on the ocean.
2. Checking the storm report.
3. Practising your lost-at-sea balancing technique.
4. Reading about the utterly astonishing devastation caused by the 1883 eruption.
5. Asking if it's alright to scree jump on the way back down the mountain.

Inspired: The vividly red sky in Edvard Munch's famous painting *The Scream* (1893) is thought to show the atmospheric conditions over Norway caused by the Krakatua eruption of 1883, the year Munch recalled in the artwork.

WEST KALIMANTAN, BORNEO

Story: *The Heart of Borneo*, p210.

Location: Betung Kerihun National Park lies in the far interior of West Kalimantan at the headwaters of the Kapuas River.

Getting There: The park can be accessed by land, air and water from Putussibau. Choose a method that suits your sense of adventure.

Movement: Crossing West Kalimantan is an incredible experience however you do it. The sheer magnitude of the island is mind blowing as you navigate along the twisting Kapuas River and many of the province's 100 other rivers.

Geography/Geology: The park covers an area of 800,000 hectares and comprises diverse habitats rich in biodiversity. Among the lowland Dipterocarp forest, wet hill forest, montane forest, moss forest and some swamp forest, can be found numerous endangered and unique species. Scientists believe that there are many more, as yet undiscovered, plants and animals in the jungle.

History: The earliest evidence of human occupation on Borneo is from about 50,000 years ago. The current indigenous population, the Dayaks, are descended from the Proto-Malay who came to the island via the Malay Peninsula. Under their stewardship, the forests were able to maintain the highest species diversity of any terrestrial ecosystem. With the introduction of industrial logging this has changed dramatically. Current estimates predict that Borneo's rainforests could disappear by 2010.

Things to Do/Highlights: The first sight of one of the 'old men of the forest', an orangutan, will touch your heart forever. Pay a visit to a local 'longhouse' and share the hospitable warmth and rice wine of the native peoples.

Proximity to Civilisation: Pontianak, the capital of the province, is about 600km away, and there's an awful lot of wilderness in the other directions.

Don't Go Without:
1. Leech socks – handy if you don't want to play host to bloodsuckers.
2. A sarong – locals were onto them well before David Beckham.
3. Light waterproof jacket – an encounter with rain is extremely likely.
4. Hiking practice – you'll need to be a strong walker if you intend to make it into, and back from, the interior.

5. Learning not to be squeamish – some locals still hang skulls collected by their head-hunter ancestors outside their homes.

Inspired: The city of Berkeley, California, designated the Borneo village of Uma Bawang as its official sister city. In 1991 Berkeley residents founded the Borneo Project to assist diverse tribal groups in their struggle for human rights recognition, rainforest protection and sustainable community development.

WITTENOOM, AUSTRALIA

Story: *I Went to Wittenoom and Survived*, p222.

Location: 1450km north of Perth, Western Australia's capital, in the heart of the Hamersley Range.

Getting There: Drive through the near-empty town of Wittenoom past shire warning signs for about 8km to reach majestic Wittenoom Gorge.

Movement: The health department of Western Australia advises driving to Wittenoom Gorge with the windows and vents closed to avoid inhalation of blue asbestos dust.

Geography/Geology: Wittenoom lies on the northern boundary of the beautiful Karijini National Park – land owned by the Innawonga, Kurrama and Punjima peoples. The main features of the park are its ancient gorges, where rain has etched ravines into the spinifex-

carpeted landscape, forming dramatic outcropping and tiered rock formations.

History: Blue asbestos was mined in Wittenoom between 1943 and 1966. From 1978, the government has spent $1.4 million to phase out the town. Negligible levels of airborne asbestos were recorded in 1995–96. The health department of Western Australia considers airborne blue asbestos fibres in and around Wittenoom to be a clear risk to residents and to people visiting the area, and warns that symptoms may take several years to manifest.

Things to Do/Highlights: 'The Mile' is an arduous half-day trek for wannabe Indiana Joneses or Lara Crofts, which starts at Wittenoom Gorge and wends through four spectacular gorges inside the Karijini National Park.

Proximity to Civilisation: Wittenoom is about four lonely days' drive north of Western Australia's capital, Perth.

Don't Go Without:
1. A high-clearance vehicle if visiting the gorge.
2. Driving with the car windows closed and vents sealed.
3. Considering taking an asbestos mask.
4. Informing the local ranger if you intend to trek through the gorge.
5. Your own power source – in 2005 the electrical power supply to Wittenoom was switched off to force residents to leave the area.

Inspired: The first track on the album *Blue Sky Mining* by Aussie band Midnight Oil was inspired by the book, *Blue Murder: Two Thousand Doomed to Die – the Shocking Truth About Wittenoom's Deadly Dust* (1989), by Ben Hills, which investigates the history of the blue asbestos mine in Wittenoom.

LASSETER'S CAVE, AUSTRALIA

Story: *An Australian El Dorado*, p226.

Location: Lasseter's Cave is a low rock formation nestled in Australia's majestic red centre 135km from the Uluru-Kata Tjuta National Park.

Getting There: Take the Docker River Rd towards Uuru. Permits from the Aboriginal Central Land Council are required to travel the road to Lasseter's Cave.

Movement: Motorised vehicle is the only way to go. Unless you are a professional explorer, attempting to traverse this terrain on foot is asking for trouble.

Geography/Geology: Geologists believe that the discovery of 1130-million-year-old igneous rocks in Mordor Pound indicate that the Red Centre was connected to North America until around 600–700 million years ago, when the Australia–North America super-continent was split by subterranean forces to start forming the Pacific Ocean. The term Red Centre is a reference to the red soil that characterises the region.

History: Harold Lasseter first travelled west from Alice Springs on foot in 1897, seeking work in the goldfields of Kalgoorlie. He failed to reach his intended target but claimed discovery of a gold reef in unexplored lands. He returned in 1930, and perished during the search.

Things to Do/Highlights: Visitors who venture into the outback travel in search of solitude and can expect to find it in abundance. Of course, stumbling across the fabled gold vein would be a unexpected bonus.

Proximity to Civilisation: Lasseter's Cave is approximately 650km drive from Alice Springs, hopeless solitude for a man who must have known his time was nearly up.

Don't Go Without:
1. Respecting Aboriginal culture – access to the Red Centre is a privilege granted by the traditional custodians of these vast surreal lands.
2. A wide-brimmed hat – even in winter you will need protection from the scorching sun.
3. Being totally self-sufficient – venturing into the outback without full food and water provisions is irresponsible and dangerous.
4. Taking a crash course in gold vein spotting – just in case.
5. Total sunblock.

Inspired: Australian children's author Mark Greenwood wrote *The Legend of Lasseter's Reef* (2003) to inspire a new generation of young historians and adventurers.

28°S 137°E
LAKE EYRE, AUSTRALIA

Story: *Where Water is the Exception*, p230.

Location: The Warburton Creek originates at the Goyder Lagoon, running 250km along the eastern side of Australia's Simpson Desert before reaching Lake Eyre.

Getting There: Access the creek by car through one of several cattle stations along the Birdsville Track. The shore of Lake Eyre can be reached at ABC Bay in the west, and in the south via Muloorina homestead. Most roads are passable for 2WD, but be sure to tighten all nuts first.

Movement: It is a rare occurrence for there to be enough water in the creek to float a canoe. Camel treks or 4WD safaris are more common during winter.

Geography/Geology: Lake Eyre is the final destination for rain that falls within the Lake Eyre Basin, which covers one sixth of Australia, roughly 1.2 million sq km. Rainfall in the region is unpredictable and must be considerable to activate the rivers and creeks, including the Warburton. When the lake does flood, plants, marine life, birds and other animals briefly flourish before the waters evaporate.

History: The Arabunna and Dieri Aboriginal peoples have lived in the vicinity of Lake Eyre for at least 10,000 years. In 1964, British speed ace Sir Donald Campbell took advantage of the flat, hard salt crust to set a new world land speed record with the jet propelled *Bluebird*.

Things to Do/Highlights: To witness the beauty that is the transformation of the 'dead heart' of Australia into a colourful, luscious environment that attracts thousands of birds and other animals is simply beyond imagination.

Proximity to Civilisation: Warburton Creek is hundreds of kilometres from anywhere. The only human contact you are likely to have is watching planes fly overhead.

Don't Go Without:
1. Head net – the flies are relentless in their pursuit of human sweat.
2. Mud skis – if you plan on getting from the Groove to the shore.
3. Satellite phone or two-way radio – your only hope of rescue in an emergency.
4. Jerry cans – the extreme heat means that only heavy-duty containers can protect water from evaporating into thin hot air.
5. Sandboard – the dunes on the south side of Lake Eyre are ripe for riding, just lookout for thorn bushes at the bottom.

Inspired: For the IMAX movie *Australia Land Beyond Time* (2001), the crew camped on an island in the middle of Lake Eyre to capture some of the most memorable day and night footage for the film.

59°N 153°E
BABUSKHINA, RUSSIA

Story: *Cold Toes in Babushkina*, p234.

Location: By road Babushkina is 1000km northeast of Moscow and more than 280km from the nearest town of Vologda.

Getting There: Take an overnight train north from Moscow to Vologda, one of the old 'Golden Ring' cities of Russia. Take a bus north from Vologda to Totma and onto Babushkina. Or just keep going to the northern city of Arkhangelsk, re-route to the Urals, Kola Peninsula…

or to wherever you are invited along the way.

Movement: You won't find any snowmobiles in this village, so stamp your feet to get the blood flowing and start walking.

Geography/Geology: The area around Babushkina is rugged and unforgiving. Hundreds of rivers crisscross the land, giving rise to forests and a surprising amount of vegetation.

History: Slavs have mingled with the various Finno-Ugric groups of forest- and tundra-dwelling people for millennia. There were many thousands of isolated hamlets based on the fur and fish trade. Many villages were wiped off the map during collectivisation under Stalin but those that remain are as timeless as the land itself.

Things to Do/Highlights: Chance meetings with amazing locals will lead to many unexpected (and drunken) nights. Younger travellers may also suffer the hilarious indignity of being publicly berated by fierce old women for not dressing appropriately for the extreme conditions. At night the air is so clear that it's like looking at the stars through a telescope.

Proximity to Civilisation: The nearest town is Vologda more than 280km away.

Don't Go Without:
1. Valenki (felt boots) – traditional winter boots made from a mixture of lambswool and cows hair.
2. Hat – old women (babushkas) will not hesitate to tell you off if you go out without one.
3. Drinking practice – your liver should be well-trained before you arrive.
4. A flannel so you can wash without always having to get naked.

5. Pencils – in winter the ink in a pen will freeze to make keeping a journal impossible.

Inspired: Heavy drinking – homemade vodka/wine before breakfast is the norm in winter. The Kate Bush song 'Babushka' sounds like it could have been inspired by Babushkina, but was in fact based on the Russian word *babushka*, meaning grandmother.

45°S 166°E

DUSKY SOUND, NEW ZEALAND

Story: *On the Dusky Track*, p238.

Location: The Dusky Track is in the 12,519-sq-km Fiordland National Park, 110km from the New Zealand ski resort of Queenstown.

Getting There: Hop on a speedboat to cross Lake Hauroko and find yourself on an isolated corner of the lake.

Movement: The only way out from Lake Hauroko is to walk to Lake Manapouri, five to seven days away. Strap on your pack, enjoy the views and don't mind the mud.

Geography/Geology: Dusky Sound is an exceptionally massive fjord, measuring in at 40km in length and 8km wide at its widest point. The diversity of the terrain is matched by an impressive array of wildlife.

History: Dusky Sound was named by Captain James Cook, who first spotted it at nightfall on his maiden voyage to New Zealand in 1770. The Maori already knew it as Tamatea, named after their own famed explorer. The first Westerner to attempt an overland crossing was Sir Thomas MacKenzie, in 1884 and 1886. The loss of his compass on one of his trips, however, caused him to compile a map showing the Seaforth River and the MacKenzie River running parallel into Dusky Sound. Later exploration proved that there was but one river.

Things to Do/Highlights: If you're really lucky and keep a careful watch you could be rewarded with the site of a real life loose moose. Failing that, the trail will take you across some of the wildest backcountry in a land famous for its outstanding natural assets.

Proximity to Civilisation: Halfway along the 84km trail you'll find yourself three days' walk from the nearest settlement, which will no doubt conjure up thoughts of being on your own Hobbit quest.

Don't Go Without:
1. Endurance – you'll be out in the bush for several days so toughen up.
2. Wet weather gear – you can expect rain and flash floods as a matter of course.
3. A two-way radio so you can call for help if things go awry.
4. Two compasses, in case one goes walkabout.
5. Reading or watching *The Lord of the Rings*.

Inspired: It is believed that the first painting of a Maori by a professional European artist was made by William Hodges (1744–97), who accompanied Captain Cook on his second voyage to New Zealand in 1772. The artwork depicts a warrior standing on a rock in Dusky Sound.

MOON

Story: *Where Dreams and Endeavours Collide*, p242.

Location: The moon is 384,403km from Earth and is the second brightest object in the sky after the sun.

Getting There: It's only three day's from the earth but the Moon has not been visited by humans since the 1970s.

Movement: When you've had enough of moon walking, jump on board the original interplanetary Sports Utility Vehicle – NASA's Moon Buggy.

Geography/Geology: Exactly how the moon was formed is still the subject of intense debate. However, the consensus at present is that sometime around 4 billion years ago the Earth collided with a very large object – possibly greater than Mars – and that the Moon was formed from material ejected as a result of this collision. In alignment with this impact theory, most rocks taken from the Moon's surface are between 4.6 and 3 billion years old. The oldest terrestrial rocks are rarely more than 3 billion years old.

History: The first manned mission to the moon arrived on 20 July 1969. Two astronauts, Neil Armstrong and Edwin 'Buzz' Aldrin, touched down in the lunar module *The Eagle* and walked on the surface, while Michael Collins waited for them on board the command module *Columbia*. Over the next 3½ years 12 NASA astronauts walked on the moon, before cuts in funding and waning public enthusiasm halted manned lunar expeditions.

Things to Do/Highlights: Curiously the most memorable experience shared by those who have been to the moon is casting a wistful eye back towards whence they came.

Proximity to Civilisation: A handful of people live semi-permanently on the International Space Station but if anything major goes wrong, rescue would be impossible.

Don't Go Without:
1. Zero gravity training to get through the flight.
2. Enough fuel for the return leg.
3. Checking there are no rips in your space suit.
4. A flag – to uphold the questionable tradition of staking a claim to new land for one's country.
5. A video-phone – so you can add the footage to your blog when you get home.

Inspired: The fact that the first words spoken by US astronaut Neil Armstrong as he set foot on the lunar surface can be recited verbatim by millions of people who were not even born at the time, is testament to the moon's hold over humanity's collective imagination.

IMAGE CREDITS